European Women and
Preindustrial Craft

EUROPEAN WOMEN

and

PREINDUSTRIAL CRAFT

EDITED BY

Daryl M. Hafter

INDIANA UNIVERSITY PRESS
Bloomington and Indianapolis

Manufactured in the United States of America

Library of Congress Cataloging-in-Publication Data

European women and preindustrial craft / edited by Daryl M. Hafter.

p.   cm.

Includes bibliographical references and index.

ISBN 0-253-32755-5 (cloth : alk. paper). —

ISBN 0-253-20943-9

(pbk. : alk. paper)

1. Women—Employment—Europe—History.   2. Women textile
workers— Europe—History.   3. Industries—Europe—History.
I. Hafter, Daryl M., date

HD6134.W65   1995   331.4′094—dc20   94-29439

1   2   3   4   5   00   99   98   97   96   95

Contents

Introduction
A Theoretical Framework for Women's Work in Forming the Industrial Revolution

Daryl M. Hafter

The subject of this collection of essays is central to our continuing reassessment of the history of economic modernization and the place of women in work and production. We no longer think of the Industrial Revolution as a total and abrupt move to a factory economy which took place between 1750 and 1815, but it has taken longer to realize that industrializing was not a solely masculine endeavor. What were the women doing while the men became factory workers? Historians such as David Landes and François Crouzet demonstrated that innovation spread from England to the rest of Europe more gradually and unevenly than had been assumed.[1] E. P. Thompson led the way to understanding the role of class cohesion in terms of working-class acceptance of and resistance to industrial mores.[2] Despite the work of these and other historians, a fundamental understanding of the dynamics of industrialization could be achieved only with the documentation of women's place in the economy.

Research in the field of women's history, particularly on women's economic functions throughout history, has revolutionized our comprehension of the process of modernization. Natalie Zemon Davis pioneered in bringing to historians' awareness the importance of early urban female workers. Focusing on the craftswomen of Lyon, Davis demonstrated that they participated in a wide variety of work and that their work identities were flexible. Shut out of most apprenticeships, forced to pick up whatever task presented itself, and expected to change jobs to accommodate their husbands' trade, Lyon's women workers were at the bottom of the scale. Yet Davis reported that the sixteenth century witnessed the closing of masterships to women in trades such as barbering, implying that more egalitarian status may have existed earlier.[3] Franklin Mendels showed that the protoindustrial era blended farming and piecework done as cottage industry.[4] Louise A. Tilly and Joan W. Scott gave us a framework for thought with the demonstration that economic life depended on family cooperation, even into the nineteenth century.[5] By providing labor, by their choice of technology, and by their skill, women workers were able to advance or retard new technology, to speed up the move toward mechanization, or to help preserve traditional ways of life.

As historians documented the widespread participation of female workers, their study of economic organization led to the development of gender theories of labor. It has taken nothing less than deconstructive analysis to show the important effects that gender has had on the process of industrialization. Study of economic development does not stop at identifying women's presence in history; it goes on to show that economic organization follows certain paths precisely because of the attributes that women are believed to have.

Gender theories of economic action begin with the assumption that whatever men and women do in their daily lives, their choices are constrained by gender roles which are socially constructed. As Joan W. Scott wrote, "Gender is a constitutive element of social relationships based on perceived differences between the sexes, and gender is a primary way of signifying relationships of power."[6]

When this approach is applied to economic organization, it forms the basis for new theoretical interpretations of women workers' role in the industrializing process. Feminist scholars of economic history have pointed out how incomplete the earlier studies of industrialization were because they did not use gender as a tool for analysis. As Sonya O. Rose wrote, scholars tried to explain the events of the Industrial Revolution by "biology or economics."[7] Instead of asking *why* women automatically received lower pay than men or why women workers never supervised men, traditional scholarship assumed that this was "natural." Rather than trying to discover how women became relegated to a particular set of jobs, the traditional economists took this configuration as a given and used it to describe emerging capitalism. Marxist theorists, too, while taking account of gender divisions, tended to view patriarchy and capitalism as separate, rather than examining how gender-laden both are.[8]

By focusing on the transitional period of 1750-1850, when European society redefined the attributes of males and females, we join theorists in perceiving a new awareness of the effects of gender on economic life. In the early modern era, the ideal wife worked in the home or outside to help support the family. By the late eighteenth century this standard had changed, with the wife now separated from market production, occupying a purely domestic function. As the home ceased to be considered a place where the family created products for sale, wage labor was thought to rest solely on the efforts of the husband. Thus the ideal of womanhood exchanged the traits of industriousness, strength, commercial savvy, and public assertiveness for the qualities of dependence, domesticity, modesty, and delicacy. The ideal of manhood changed from the expectation that work should be found for men's wives to hostility toward women workers and the idea of female wage earners. Nevertheless, certain gender assumptions about women's work carried into the industrial era, their linkage to a new female ideal throwing into relief the constructed nature of perceptions of female behavior.

What is specifically important to us in this context is tracing how accepted notions of gender became instruments with which entrepreneurs structured new forms of capitalist industry. Women who had performed craftwork at home in the early economy became crucial to the finishing process of mechanized factories.[9] Capitalist employers considered it "natural" that women should earn less than men.[10] The employers retained this practice to enhance their own profits.

Our general paradigm for the preindustrial era shows women workers linked to the family economy, which functioned as a unit, as Louise A. Tilly and Joan W. Scott demonstrated, to produce goods and reproduce future workers. A number of possibilities for the family economy existed simultaneously, depending on the region, the goods produced, local customs, and the pressures of merchant capitalists. Agricultural families spent a portion of the year manufacturing goods or parts of them in a putting-out system. They might work together or separately, and sometimes they might largely abandon their farming pursuits in favor of craftwork. It was possible for craft manufacture to be so successful that it retarded technological modernization in a region.[11] Urban guild families cooperated in turning out regulated products; people without guild ties became skilled or unskilled laborers, pooling their earnings to enable the family to survive. Women as well as men left the household to find sources of earnings; they sent their children out to scavenge, to find casual work, to beg, or to steal. As Olwen H. Hufton has shown, it was an imperative of early modern economic life that every person contributed to his or her own upkeep.[12]

Seen in every street and workshop, the woman worker became a habitual figure both on the farm and in the urban center. Her gender role included constant labor at productive work rather than genteel occupation in the home. But even though her work constituted not the unpaid domestic tasks that Marx pointed to but employment in the public sphere, it was still a function of her gendered status that her efforts earned less than a man's. Thus society was willing to let women workers perform skilled tasks, but insisted that these activities should be paid on a low scale. As Rose wrote, wages were determined by who the worker was, and they often had no relation to what the worker did.[13]

Even in circumstances when women could not be found to fill essential jobs, prospective employers still offered them low wages. The drawgirls of the eighteenth-century silk industry in Lyon, France, illustrate this resistance to market pressures. The silk weavers complained that a lack of workers to pull the cords advancing the brocade looms caused them to fill their contracts late, but not one voice can be found in the guild tracts suggesting that the solution was to offer higher wages. Nor did anyone suggest the use of boys for this task, since in Lyon the post was firmly associated with young women.[14] Although many circumstances in the preindustrial era gave women and men access to similar tasks, urban and rural tradition also imposed sex-specific work on others.

Jobs continued to be divided on the basis of the sex of workers into the industrializing era. But by the nineteenth and twentieth centuries, the terms of the struggle between labor and management were changing. In order to lower the cost of production, entrepreneurs introduced machines or other functional changes in some operations that men performed, and they redefined the jobs as women's work. This attempt at deskilling met with a variety of protests from male workers. As Ava Baron has shown in a study of the printing industry, male printers traditionally had monopolized typesetting and casting, calling it so physically hard and intellectually demanding that only men could do it. When the industry adopted the Linotype process and employers started replacing male with female workers, the men felt their prestige as males to be undercut. "Earlier, men had claimed that the work itself was masculine; after the Linotype, in contrast, they claimed that there was 'no sex in labor.' *Work* did not embody gender; only *workers* did, and some workers could do work that others could not."[15]

In the nineteenth-century industrializing process, the definition of women's work was sealed as hidden, auxiliary, and secondary to the economy. This assertion has been cogently argued by Wally Seccombe, who demonstrated that the "male breadwinner wage" was both an artifact of gender beliefs and also an enforcer of them. It was the skilled trade workers, he believed, who confronted the exploitation of factory work with a demand that their wage be sufficient to keep their wives in the same state of idle domesticity that their bosses' wives enjoyed. The male English trade unions opposed the competition of women workers, whose low wages jeopardized their own jobs, by insisting that the place of women was at home. To put teeth into this demand, they generated a campaign for a man to be paid enough to support his family. Not only did this view set male and female workers in competition with each other, it also posed an impossible goal for working-class families whose husbands could never earn this much. The women forced to labor to make up the difference did so as marginalized, denigrated persons.[16]

For this reason, documentation of their activities in the industrializing process has seemed unimportant. The measure of economic progress was considered to be found in factory work and in the technological advances located there. Such trades as home sewing of garments, shoe construction, and watch assembly were considered incidental to productivity. However, recent investigation, of which this book is a part, has begun to show that women's work was essential to technical change. *A Woman's Hand in Industrializing Craft* tests and verifies this insight. It shows how, by working in the home, in rooms as sweated workers, or in large workshops, women helped to bring about the industrial society.

Women's work has had both radical and conservative effects. In one situation, female employment might foster the use of new technology; in another, it might enable old practices to continue. Female work might be a destabilizing force or a means of preserving family unity. The meaning of women's work emerges only from its context. For this reason, focusing on individual industries is essential. This book presents ten case studies that show how women's work contributed directly and indirectly to industrial modernization.

Five themes focusing on the relation between technology and society unify the questions in this book:

1. The relationship of women to technical skill underlies any discussion of female employment. What industrial tasks did women perform in the past? Was female employment limited exclusively to low-skill activity? Was official training available to women? Could workers acquire specialized techniques only through formal apprenticeships?

2. We have come to define work in terms of market production. This has led us to the dichotomy that male workers produced for long-distance, wholesale markets, while female workers made commodities for local, retail trade. Was this true for the preindustrial period? Did it prevail in the industrial era?

3. Closely linked to these earlier themes is the question of whether women were "naturally" unsuited to understand and work with mechanical devices. Did this idea start in the era of craft production? What social ideals did the notion of women's lack of mechanical ability satisfy?

4. We are now aware that women's craftwork persisted through the nineteenth-century industrializing era and even into the twentieth century. What economic function did their home employment have for entrepreneurs and for technological advance? What criteria did women use for choosing production in the home over factory employment? What economic effects did their choices have?

5. Finally, all of the case studies call for a review of female work in its social context. How does our analysis of the industrializing process change when we view it as a social structure of reciprocal gender roles? What kind of work did society consider appropriate for women to do? What about the value of a woman's wage for the family? Why was it acceptable for women to perform industrial work in the home but not outside? To what extent are these definitions based on technical considerations? To what extent on social norms?

The essays in this book continue the groundbreaking reinterpretation of particular industries in light of the five major themes set forth above. The chapters on the early period focus on women's access to new technology. Reed Benhamou analyzes the Montpellier verdigris industry, which produced copper acetate for use in dyes, paints, and medicines. This craft was run entirely by women, who passed on the "secrets" of manufacture from mother to daughter. When men tried to enter the lucrative trade, the women refused to share trade information and kept them out by making fun of their ignorance. Inger Jonsson shows how farm women monopolized the "high-tech" process in flax processing in eighteenth- and nineteenth-century Sweden. As unofficial apprentices, they performed the traditional women's part of the work, even when a new water-powered "scutching wheel" transformed it into skilled employment.

Walter Endrei and Rachel P. Maines trace the spread of the two-headed Saxony spinning wheel, which doubled the production of thread. When technical improvements brought it to the forefront of hand-spinning technology, women continued to use it in Eastern Europe. Their skill contributed to the region's resistance to adopting the simpler and more productive Arkwright frame when it was developed. Daryl

M. Hafter demonstrates that wives of guildmasters in the silk industry of Lyon wove a quarter of the textiles produced by the home workshops. Without formal apprenticeship or recognition, these women mastered the complex and prestigious weaving process. Their tradition of work stimulated women's employment in the nineteenth century and enabled skilled male masters to maintain their profession and status in the industrial era.

Do these case studies document Olwen H. Hufton's "good old days"? What they show is a surprising degree of economic activity for an era in which women were not autonomous adults under the law. They challenge several assumptions: that workers acquire skill only through formal apprenticeships; that women workers' general lack of guild status automatically meant auxiliary jobs; that the preindustrial society itself considered female labor peripheral to the economy. Reappraising the structure of preindustrial work contributes new insights into how the Industrial Revolution got its start.

The last six chapters in this volume examine the varied contributions that female work made to areas of production that have received less scholarly attention. These essays reveal that craft industry persisted longer than we had thought. Hand manufacture contributed both skills and patterns of social behavior to the new industry. Following earlier practice, women workers brought their activity into the unevenly mechanizing field, with some surprising results.

The authors in this section of the book present substantive, detailed analyses of manufactures that continued to tap female handwork long into the industrial era. John Sweets demonstrates how the persistence of traditional views of women's roles in the hand lace industry of Le Puy prejudiced industrialists and government inspectors. Women were responsible for most aspects of this business, from distributing the thread to making up sample patterns. Contemporaries justified paying women lower salaries by characterizing their work as incidental. Sweets points out a nineteenth-century historian's oxymoron in calling lacemaking "an essential supplementary resource." Meanwhile male merchants reaped the fortunes that hand lace earned in an international market through the 1870s.

We have become accustomed to viewing technological advance as an impersonal process, driven by the inevitability of machine improvements; but a close look at the context of the economy will show that many considerations influenced whether production would become mechanized. Examining the relationship between women workers and the adoption of machinery underscores this assumption. Women's choice of technology was not automatically predictable. Whitney Walton contends that nineteenth-century Lorraine embroiderers resisted both the technological advance of working with embroidery frames and regulation by means of workbooks. These young rural workers preferred the less tiring technique of hand embroidery and the flexibility of working on family farms. Their handmade products competed successfully until the Swiss adopted new machines which were operated by men assisted by the rest of the family. This pattern suggests that the date assigned to the completion of the Industrial Revolution should be shifted to the mid-nineteenth century.

As Pierre Caspard shows, the calico-printing industry exemplified the flexible use of women's and children's labor as handcraft was employed alongside mechanized technology. One of the major industries of the eighteenth and nineteenth centuries, the popular calico manufacture developed hand painting of cottons as a woman's specialty in order to offset the increasing cost of block printing by the males. Here the female labor, which was actually supervised by women managers, was suppressed when copper-rolling technology made the hand painters redundant in the 1840s. There is no doubt that entrepreneurs benefited from the women workers' skill and their willingness to accept lower wages.

It is a testament to the complexity of sex-role applications that we can find male and female activities viewed differently according to place and time. In Patrizia Sione's study of silkmaking in the Como region of Italy, the nineteenth century saw women's skilled domestic work of reeling as a background to their induction into the important silk factories. As Sione writes, "The adoption of machinery did not destroy these skills, as the work process was not substantially altered by the concentration in small mills or by application of steam power." Rather, as agricultural incomes declined, women entered factories in ever greater numbers. There they continued to process silk with their customary skill, but in the industrialized setting their wages were kept low. Silk manufacture, especially the weaving, eventually moved to the cities. But the higher wages there induced entrepreneurs to relocate it again to rural areas. Eventually a mixed system of power and hand looms and hand processing enabled women to maintain their skills and to work cooperatively with their husbands or other heads of workshops in order to contribute to the family wage.

Jean Quataert's study of the textile workers in the Oberlausitz district of Germany between 1780 and 1860 also shows how the mixture of hand and machine energy enabled a district to survive the decades of industrialization without being transformed into a total factory economy. Taking advantage of traditional linen-weaving skill, entrepreneurs there introduced the processing of cotton, which they were able to sell at home and to export in competition with English textiles. State support of handwork also helped the mixed economy to thrive. Most important, the Oberlausitz weavers used flexibility in gender roles and in their techniques of selling and smuggling their goods in order to survive.

The endurance of traditional manufacture contributed to the maintenance of social peace by enabling artisanal and farming households to survive. In this way, the structure and ideology of society did not appear to be shaken to an unacceptable extent. In large measure, female workers provided the means of bridging handicraft and mechanization with their flexibility. Flexibility has been considered a hallmark of women's work in the preindustrial era. The pattern continued through the Industrial Revolution. Tessie P. Liu shows why certain female homeworkers in the lingerie trade of Chollet accepted low-wage factory or cottage labor. The key to their work was that it allowed the father of the family to remain an artisan of prestige. Wives and daughters, whose work identity was secondary, performed sweated labor in order to enable the men to remain hand-loom weavers. By working for wages themselves, the women enabled their male relatives to escape being proletarianized; they helped to maintain the professional identity of the men and their households.

In order for women to perform this function, their work had to be invisible to society. Tessie Liu's trousseau makers, earning from one-third to one-half of the family income, kept the hand-loom families intact. John Sweets's lacemakers did the same, bringing in a similar proportion of the family funds. In both cases, their wages were considered merely supplemental. They were earning "the little luxuries and frills" to make the home more comfortable; they were not challenging the ability of male heads of households to support, and therefore dominate, the family. In preindustrial times, every individual was expected to earn a living. After the Industrial Revolution, the need stayed the same but the ideology changed. A notion of separate spheres defined women as competent only at home. Direct participation in the market economy went against women's "nature" and their role of domestic nurture.

Women's opportunities and choices were thus shaped by the conception of a moral order. The issue of factory work vs. homework drew on nationalist feelings of family protection and pronatalism. Needlework, for instance, had connotations of morality, especially when it was performed in the home. In this way women's economic gain was veiled by their cultural function. Moreover, because the domestic sphere became a cultural opposite of the machine-filled workshop, any work performed there was considered "women's work," by definition unskilled, appropriately low-paid employment. Even men who worked in homelike settings in Chollet came to be denigrated as amateurs.[17]

With this variety of patterns, the chapters in this book document how men and women used all the ingenuity at their command to weather the transition from artisanal shop to mechanized industry. Modern scholars need to scrutinize the semiotics of women's work to see how past ideology was preserved and altered by past necessity. We need to understand how women's adoption of new technology in certain situations and rejection of it in others helped to maintain social peace in an era of profound economic dislocation. We must document what elements were retained from the preindustrial period and how female workers actually related to the evolving technology of the early Industrial Revolution. The essays here make possible this kind of investigation. From historic inquiries will come a much-needed perspective on issues relating to women and technology in the twentieth century.

Notes

1. David S. Landes, *The Unbound Prometheus: Technological Change and Industrial Development in Western Europe from 1750 to the Present* (Cambridge: Cambridge University Press, 1969); François Crouzet, "Wars, Blockade and Economic Change in Europe, 1792-1815," *Journal of Economic History* (December 1964): 567-88; and "Encore la croissance économique française au XIXe siècle," *Revue du Nord* (July–September 1972): 271-88.

2. E. P. Thompson, *The Making of the English Working Class* (New York: Pantheon, 1964).

3. Natalie Zemon Davis, "Women in Crafts in Sixteenth-Century Lyons," *Feminist Studies* 8 (1972): 49-53.

4. Franklin Mendels, "Proto-industrialization: The First Phase of the Process of Industrialization," *Journal of Economic History* 32 (1972): 241-61.

5. Louise A. Tilly and Joan W. Scott, *Women, Work, and Family* (New York: Holt, Rinehart and Winston, 1978).

6. Joan Wallach Scott, "Gender: A Useful Category of Historical Analysis," in Scott, *Gender and the Politics of History* (New York: Columbia University Press, 1988), p. 42.

7. Sonya O. Rose, *Limited Livelihoods: Gender and Class in Nineteenth-Century England* (Berkeley: University of California Press, 1992), p. 4.

8. For a brief discussion of the historiography of economic theories on gender, see Veronica Beechey, "Introduction," in *Unequal Work* (London: Verso, 1987). Ideas of Heidi Hartman and Cynthia Cockburn are analyzed on pp. 10-11.

9. See Maxine Berg's discussion of the burgeoning of domestic piecework at the beginning of the factory era in *The Age of Manufactures: Industry, Innovation and Work in Britain, 1700-1820* (New York and Oxford: Oxford University Press, 1986), pp. 146-49.

10. Rose, *Livelihoods*, p. 13.

11. See Gay Gullickson, "Agriculture and Cottage Industry: Redefining the Causes of Proto-industrialization," The *Journal of Economic History* 43, no. 4 (December 1983): 831-50.

12. See especially Olwen H. Hufton, "Women and the Family Economy in Eighteenth-Century France," *French Historical Studies* 9 (Spring 1975): 1-22.

13. Rose, *Livelihoods*, p. 10.

14. For further discussion see Daryl M. Hafter, "The 'Programmed' Brocade Loom and the Decline of the Drawgirl," in *Dynamos and Virgins Revisited: Women and Technological Change in History*, ed. Martha Moore Trescott (Metuchen, N.J.: Scarecrow Press, 1979), pp. 49-66.

15. Ava Baron, "Contested Terrain Revisited: Technology and Gender Definitions of Work in the Printing Industry, 1850-1920," in *Women, Work, and Technology*, ed. Barbara Drygulski Wright et al. (Ann Arbor: University of Michigan Press, 1987), p. 70.

16. Wally Seccombe, "Patriarchy Stabilized: The Construction of the Male Breadwinner Wage Norm in Nineteenth-Century Britain," *Social History* 11, no. 1 (January 1986): 53-76.

17. Jean H. Quataert, "The Shaping of Women's Work in Manufacturing," *American Historical Review* 90 (December 1985): 1122-1148.

PART I
Handicraft and Invention in the Eighteenth Century

Reed Benhamou 1

Women and the Verdigris Industry in Montpellier

The history of women's work is frequently a history of exploitation: menial tasks, arduous labor, health risks, inadequate wages, and severely limited opportunity. Occasionally, however, this dreary account can be leavened with episodes of individual or collective achievement. This presentation, which focuses on the verdigris industry in the south of France, provides such leavening. It is a success story, a report of a financial golden age during which many women became entrepreneurs, and a few developed lucrative, and legally protected, power bases.

To a certain extent, it is ironic that this economic Eden should have developed in France. Granted, France is a country with traditional interest in the female; but this interest has not been generally translated into concern for her occupational or economic fulfillment. By and large, those women who sparked the French imagination were aristocratic, intellectual, literary, sensual, and/or fictional. The predictable result has been that we know more about the inventive Marguerite de Navarre and the inventive Manon Lescaut than we do about the hundreds of thousands who contributed the labor upon which much of the French economy was built.

The nature of their contribution—that is, the range of the occupational roles open to them—is not well known. In *Histoire et sociologie du travail féminin*, Evelyne Sullerot, citing Etienne Boileau's thirteenth-century *Livre des métiers*, mentions that fifteen of the medieval trades were considered "uniquely feminine," and finds the conventional irony in the fact that many of these trades revolved around gold and silk, "two of the most precious and sought-after materials of the time." Referring to the same source, Eileen Power makes a more modest claim: of one hundred crafts practiced in medieval Paris, five were performed by craftswomen alone, although in many others women worked alongside men.

The demographic realities of the Renaissance, when peace and prosperity brought more men into the labor force, spelled an end to even this restricted influence: "women lose one after the other the prestigious trades which had been theirs," Sullerot writes, "and the working of the precious materials of gold and silk escapes them."[1]

In any case, relatively few women had been involved in producing luxury goods

3

from these luxury materials. The majority—in the Middle Ages as throughout the preindustrial era—contributed strength rather than creativity or intelligence to the French labor force. Agriculture was at once the biggest and most anonymous employer. Regional industries, particularly those based on textiles, absorbed many others, primarily for tasks requiring cheap muscle or constant attention. Other occupations are briefly listed by Albistur and Armogathe in *Histoire du féminisme français*; these and more are frequently depicted in the French encyclopedia edited by Diderot and D'Alembert in the middle of the eighteenth century. While not mentioned in the articles which the plates illustrate, women are shown as performing over 140 tasks, preponderantly in basic industries such as glass, wax, and metals; in the production of decorative goods and accessories; and, of course, in areas related to clothing and textiles.[2] In many instances, because of the stringent guild rules that regulated French crafts, women would have been so employed because they were the wives or daughters of the craftsmen in charge rather than because they were licensed craftspersons.[3]

Remuneration for these tasks was seldom good, and only rarely equal to a man's. Sullerot reminds us that as a group, women saw their wages fall from three-quarters to two-fifths of a man's earnings between the beginning of the fourteenth and the end of the sixteenth centuries. Charles-Roux et al., consulting as had Sullerot data compiled by Georges D'Avenel for his *Histoire économique de la propriété*, found some improvement in the seventeenth century, when the average daily wage for female labor varied between 60 and 71 percent of that for men.[4] Turning ourselves to D'Avenel, we see that the eighteenth century (the period emphasized in the present study) was an extension of the seventeenth. The average annual wage of an eighteenth-century craftsman, D'Avenel finds, was 288 livres; in general, a woman earned 60 percent of that. One pleasant exception was the case of female grape pickers in the Lorraine, whom he reports as earning the same as their male coworkers. The Lorraine was an economic anomaly, however; much more typical was the Herault, where female pickers were paid only half a man's wage. Moving from viticultural dayworkers to small craftspersons, D'Avenel cites female mattress makers who earned one-third a man's rate—this in 1791—although part of that difference was geographic, the men working in Paris and the women in the provinces.[5]

It is against this background of limited economic opportunity that we must consider the case of verdigris producers.

Most of us are familiar with only one form of verdigris, the copper carbonate that discolors copper cookware and gives bronze statuary its green patina. It seems not only that verdigris appears without help from humankind, but that it appears despite our best efforts to prevent it. The verdigris that concerns us here, however, is the deliberately cultivated copper acetate caused by the action of acetic acid on copper. The intentional production of copper acetate is an ancient practice: the eight common methods of production listed in Pliny's first-century account imply an already long tradition. More recently, replaced by other substances, it has so faded from public awareness that the brief description of its uses found in the *En-*

cyclopedia Americana may be unique among popular information sources.[6] For several hundred years, however, it was widely used in dyes, paints, and medicines, and, as a desirable and exportable raw ingredient, it figured in the French economy from at least the end of the thirteenth century to the early years of the twentieth.[7]

The basic materials of verdigris production are copper, grapes, and wine; the basic factory is an earthenware jar and a cool place to keep it. Perhaps for this reason, although verdigris was occasionally cultivated as far north as Grenoble, production quickly localized to Montpellier, where the climate and the nearby vineyards created an ideal work environment.

It appears to have always been a cottage industry but not, at its origins, necessarily the women's industry it was later to become. In his examination of fourteenth-century tax records, Jean Combes found that production was controlled by a wholesaler who brokered the output of various workers. These were occasionally designated as "laborers"; but it was more common to find that they held occupations such as carpenter, shoemaker, haberdasher, or coiner. Some degree of financial flexibility was necessary to purchase the copper (then, as later, imported from Sweden), the wine, and the jars. Deals were struck and investments made, however: a cattle breeder and his wife contracted for copper, promising to pay its weight in verdigris within four months; a carpenter and his wife went into debt for 102 pounds of copper, as did a shoemaker's widow and her two brothers-in-law. These were not the only wives and widows to figure in the accounts; over the centuries, they would come to greatly outnumber the men.[8] They were also more likely to control the jars and copper (and thus the manufacture itself), since these were often part of their dowries and estates.[9]

On its face, verdigris production appears to have been more tedious than difficult, but successful cultivation required a sensitivity to changes in appearance, temperature, and odor that could come only with initiation and experience. The importance of making accurate judgments on the basis of minute evidence will be seen as we follow the various steps in the process as these were recorded by eighteenth-century encyclopedists.[10]

Generally speaking, verdigris was produced by placing copper strips between layers of fermented grapes in an earthenware jar and leaving them until the acid in the grapes caused the copper to develop the crystals that would ripen into verdigris. The process was not automatic, and individual makers brought their own variants to it.

New copper strips, cut from twenty-one-inch disks and hammered smooth by the metalsmith, could be used immediately; but many growers first buried them for a few days in verdigris, saying that this "seasoning" kept them from overheating when they were introduced into the jars. Seasoned or not, the strips lasted through several production cycles, becoming more efficient (i.e., producing more verdigris) as they aged.

New pots, made of porous, partially fired earthenware, were moisture-proofed by being soaked for a week to ten days in wine vinegar. They were then scrubbed in the same liquid to cleanse them of any tartar deposited by the wine. Old jars were preferred, but they needed to be thoroughly scrubbed with sand and vinegar at regular intervals. As Chambers's anglicized spelling implies, "verdegrease" is mucilaginous, and an excess of its fatty residue impeded new formation.

The wines used in the process were selected for their strength, judged on the basis of how easily they would burn (wines were accepted or rejected on the basis of their "fire"). Such strength was lacking in wines that were either white, sweet, or old; and so the verdigris producer fed her crop on the same wines that were sought by connoisseurs.

The grapes were prepared by a lengthy process that began with their selection in the vineyards at harvest time. They were then sun-dried, a process that involved frequent turning and an absolute avoidance of any water or oil, and then compacted in a press "at the top of the house." (The reason for this location is not explained, although it may lie in the fact that the top of the house might be less damp than the basement *cave*. The indication of a multistory house is interesting, and reinforces the idea that the growers enjoyed a slightly elevated social status, first noted in Combes's account of medieval producers.) Once pressed, the grapes were soaked in wine vinegar until they had doubled in size. A basement location was preferred for this and subsequent operations, although some producers (perhaps those who for socioeconomic reasons lacked a *cave*) worked on the ground floor of their houses.[11] The grapes were then packed into large balls, covered with three pots of wine, sealed in earthenware jars, and left to ferment. Opinions and practices varied; some growers stirred the wine at intervals they felt to be dictated by the ambient temperature and humidity and the heat produced by the fermentation process itself, while others allowed the process to go forward undisturbed until they sensed it had run its course.

Being able to judge the fermentation process accurately was extremely important since it determined when the copper could be introduced into the jars, and several methods had evolved for making these decisions correctly. Some producers looked for dampness on the underside of the urn's lid, others checked for crystal formation when a heated copper plate was suspended over the grapes. A third approach was to examine the top layer of grapes for the iridescent film the growers called "a kind of dew."

When fermentation was judged to be complete, the grapes were drained for a few days and then layered by placing around 100 heated copper strips in the urns. In about a week, crystals developed (or, as the producers said, "cottoned") on the strips. The copper had to be withdrawn from the urns at this point, since if crystallization became too advanced, the growths attached themselves to the grapes and were extremely difficult to harvest.

The crystal-covered copper strips were then placed in racks where they were dampened with wine vinegar (or water, although this was illegal) over a three-day period, a process known as "feeding the verdigris." "Feeding" was repeated at weekly intervals for about a month, or until efflorescence was complete and the strips showed the desired blue-green, spongy growth.

The fully developed verdigris was then scraped from the multitude of copper strips by groups of women working around lipped hexagonal or octagonal tables, a task frequently done at night when other chores, and housework, were finished.[12] The final stage in which the producers were directly involved was packing the verdigris into bags and passing it on to the commissioned brokers who would oversee its inspection and sale.

The product had to meet strict standards. It was not unusual for a district supervisor to reject a shipment and order the defective material to be publicly burned in the presence of its maker.[13] If the crop was passed, it went to merchants who prepared it for resale. A good deal of it was exported to Holland, where it was used to make the dark green, weather-resistant paint that protected Dutch houses from the sea air; the rest was used in dyes, inks, and a range of pharmaceutical products from eyewashes to escharotics.

Production of a crop of verdigris might take as long as ninety days, but efficiency was gained because cultivation ran on more than one cycle. Most growers had as much copper in reserve as they had in production; and once the strips were taken from the urns to be drained and "fed," three pots of wine were once again poured over the grapes so that they might again ferment. Reserved copper was added when fermentation was once more at its height, and another crop was on its way to market. The need for efficiency, and the amount of work involved in this essentially year-round industry are obvious, especially when we consider that some growers manipulated as many as 500 pots and 100,000 strips of copper.

The population of growers was almost totally female, although, as we have seen, men were involved at the dawn of the industry. By the beginning of the eighteenth century, however, men were only occasional producers, and then in the indirect sense of paying for materials. At a time when men were excluding women from even that most female of occupations, midwifery,[14] their absence from this trade invites question. It may well be that, unless a man was dealing with members of his own family, he found little profit in the industry. Women were much more likely to have been initiated to its secrets as children, simply because it is more likely that girls would have remained close to their mothers once they had reached an age at which they might be of help to the family. Excluded from this early training, men were easily exploited by an unscrupulous female workforce:

> Most of the women who make verdigris for [male] factory owners, most of whom know nothing about how to prepare it, can make them believe anything. If they make a mistake in judging the fermentation, they will go ahead anyway, even though the copper will hardly dissolve, and will say that the wine wasn't good, or give any other excuse that will save them the reproaches the owner has the right to make.[15]

Ridicule was another weapon in what may have been a guerrilla war against masculine encroachment. Fabre quotes an eighteenth-century writer to the effect that "if there were any men who wanted to keep their wives, they were jeered, and the women taunted them for doing work that threatened their masculine dignity."[16] It is possible that a threat to more than dignity was implied. Verdigris is a notoriously unsafe substance, as we shall see, and might well have had the reputation of causing impotence in addition to a long list of other ailments.

Fear of verdigris poisoning was certainly justified. The French periodical press of the time frequently carried articles describing sickness and even deaths caused by verdigris. A dog was reported killed by eating tripe served from a copper pan (1754), and copper cookware was decried that same year. The author found it "singular" that Sweden, the major exporter of copper, itself forbade the use of copper pans. Copper fountains, an important source of water for most of the Paris population, and the copper cauldrons in which beer was brewed were denounced in 1757. And the *Supplément* to the *Encyclopédie* described how a family had died from eating bread baked in an oven fueled by wood coated with verdigris-based paint.[17]

Nineteenth-century scientists, with rising interest in public health, experimented on animals: a dog, which could vomit, was finally killed when it ingested verdigris-laced food for a third time; a rabbit, which could not vomit, died straightaway. The urine of verdigris producers was tested and was found to contain copper, proof that this metal was being absorbed. Researchers interviewed and examined around sixty producers, evaluating their working conditions. Proper hygiene was certainly lacking. The workers spent most of the day with their hands and arms immersed in verdigris-laden liquids. Their faces, hair, and bodies were covered in verdigris dust. Washing-up did not take place until the workday was over and the women were ready to go home. Many women brought infants to the workplace and nursed them from verdigris-dusted breasts. The situation seemed ideal for studying the extent of the anorexia, raging thirst, nausea, uncontrollable vomiting, diarrhea, anemia, and abdominal pain that were, with death, the inevitable results of copper poisoning.

The scientists found nothing of the sort. The worst health problems were an occasional sinusitis caused by a sensitivity to the dust that hung in the air and an even less frequent urge to vomit because of the somewhat sickly odor of the product. Menstruation was normal, and the mothers delivered healthy babies. Young women showed a pleasing plumpness, octogenarians an enviable strength and lucidity. For reasons the researchers could not explain—perhaps the slow and constant exposure to verdigris gave a kind of immunity—these women were absolutely resistant to the well-documented dangers of verdigris poisoning.

The finding was not new. An eighteenth-century observer had recorded that verdigris-related sicknesses were nowhere mentioned in the annals of the industry; and he offered the opinion that the fumes of the wine vinegar used in production neutralized the pernicious effects of the copper. As rational investigators, the researchers expressed only wonder at the phenomenon;[18] it is not hard to imagine that in a more superstitious age, women who could handle poisons with impunity were regarded with some awe.

Precious as good health might be, women produced verdigris for a more basic reason: money. Verdigris had many advantages over other cottage industries. It required little start-up capital, and that could be borrowed against future earnings and paid back in kind rather than cash. It needed neither special facilities nor exotic materials and equipment. Everything required for the making of it could be reused, even the grapes and the wine. Its tasks could be scheduled around housework and childcare. It was labor-intensive, but production could go forward with few workers, and these were mostly family members, committed to successful practices and working for their keep and not for a salary. And it could be profitable on any scale. Small wonder that it was commonly believed that with verdigris, a woman could not only preserve her *dot*, she could double her money.[19]

In good times this could happen; but times were not always good. "The gains were . . . irregular, production and profit varying with the weather, the price of wine, and the stability of the market."[20] Production fell when cold winters impeded the oxidation of the copper; demand dropped when war made enemies of importers; and cost rose when the government imposed stiff import duties on copper in the nineteenth-century.[21]

Of these factors, war was the most serious impediment to profit. The bulk of production went into paints and dyes, coloring agents for the luxury trades of textiles and furnishings that, more than others, required peace for their advancement. The demand for verdigris in eighteenth-century pharmaceuticals was probably constant, but the number of products that used it as an ingredient was limited: "Lanfranc's eyewash, Metz's green balm, Egyptian unguent and that of the apostles, divine plasters, and manus Dei."[22] In 1755, reflecting the tensions that were soon to erupt in the Seven Years' War, over a third of the producers went out of business. In 1773, "none of the producers are making money because wine and copper are excessively high, and there is no demand"; again, many producers shut down.[23]

Not all did so, and certainly not all did so permanently. Verdigris production could be interrupted with relative ease: once the last crop was marketed, the jars could be scrubbed and the copper laid aside; even the wine could be stored. Tied as much to the cycles of the earth as to the movements of nations, cultivation could begin again with the next grape harvest. Times of slow financial gain were not always times of panic: even in 1773, "well-off growers, and those who are obsessed with making verdigris, are holding out, and do not cease buying copper." A good deal of the purchase price of this raw material reportedly came from "husbands, who are financing an industry that often runs at a loss—a fact their wives are not always careful to tell them."[24] Tables in the civil archives of Montpellier show the rise and fall of eighteenth-century production, if not profit: a low of 348,247 livres in 1748, rising to 1,011,145 livres in 1755, a second low of 377,508 livres in 1760, an all-time high of 1,155,982 livres in 1776, followed by three more years of substantial (over 900,000 livres) output.[25] A comparable quantity—600,000 kilos—was produced in 1865.[26]

The eighteenth-century wholesale price of verdigris varied with the international situation, dropping to 12 to 13 sous per pound in times of war, rising to 17 or 18 sous in times of peace. Many of the growers, "the wives and daughters of *bourgeois* [and] artisans," could use their profits as supplementary income (although, as we have seen, the "obsessed" might be as likely to view their husbands' incomes as supplements to their own profits). Others, such as the "few peasant [families]" in the industry, "knowing no other trade, have only this for their support."[27] (Bought relatively cheaply, verdigris was severely marked up when resold: a 1773 manual on paint processes and materials gives a price of 2 livres 15 sous for approximately 1/32nd of a pound of a verdigris "brick" [the compacted form in which it was generally marketed], and 3 livres for the same amount of pulverized verdigris.)[28]

In the mid-nineteenth century, dealers paid between 180 and 210 francs a kilo, resulting in sales ranging from 1,080,000 to 1,260,000 francs.[29] A commentator of the time, perhaps deprecating the importance of this feminine industry to the economy, said slightingly, "84 pots suffice to buy the clothing of a *bourgeoise* and her daughters."[30] A century earlier, the contribution of the growers to the community at large was more frankly acknowledged: "From time immemorial, the manufacture of verdigris has been seen as having tremendous importance for the city of Montpellier, as much for its use of the local wines as for the number of families it supports."[31]

With both personal and community well-being at stake, it is not surprising that manufacturers would seek production shortcuts, or that buyers would seek guarantees of the substance's quality. Conflicts were not uncommon. We have already seen that unacceptable verdigris could be destroyed before the eyes of its unfortunate maker; it was also possible to be sued in civil court, as was a widow who was named a codefendant with the wholesaler when her verdigris failed to satisfy a coachmaker who used it in his enamels.[32] Such faulty products, it was felt, call the integrity of French manufacture as a whole into question.

Accordingly, the government set up an inspection system in July 1711 that defined how verdigris was to be produced, and forbade the use of additives (such as potassium bitartrate, found in wine) to speed efflorescence, of water (rather than wine or wine vinegar) for "feeding," and, not unnaturally, of fillers (used to increase selling weight). The compaction of verdigris powder into the bricks in which the product was sold was given over to bonded *pétrisseurs* (literally, kneaders or molders). These were generally, but not always, men, and, like the members of other occupations in eighteenth-century France, they tended to be related: in 1753, three of four *pétrisseurs* certified were related.

Finally, the government interjected between the makers and the market a number of commissioned brokers whose responsibility it was to collect the verdigris from the growers, oversee its compaction, guarantee its purity to the intendant administering the district, find buyers for the product, and deliver payment to the manufacturers. These brokers, all women, immediately became forces to be reckoned with.

Their integrity and impartiality were supposedly ensured by a prohibition against their producing, warehousing, or selling verdigris on their own account. The familial nature of French trades, however, made it possible to circumvent the letter if not the spirit of the law, as did the brokers' privilege of asking relatives and female friends for help in their time-consuming tasks. Almost certainly, some of the brokers profited by their families' production, and families were rewarded by the almost hereditary nature of the post: by the late 1760s, several of the brokers were the third of their line, daughters or nieces of former officeholders in the profession. This descent was so common that appointments made for other reasons were justified: for example, one woman, although an outsider (*pas de race*), was rewarded with a commission for having served as a wet-nurse to the child of a local dignitary.

Once in position, a broker competed with her sisters for business, and the infighting was frequently nasty. Appalled, one district administrator wrote, "Although they may come from a good family and have a comfortable income, they are essentially fishwives who will sell one another for a profit of five sous." Another said, "It's a good thing there aren't many of them. They are so jealous of one another's gains that they will destroy themselves rather than lose a client."

The less successful might also form uneasy coalitions and turn to the law if one of their number gained too much power. The report of one ultimately unsuccessful suit reveals both the possibilities and responsibilities of the position.

In 1753, seven of the eight brokers petitioned to have the eighth removed from office, claiming that, since the daughter who had been helping her had moved out of town, she would no longer be able to service her clients. The transparency of the ploy ensured its failure, as did the loyalty of the defendant's clients. This was a considerable number: "three-quarters of the Montpellier producers, whom she had known how to attract and keep . . . by the quality of her advice, her loans to women needing copper and wine, and her cash advances on verdigris sales." She had been a broker for forty-two years at the time of the suit, and these practices had brought her a lifetime income of over 50,000 écus (150,000 livres).[33]

This translates into an annual income of 3,570 livres, a sum roughly twelve times the annual wage of the average craftsman (to use D'Avenel's estimate), and reveals the financial benefits a single-minded broker could wrest from her commission. There is no hint in the archival records that any broker used these funds in an attempt to rise in social status, even had that been possible in a country so conscious of social origins as France.

The comments on the manner, and manners, of these brokers, cited above, imply in fact that their interest was more in making money than in what it would buy. Still, it is interesting to compare this average income with those reported by Jean Sgard, who found that daily workers might earn between 100 and 300 livres; skilled craftsmen, teachers, and editors between 300 and 1,000 livres; and university professors, government appointees, and royal tutors between 1,000 and 3,000 livres. A determined broker could thus surpass the earnings average, not only of those in her own social class but of those with more prestigious, intellectual callings. (Diderot himself, for example, earned only 1,500 livres a year in 1751 for his beginning work on the *Encyclopédie*.)[34] This reality may go far to explain the care with which various government administrators expressed their dismay with the brokers' behavior.

The Revolution that eventually brought opportunity to so many ended the brokerage positions by which a few had been allowed to gain real financial influence. Even before the positions were abolished, however, there had been a revolution in the method by which verdigris was produced, thanks to the serendipitous discovery (or rediscovery)[35] credited to a local grower, or, rather, to her donkey. The tale con-

tains too many concrete details to be anything but apocryphal, although it was seriously reported in the literature of the time and as seriously repeated a century
later;[36] as such, it is probably more revealing for the attitude it displays toward dis-
coveries made by women than for the accuracy of its content.

The story concerns Mme Rose Refreger, the wife of Jean Bertet, a wigmaker. Like
many of her neighbors, she supplemented the family income by cultivating verdigris; and, like them, she fed her donkey the skins of the fermented grapes. In December 1777, distracted by a visitor, she dropped grape skins and some copper strips
she was carrying into the donkey's manger, where the beast nosed some of the skins
over the copper and ate the rest. A few days later, Mme Refreger found her missing
copper, and to her delight and astonishment, she found as well that it had developed a handsome coat of verdigris. The story, whispered by Mme Refreger to her
friends, was soon known to the community of growers, all of whom quickly abandoned the techniques of a lifetime and adopted the new approach, which consisted
of simply burying copper in grape skins and allowing nature to take its course.

However the change in production method came about, it is true that verdigris
producers in the nineteenth century greatly modified the approach taken by their
grandmothers, and that, so simplified, the industry continued "with an activity almost equal to that of the period prior to the Revolution."[37] The eighteenth century
writer who had first publicized the new method felt that the verdigris it produced
was comparable in quality to that grown in the traditional, time-consuming manner. A nineteenth-century critic, however, saw "with regret that the quality of this
product is deteriorating," and wished that the inspection system, "which assured
the quality and reassured the buyer," could be reinstated.[38]

This did not happen, of course, but production itself continued until the First
World War. When interviewed, one former producer attributed its disappearance
"to the more modern methods developed by the Americans."[39] Perhaps politics colored her statement, since in both dyestuffs and pharmaceuticals, the two greatest
users of verdigris, the Germans led the Americans in the early part of this century.
When production stopped, the old retired and the young workers "went to . . . embroider silk hosiery."[40] It is evident now that this was a trade with no future, and
surely as evident then that work in a regimented factory offered none of the financial and personal independence that had marked the cottage industry.

The production of verdigris might be described as a quintessentially preindustrial
occupation: other than its copper, readily available through trade, it required only
local, and predominantly agricultural, materials; it was labor-intensive; and it uti-
lized no machinery of any kind for its success.

It might also be described as a quintessentially feminine occupation, not only in
the obvious sense that almost all of its workers were female, but because it relied less
on skill than on heightened sensitivity, that is, to use the cliché, on "feminine in-
tuition." What Branca has said of another female industry, cheesemaking, is true of
verdigris production as well: "Knowledge was purely empirical, the art . . . handed
down from one generation to another. Here, as in most aspects of women's work,
there was little formal training and no concept of skills."[41]

The contemporary attitudes toward the special fitness of women for this work can only be guessed at. Both eighteenth- and nineteenth-century writers on the subject found the fact that the labor force was female to be worthy not only of comment but of repetition (Saintpierre reminds his readers almost from one page to the next that "the work is almost exclusively performed by women");[42] but neither value judgments nor speculation on the phenomenon entered their reports.

Certainly men could have done the work, but the fact is they did not. The ridicule offered as a reason by one of the commentators seems an insufficient reason unless, as was said above, it reinforced fears males might have had about the effects of the substance on their physical safety or sexual ability. Such fears did not keep men from involvement with toxic materials in other crafts, however—gilders worked with mercury in the production of ormolu even though its pernicious effects were recognized.[43] One is left with the admittedly unsatisfactory notion that in France, with its respect for tradition in the crafts, verdigris may have been a female trade simply because it had always been a female trade.

There is an indication of male opinions about verdigris workers in the anecdote about Rose Refreger, a story which implies that women were not capable of conceiving of more efficient methods, and that only chance in the shape of a donkey brought renewal to the industry. Jacques Montet, the eighteenth-century observer, had already deplored the resistance to technology shown by his informants when they rejected the thermometers he had offered as a means of judging the fermentation process.[44] The anecdote, however, had to demolish one myth in order to create another: the mutual suspicion attributed to women in the verdigris industry by eighteenth-century government workers had to be ignored so that the technique could be spread through the whispered back-channels of women's talk.

Perhaps more to the point, however, is the tacit acknowledgment of women's grasp of this craft found in the government brokerage commissions created in the early eighteenth century. To place women in such a position of influence—and, especially, to keep them there when the extent of their influence, and its financial possibilities, were made clear—obviously implies that the processes of verdigris production were comprehensible only to the initiated. Men could certainly tell whether the finished product was good or bad, because its quality affected their own work. To ensure that the processes used were those required by law, however, and to gain the workers' acceptance of these regulations, appeared to require the inside information available only to, and through, women. The value of the finished product was apparently enough, especially in mercantilist France, to overcome any distaste district administrators may have felt about dealing with "fishwives," and wealthy fishwives at that.

Certainly it is the wealth, or at least the financial independence, that verdigris made possible that gives the story of this craft its special interest. The methods by which knowledge was acquired and used are in no way unique; the recompense they brought is. In exercising this craft, and in so efficiently protecting it from male encroachment, by whatever means this was done, a group of women were for generations largely or completely self-supporting, able to start and direct businesses and, in certain cases, to gain real financial advantage and influence at a time when this was generally limited to the male aristocracy. The product they made has been superseded by modern materials; the opportunities it offered are only slowly becoming available to other women, in other fields.

Notes

An earlier version of this essay appeared in *Technology and Culture* 25 (April 1984): 171-81.

1. Evelyne Sullerot, *Histoire et sociologie du travail féminin* (Paris: Gonthier, 1968), pp. 56 and 62-63; Eileen Power, *Medieval Women*, ed. M. M. Postan (Cambridge: Cambridge University Press, 1975), p. 62.

2. Maité Albistur and Daniel Armogathe, *Histoire du féminisme français du Moyen Age à nos jours* (Paris: Editions des Femmes, 1977), pp. 179-80; *Recueil de planches sur les sciences, les arts libéraux et les arts méchaniques*, 11 vols. (Paris: Briasson, 1762-72). Additional insight into French female employment is provided by Elise Boulding, *The Underside of History* (Boulder: Westview Press, 1976), pp. 480-522; and Patricia Branca, *Women in Europe since 1750* (New York: St. Martin's Press, 1978), pp. 18-29.

3. Etienne Martin Saint-Léon, *Histoire des corporations de métiers depuis leurs origines jusqu'à leur suppression en 1791* (Paris: Guillaumin, 1897).

4. Sullerot, p. 62; E. Charles-Roux et al., *Les femmes et le travail du Moyen-Age à nos jours* (Paris: Editions de la Courtville, 1975), p. 64.

5. Georges D'Avenel, *Histoire économique de la propriété . . . depuis l'an 1200 jusqu'en l'an 1800*, 7 vols. (Paris, 1898; reprint ed., New York: Burt Franklin Research Source Works Series 236, 1968), vol. 3, pp. 491-524, 550-64, and 607-12.

6. Pliny, *Natural History*, trans. Harris Rackham, 9 vols. (Cambridge: Harvard University Press, 1947-63), vol. 9, pp. 209-15; *Encyclopedia Americana* (Danbury: Grolier, 1981), s.v. "Verdigris."

7. Jean Combes, "Le Verdet à Montpellier dans les derniers siècles du Moyen Age," *Bulletin Etudes sur Pezenas et l'Herault* 12 (1981-84): 23; Ghislaine Fabre, "Le Verdet en Languedoc à l'époque moderne," ibid., p. 38.

8. Combes, pp. 27-30, especially notes, 27, 37, and 49.

9. J. Thuile, *La Céramique ancienne à Montpellier* (Paris, 1943), p. 34, note 19; Fabre, p. 33.

10. *Encyclopédie, ou Dictionnaire raisonné des sciences, des arts et des métiers* (Paris: Briasson, 1751-72), s.v. "Verd-de-gris, ou verdet"; *Chambers' Cyclopaedia: or, An Universal Dictionary of Arts and Sciences* (London: D. Mid-winter, 1738), s.v. "Verdegrease."

11. Jacques Montet, "Mémoire sur le ver de gris," in *Histoire et mémoires de l'Académie Royale des Sciences 1750* (Paris, 1754), p. 400. Montet's memoir of 1750, and another of 1753 (see n. 13), were the basis of the article in the *Encyclopédie*, also written by Montet.

12. Jacques Montet, "Second mémoire sur le verd de gris," in *Histoire et mémoires de l'Académie Royale des Sciences 1753* (Paris, 1757), p. 609.

13. Montet, "Mémoire sur le verd de gris," p. 412.

14. Albistur and Armogathe, p. 179-80.

15. Montet, "Second mémoire," pp. 620-21.

16. Fabre, p. 33.

17. *La Nouvelle Bigarrure* 11 (January 1754): 37-42; *Annonces, affiches et avis divers*, Janu-

ary 2, 1754, n.p.; *Année littéraire* 6 (September 24, 1757): 199-201; *Supplément au Dictionnaire des sciences, des arts et des métiers* (Amsterdam: Rey, 1776-77), s.v. "Cuivre."

18. G. Pecholier and Camille Saintpierre, *Etude sur l'hygiène des ouvriers employés à la fabrication du verdet (vert de gris, acetate basique du cuivre)* (Paris: Asselin, 1864), pp. 10-34; Camille Saintpierre, *L'Industrie du Département de l' Hérault, Etudes scientifiques, économiques et statistiques* (Montpellier: Imprimerie Typographique de Gras, 1865), p. 32; and Jacques Montet, "Troisième mémoire sur le verd-de-gris," in "Mémoires de mathématiques et de physique présentés à la Société Royale des Sciences, et lûs dans ses assemblées, 1779" (manuscript of June 1, 1780, edited by Poitevin), pp. 356-57.

19. *Archives civiles—Serie C* (Montpellier: Ricard, 1887), c. 1691.

20. Ibid.

21. Joseph Berthele, *Archives de la ville de Montpellier* (Montpellier: Roumegous and Dehan, 1928), vol. 5, p. 337.

22. *Encyclopédie*, s.v. "Verd-de-gris, ou verdet."

23. *Archives civiles*, c. 2696.

24. Ibid.

25. Ibid.

26. Saintpierre, p. 39.

27. *Archives civiles*, c. 2692.

28. Watin, *Supplément à l'Art du peintre, doreur, vernisseur* (Paris: Grange, 1773), pp. 359-60.

29. Saintpierre, p. 39.

30. Felix Platter, quoted by Fabre, p. 33.

31. *Archives civiles*, c. 2690.

32. Ibid., c. 2689.

33. Ibid., c. 2689, 2692, and 2694.

34. Jean Sgard, "L'Echelle des revenus," *Dix huitième siècle* 14 (1982): 425-27.

35. Pliny, vol. 9, p. 209.

36. Montet, "Troisième mémoire," pp. 339-40; Louis-Sébastien LeNormand, *Manuel du fabricant du verdet* (Avignon: Seguin, 1813), pp. 69-72.

37. Berthele, p. 337.

38. Ibid.

39. Fabre, p. 38.

40. Ibid.

41. Branca, p. 20. See also Ivy Pinchbeck, *Women Workers and the Industrial Revolution, 1750-1850* (1930; reprint ed., London: Frank Cass, 1969), pp. 10-11. Interestingly, the eighteenth-century *Encyclopédie* makes no mention of female cheesemakers, and its plates show only men engaged in this occupation.

42. Cf. Saintpierre, pp. 32 and 38.

43. Reed Benhamou, "Furniture Production in 18th-Century France: An Interactive Process," *European Studies Journal* 1 (1984): 46–47.

44. Montet, "Troisième mémoire," pp. 622-24.

Women Flax Scutchers in the Linen Production of Hälsingland, Sweden

The water-powered scutch, or lintmill, was an important labor-saving invention in the production of linen in the eighteenth century. With this new technique, at least some of the laborious operations in the process of turning flax into linen were facilitated. The mechanization of braking and scutching was an obvious success, as the lintmills rapidly became widespread in those countries which are known to have had a significant linen industry. Like every other task in the manufacture of linen, braking and scutching were also characterized by a gender division of labor. However, although the technique was much the same in all types of lintmills, the gender division of labor was not.

In the area of my own research, the county of Hälsingland in Sweden, the braking of flax was performed mainly by men, and the scutching was entirely women's work. This was not, however, the case everywhere. In many countries scutching seems to have been an exclusively male preserve, and in some areas in Ireland, for example, there actually were no women at all working in the water-powered lintmills. Even more interesting, scutching was considered to be highly skilled work, not only in those areas where it was performed by men, but also in Sweden, where it was performed by women. A study of the water-powered lintmills could therefore prove to be a useful starting point for a discussion of technique, skill, and the gender division of labor in the preindustrial society.

The question of technique, skill, and the division of labor is not new. There has been a lot of research undertaken in this field by labor historians, sociologists, and others interested in the history of work and work relations. Not many of the studies have paid any attention to the question of gender, however. But since the 1980s, a growing number of researchers have stressed the fact that gender is an essential concept to consider in analyzing technical development, work, and the question of skill.[1] The subject has not yet been investigated in all its complexity, and more aspects are still waiting to be brought to light.

For one thing, there is a gap in our knowledge when it comes to preindustrial society, as hitherto attention has been given mainly to modern society and industrial work. The studies that exist on earlier periods refer primarily to craftspersons and artisans. There has been, however, a growing interest in the work and working conditions of the preindustrial rural society, an interest that originates largely from the international debate on protoindustrialization. In that context it has become interesting to discuss problems concerning technique, skill, and the division of labor, even though the production takes place in a rural surrounding. Linen production of the eighteenth and the beginning of the nineteenth centuries fits very well into the concept of protoindustrialization, and by studying the work in the water-powered lintmills, I hope to contribute to our understanding of these problems.

The Cultivation and Dressing of Flax in Hälsingland

Before industrialization, the method of preparing flax was common knowledge, and the technique differed only slightly from one place to another. Flax growing in Hälsingland was, up to the nineteenth century, part of a system of crop rotation consisting of grass or fallow, flax, different types of grain, and then again fallow. When the land in fallow was to be used for growing flax, it had to be plowed in the autumn and harrowed in the spring. Sowing, which usually took place at the end of May or the beginning of June, demanded a good sower and calm weather, as the seed is very light and difficult to handle. In contrast to many other flax-growing countries, there was seldom any need for weeding the flax field in Hälsingland because of the special kind of land used for this purpose.

The cultivation of flax was probably the least labor-intensive part of the process, while all other tasks demanded enormous efforts. Flax is an extraordinary crop in that it has to be pulled up by the roots. This work, which started at the end of August or the beginning of September, was extremely laborious as it was performed wholly by hand. Therefore, even if everyone on the farm, both men and women, participated in the harvesting, the number of workers was still insufficient and extra hands had to be hired.

In order to make the flax easy to handle, the seed was rippled off immediately after the harvest. The seed could be used for feeding cattle, but it was also sometimes used for sowing. Flax growers in Hälsingland, however, bought most of their linseed from abroad. The rippling was performed by two persons standing or sitting on each side of a ripple, which can be described as a big iron comb that is fastened to a wooden seat. Handful by handful, the flax was pulled through the ripple until the seed fell off onto the ground.

Next it was time for retting or watering. By sinking the flax into water for about two weeks, it was possible to dissolve a kind of glue which attached the fiber to the wooden parts of the stalk. The flax was tied together on a framework of wooden bars, resembling a raft, before it was sunk with the help of heavy stones. The retting process had to be supervised carefully because flax that had been watered too long produced linen of inferior quality. On the other hand, there could be problems with removing the fiber from the refuse if it was not retted enough. When the flax had been lifted out of the water it had to be dried, which in Hälsingland was done on drying racks or fences.

Although the fibers no longer were stuck to the stalk, they were not totally separated from the unusable woody parts. To start with, that woody stalk had to be crushed by braking. The methods used to brake the flax differed slightly from one area to another, and before the water-powered lintmills this process was performed by hand. It was considered to be very hard work beating the flax with a heavy wooden mallet against a stone as it was done in Hälsingland.

When the wooden stalk was crushed to pieces, these pieces of "shoes" had to be removed or scraped off the fiber. Even this work could be done in somewhat different ways. In Hälsingland, a "scutching knife" and a "scutching chair" were used for this purpose as long as the scutching was performed by hand. The "scutching chair" was a wooden post over which the flax hung. The scutcher held one end of the flax firmly against the post and with the other hand dressed the flax by swinging the "scutching knife," a kind of wooden paddle, against it, thereby making the "shoes" fall to the ground. Now and then the scutcher had to change her grip to be sure that all parts of the flax were dressed. In this condition the flax was ready to be sold as raw material, but if it was destined to become linen, there still remained several stages in the production.

The next stage in the process was heckling. By pulling the flax through a heckle, which could best be described as a kind of "iron brush," the long, fine fibers could be separated from the shorter, more coarse ones. This was important as different fibers produced different yarn, which in turn resulted in different types of fabrics.

As the spinning and weaving are more well known procedures, I will not go into a description of them. It could, however, be of some significance to know that the spinning wheel was not widespread in the northern part of Sweden, where Hälsingland is situated, until the beginning of the eighteenth century. Some writers even argue that the diffusion of this new spinning technique played an important role in the expansion of flax growing during this period, as the spinning wheel made it possible to spin greater quantities in less time than before.

Considering this laborious process, it is not hard to understand why the linen industry had such a small chance of standing up against the challenge from the cotton industry, especially since cotton fabric had many preferable qualities compared to linen. There of course were attempts to rationalize the production of linen, and the water-powered lintmills are an early example of this. But when it came to important developments concerning the mechanization of the spinning and weaving process, the cotton industry had a small but crucial lead. It was not until the 1790s that the technical problems of constructing a flax-spinning machine were finally solved, and a power loom for linen was still some decades away from use in the English linen industry.

In Hälsingland, a Swedish county with an old and considerable linen industry, the first and only factory for the spinning of flax was not established until 1897. By then the industrialization of Sweden was already in full progress, and the cotton factories had had a long time to expand their production since they first were introduced into Sweden in the 1820s. As a matter of fact, linen production never came to be of any importance in Sweden's industrial development, and Hälsingland took a totally different path into the industrial society. Not only had the county long been producing linen, but it also had extensive woods, which in the mid-nineteenth century became a valuable starting point for a flourishing lumber industry including sawmills and pulpmills.

The Water-Powered Scutching Mill or Lintmill

If the mechanization of spinning and weaving came too late to save the linen industry, the water-powered lintmill was an invention that came at exactly the right time. Not only in Sweden but in most major linen-producing countries, the growing of flax experienced a boom during the eighteenth century. Many factors, including a growing market for linen products, played a part in this expansion. In the case of Sweden, this was a period of immense activity in the reclamation of land. If the supply of arable land was extended, more flax could be grown without interfering with the growing of corn. The Swedish official policy of the time, which in a mercantilistic spirit was eager to replace as many imports as possible with domestic products, also contributed to the stimulation of linen production.

Thus, on the one hand, it had become possible to increase both the growing of flax and the selling of linen products, but on the other hand, the techniques in use were a severe obstacle to the possibilities of increasing production. Two of the central bottlenecks were braking and scutching, and throughout the eighteenth century an enormous amount of energy was spent on various experiments to rationalize these parts of the process. Exactly how the new techniques were developed, as to the original stimulus and if there existed influences from one country to another, is a story that we still know only to some extent. It is, however, interesting to note that in all major flax-growing countries it was the braking and the scutching that first became mechanized, and the technical solution to this problem was pretty much the same everywhere.

Through earlier surveys of the water-powered lintmills in Hälsingland, we are well informed about both the persons who were involved in the process of invention and the contribution that each of them made. The history of the lintmills seems to be a history of a number of enterprising eighteenth-century clergymen, from the dean Olof Broman, who started the experiments with water power in the year 1700, to the vicar Samuel Berg, who completed the scutching machine at the end of the same century. It is impossible to judge to what extent the local farmers contributed to the invention because, unlike the clergymen, they left no documents behind. There is, however, no evidence of the existence of special millwrights, so we can at least assume that it was the farmers themselves who actually built the lintmills.

Even though it is a fascinating story, it would take too long to look in detail at the technical development of the braking and the scutching machine. I will therefore only summarize the principal features of this story. Mechanizing braking proved to be an easy task, and this was done early in the eighteenth century. The technique of connecting a big wooden hammer or a wooden stamp to a water wheel was already in use for other purposes, and it was easily adapted to the use of braking flax. As a matter of fact, the technique was much the same as that used to perform the braking by hand.

Dean Broman tried to do the same thing with scutching, but his construction seems not to have been wholly suited for practical use. The simple "scutching knife," attached to a water wheel which made it move backwards and forwards, was difficult to handle, and Broman himself complained about stubborn scutchers who considered his invention to be much too dangerous for their fingers and consequently refused to use it. It was not until the end of the eighteenth century that the efforts to solve this problem were successful. Through a succession of inventions by different persons, the "scutching knife" gradually was transformed into a "scutching wheel." This machine, which was much more effective than Broman's construction, consisted of twelve to sixteen flat wooden blades ("knives") which rotated rapidly like spokes in a wheel.

The technique had not yet taken on its final form, and as the blade wheel was replaced during the eighteenth century with the vertical water wheel, it also became possible for one water wheel to provide power for more than one machine. This kind of "combined mill," which could contain a threshing machine, a braking and scutching machine, and a grinding machine, became the most widespread type in Hälsingland, and many travelers were amazed by those scutching mills, with their water wheels spinning around and around in almost every little river in Hälsingland. As early as 1764 it was possible to count eighteen flour mills and eight scutching mills in only one small river. In a way, these water-powered mills were a visible sign of the technical know-how possessed by the rural population of that time.

The buildings which housed the machines gradually were adjusted to suit the new technique. Originally the flax-dressing machines were placed in a fairly simple one-story house built of timber. By the turn of the century, however, the building had become both bigger and more specialized. The mill in its completed design had two stories, the first of which was always used for the braking stamps, while the "scutching wheel" was placed on the second floor. Figure 2 illustrates a typical water-powered lintmill from the nineteenth century.

The development of the mill also resulted in an alteration of the working place. In the new type of building the "scutching wheel" cut across the floor between the two stories and thus made it possible to arrange a place for the scutcher to sit while she performed the work. This, however, was only a minor improvement over the bad working conditions in the lintmills. The most severe problems were caused by the dust that whirled around in the air and sometimes caused the scutchers to get "mill fever." In Ireland the conditions in the lintmills were observed by factory inspectors, and a report from 1862 gives us the following picture:

> These mills as far as I am able to form an opinion, appear to me in general to be the narrowest, dirtiest and worst ventilated buildings for a labour so peculiarly dusty and distressing to the workers. As a rule, the Irish scutching mills are illbuilt, illkept,

Water-powered flax mill, exterior. Photo by Tors Erik (3Cat),
Nordiska Museet, Sweden.

unhealthy sheds packed with dangerous machinery, unfenced, revolving rapidly and
liable to entangle and perhaps destroy any person coming within its reach. As one
consequence accidents are frequent; and loss of life or limb invariably takes place
whenever an accident takes place.[2]

Accidents of this kind were not unknown in the lintmills of Hälsingland either, and
there are still people who can tell stories about scutchers who lost their fingers. In Sweden, it seems to have been primarily the scutching that was so dangerous, while there
are almost no remarks upon the danger of the braking machine. In countries such as
Ireland, on the other hand, where the braking was performed with rollers instead of
stamps, it seems to have been even more dangerous than the scutching.

The Social Organization of Linen Production
and the Gender Division of Labor

Compared to other cottage industries, linen production was seldom organized as
a putting-out system. Much more commonly, linen producers not only grew their
own flax but also were in control of both the making and the selling of their prod-

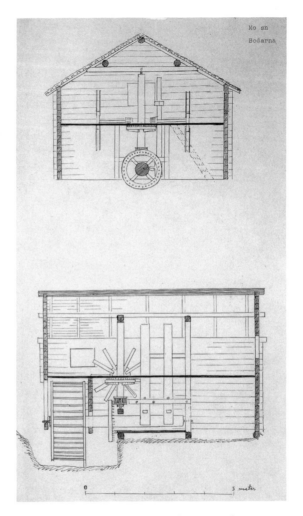

Cross-section of a typical nineteenth-
century water-powered flax mill.
Sketch by Olle Homman, 1940
(EU 16167), Nordiska Museet, Sweden.

uct. While on the one hand this model applied to the flax-growing farmer in Hälsingland, he also acted as a putting-out merchant, hiring people to work up the raw
material with which he supplied them.

This special organization can be partly explained by the fact that the need for raw
material was met by local suppliers, and in order to grow any larger amount of flax,
it was necessary for a farmer to have access to a large acreage. But at the same time

it was impossible for the farmer and his family to harvest and dress all the flax by themselves, and they were therefore forced to hire people to do it. In this way, not only the more well-to-do farmers but also crofters and smallholders came to be involved in the linen industry. This special kind of organization had some important implications for the gender division of labor in the linen industry of Hälsingland.

It is a well-known fact that people with little or no land earned their living by taking up work in the cottage industry. From other studies on protoindustrialization we also know that it was quite common for the whole family to become employed in the cottage industry, and that work which previously had been performed only by women as a consequence of a protoindustrial development could now be taken up by men.[3] In the case of Hälsingland no such changes occurred, however. Not even the introduction of a new technique, the water-powered lintmills, seems to have had any influence on the traditional gender division of labor.

When linen production increased, it was primarily for the laborious harvesting and scutching, and to some extent for the spinning and weaving, that the farmers had to rely on hired labor. This was the kind of work which had been performed by women in the days before the lintmills, and as there is no evidence of the existence of male scutchers, spinners, or weavers, we must assume that the only persons who really worked for wages in the linen production of Hälsingland were women. Why there were no employed brakers, as there were employed scutchers, can perhaps be explained by the fact that one braker could supply more than one scutcher with flax, and it may therefore have been enough if some of the men from the farm took care of this.[4] In a way, this social division of labor made it possible to maintain and reinterpret a traditional gender division of labor.

Male or Female Scutchers?

It is hard to ignore the importance of tradition, and the question of why an old pattern of labor division suddenly alters has been central to many studies on the gender division of labor. We can only speculate whether the division of labor in the Irish and Scottish lintmills was only a repetition of an earlier model, as in Hälsingland, because there is (perhaps as a consequence of insufficient sources) little available information on this. But even if that were the case, we still have to consider why there were differences between the countries at all. Technique itself is obviously not sufficient to explain why a certain task was coded as female or male, and many recent studies have shown that a technical development may alter the labor division in one case and not in another.[5]

To answer why the Swedish scutchers were women while the Irish and Scottish were men, we must therefore analyze not only the technique in a broader context, but also technique as one of many factors influencing the gender division of labor. In order to understand this, I think we have to return to protoindustrialization as a concept. There is no simple way to define this controversial concept, a concept which has given rise to a lot of interesting research as well as much theoretical discussion.[6]

Without going into the current debate, we can simply state that production in a protoindustrial area could be organized in many different ways, and that is of course what the "kauf-system" and "putting-out system" models indicate. Owing to the similarities in the conditions of growing and dressing flax and the techniques in use, it is likely that the organization of production would be much the same in different areas. This is also what the protoindustrial research has shown so far, and, as I have already mentioned, linen production seems to conform mainly to the "kauf-system" model, albeit with some variations, as in the case of Hälsingland. It would be wrong, however, to exaggerate the similarities, and the fact that linen production in different countries developed in its protoindustrial form during the same century does not mean that economic development was on the same level in these countries.

Sweden became industrialized very late, and its domestic market increased only slowly during the eighteenth and the first half of the nineteenth centuries. We can therefore assume that the linen producers in Sweden did not have the possibilities to increase their production at the same rate as their colleagues in Scotland and Ireland. Not only did the market put restrictions on the scale of production, but as a latecomer in industrial development, agriculture held the population in a firm grip in Sweden much longer than in other countries. Differences concerning to what extent the peasantry were freeholders may also have been a reason for variations in the organization of the cottage industry in different areas. The percentage of freeholders was traditionally very high in Sweden compared to other European countries.

Considering such different preconditions, due to a different market situation and a different social distribution of the rural population, it is not surprising that there were differences in the ways in which the water-powered lintmills were used in the various countries. While many of the lintmills of Scotland and Ireland can be compared to small industries which were operated almost year-round by workers who practiced scutching as a profession, the Swedish mills were nothing more than peasants' mills.[7]

In Sweden the scutching mills were used mostly in accordance with the seasonal variations of the working year on the farm. After the flax had been harvested in the early autumn, it was time for the dressing, and braking and scutching could be continued as long as the water did not freeze in the rivers. Although it was possible to use the mills again in the springtime, this seems not to have been very common, because by that time the flax should already have been worked up and transformed into yarn and linen. The linen cloth was bleached on the snow, and while the snow was still good for sleighing, farmers went away to market their cloth at the big seasonal fairs in places such as Uppsala and Stockholm. Thereafter came the spring and the summer with all the outdoor work, and it was not until the autumn that it was time for the flax again.

The fact that linen production in Hälsingland was so totally integrated into an agrarian context also explains the absence of any special professions. In contrast to many other protoindustrial areas, there are no professions connected to the textile trade listed in the parish records of Hälsingland. To judge from the records there were no spinners or weavers, not to mention any brakers or scutchers, living in Hälsingland during this period—only farmers, cottagers, soldiers, widows, and so on. But it was of course those farmers, cottagers' wives, and soldiers' widows who were actually the linen producers.

The mill owners in Hälsingland were also invisible, as they are found neither in parish records nor in any registers of taxpayers (because the water-powered flaxmills were not taxed.) From other sources we know, however, that farmers could own a flaxmill by themselves, but more common was a kind of company mill, owned by a number of farmers together—and sometimes even by a whole village. It was also possible to hire a lintmill, with the rents usually paid with a portion of the scutched flax. Whether those who hired the mill also hired their own scutchers is hard to say, because we have no written sources that give us information about agreements between the mill owner and the scutchers. From one area in Ireland we know, however, that "the farmer who sent his flax to his neighbor's mill also sent the people to be employed in scutching it. They often included his children who were expected to help just as any farmer might expect his children to help him with agricultural work that had to be done."[8] This may well be true for Hälsingland as well, although I have found no evidence of children working in the mills.

The Question of Skill

If we consider the kind of work which women and children performed in Scottish and Irish flaxmills, we again face the question of why women in Sweden were employed to do such a skilled work as scutching. What women and children were doing in the lintmills of Scotland and Ireland could hardly be regarded as skilled work—they fed the braking rollers with flax, and they assisted the scutchers by fetching, preparing, and handing flax to them. This was low-skilled and low-paid labor involving little control over the work process, the kind that we usually associate with women's and children's work in the early industrial society. But as modern research has revealed, it also reflects a gender division of labor which is a reality even in our contemporary labor market. Seen against this background, the existence of female scutchers in Sweden needs to be explained.

First of all we have to ask, in what way was scutching a task which contemporary observers in different countries considered to require years of training? In order to explain this we must understand that flax was a valuable raw material which had to be handled with care; otherwise the result would be a product of inferior quality. It was not only the quality that worried the producer, however. As the proceeds from growing flax were not significant, it was of great importance to be economical with the flax throughout the preparation process. The skill, in the case of scutching, was therefore of a special kind, which had more to do with a feeling for the material and a dexterity in handling it than with actually operating a machine. As the "scutching wheel" could rotate only at a speed dictated by the waterpower, the scutcher's work had to be adjusted both to that speed and to the quality of the flax.

On the whole, scutching seems to have been one of the most critical steps in the

Two men braking flax in a water-powered flax mill.
Photo Hälsinglands Museum, Sweden.

process, and it appears that the mechanization of this work increased the need for skill rather than the other way around. It was much more difficult to control the scutching while working with a swiftly rotating "scutching wheel" than it had been when the scutching was still performed by hand. The water-powered lintmill never became accepted in those areas of Sweden where fine and light linen fabrics were made, because people there were of the opinion that the scutching machine wore out the flax too much. In Hälsingland, however, where linen production was directed mostly to coarser linen such as canvas, the lintmill was a success.[9]

It is difficult to understand and discuss skill in an agrarian context because the concept has been developed primarily for studies of industrial work and artisans. But if we look at skill as a social construct which above all has something to do with power—for example, the power to define what kind of qualities should be considered skill—we must assume that the connection between gender and skill could vary in different times and in different societies. It is possible that, even if the agrarian society was marked by a gender division of labor, this division had less to do with skill than what came to be the case in the industrial society.

We can also interpret the gender division of labor in a way that takes into consideration both cultural and ideological aspects. The kind of work that women and men do must, in such an interpretation, also be seen as an expression of contemporary conceptions of what constituted femininity and masculinity. Thus, perhaps the scutchers in Hälsingland were female because the skill required for scutching

Women flax scutchers in a water-powered flax mill.
Photo Hälsinglands Museum, Sweden.

was considered a female skill in the Swedish context, although it was not in other countries. And the scutching may well have been female work because it corresponded to ideas about the qualities that a woman ought to have.

In order to obtain a full understanding of this special gender division of labor, we must finally ask not why women performed the scutching but why men did not. We have already stated that scutching had a long tradition of being women's work in Sweden, but there are aspects which may have caused this to change. That skilled workers and artisans have had an interest in guarding privileges which derived from their work in the form of high payment and high status is a well-known fact. Researchers have also been able to show that there is a tendency for men to take over and exclude women from this kind of work. What is more, examples from different protoindustrial areas indicate that an economically favorable development may cause men to take up what was previously women's work. Men in Hälsingland, however, seem not to have been interested in taking over the traditionally female scutching, even though it was skilled work. Neither do the mill owners seem to have been particularly interested in employing any men.

This behavior could be compared to the situation which Gay Gullickson has described in her study of a French protoindustrial area. The existence of a traditional gender division of labor prevented textile merchants there from employing women as weavers, even if, in theory, they could have done so at a lower cost. As a consequence of economic and technical developments, the preconditions of both agriculture and the textile trade changed in a way which produced full employment for men, while women had to face serious unemployment problems. "Eventually their [women's] search for work matched the merchants' and large farmers' search for workers, and a dramatic change occurred in the Caux. Women began to be hired to do men's jobs."[10]

In the case of Hälsingland this never happened, however; rather, it is as though the traditional pattern were reinforced. For one thing, scutching was never anything more than uncertain seasonal work, and in Hälsingland there was other seasonal work that must have appealed more to men, as those jobs, such as hewing and carting timber and burning and carting charcoal for the ironworks, had a long tradition of being a male preserve. Secondly, there was also a growing demand, due to the expansion of the lumber industry during the nineteenth century, for exactly that kind of labor which men in Hälsingland traditionally had performed. The linen industry, on the other hand, was in a severe decline at the same time.

It is also important to view skill not only in terms of the power to define what it should be, but also in terms of the power to maintain and express the same skill. In this respect the female scutchers in Sweden and the male scutchers in, for example, Scotland were in totally different positions. The male scutcher possessed a skilled profession, and he could probably use his position in a way that we have learned is common for this kind of work. The female scutcher was also performing skilled work, but it was not really considered to be a special profession. Women who were employed as scutchers came mostly from the lower social groups, and particularly there were many soldiers' widows among them. We can never prove that this was the case, but we have good reason to assume that these women after all did not have the same status as their male colleagues.

Taken together, these facts give us a good explanation of why the Swedish scutchers were all women. For a full answer to why this was not the case in other countries, a more detailed comparison is needed. Without having studied conditions in the linen-producing areas of Scotland and Ireland, I cannot say, for example, if the labor market for men was different there from that in Sweden, or if the scutching in those countries had a long tradition of being a male skill. Concerning the scale of production, the continuity in employment, and the question of scutching as a profession, there are, however, clearly visible differences. Rather than doing such a detailed comparison, my aim here has been to direct attention to the different kinds of preconditions that must be considered if we want to have a deeper understanding of skill, technical development, and the gender division of labor.

By this study I also hope to awaken a more theoretical interest in the question of skill and gender in the preindustrial rural society. A Swedish study of the link between protoindustrialization and the following industrialization highlights the importance of the problem. One of the subjects of the international debate on proto-industrialization has been the question of how preindustrial development contributes to the industrialization of an area. Judging from the Swedish study, one of the most important legacies of early rural industry was skilled workers. While this is an interesting result, on closer view it becomes obvious that it is mainly male skills, connected to the metal trade, that the authors are talking about.

Was there a similar development concerning female skills, or were women's special kinds of skills lost on the way to the industrial society because their jobs disappeared, or did previously female skills get a new code and become male skills? These are only some of the questions that still are awaiting an answer.

Notes

1. See, for example, Maxine Berg, "Women's Work, Mechanization and the Early Phases of Industrialization in England," in *On Work: Historical, Comparative and Theoretical Approaches*, ed. R. E. Pahl (Oxford, 1988); Cynthia Cockburn, *Brothers, Male Dominace and Technological Change* (London, 1984); Cynthia Cockburn, *Machinery of Dominance, Women, Men and Technical Know-How* (London, 1985); Martha Moore Trescott, ed., *Dynamos and Virgins Revisited: Women and Technological Change in History* (Metuchen, N.J., 1979); Joan Rothschild, ed., *Machina Ex Dea: Feminist Perspectives on Technology* (New York, 1983). For a review of works in this field, see Judith A. McGaw, "No Passive Victims, No Separate Spheres: A Feminist Perspective on Technology's History," and Joan Rothschild, "From Sex to Gender in the History of Technology," in *In Context: History and the History of Technology*, ed. S. H. Cutcliffe and R. C. Post (Bethlehem, Pa., 1989).

2. Quote from Marilyn Cohen, "Working Conditions and Experiences of Work in the Linen Industry: Tullylish, County Down," *Ulster Folklife* 30 (1984): 3-4.

3. See, for example, Gay Gullickson, "Love and Power in the Proto-industrial Family," in *Markets and Manufacture in Early Industrial Europe*, ed. Maxine Berg (London and New York, 1991); Jean H. Quataert, "Combining Agrarian and Industrial Livelihood: Rural Households in the Saxon Oberlausitz in the Nineteenth Century," *Journal of Family History* 10, no. 2 (1985); Jean H. Quataert, "Teamwork in Saxon Homeweaving Families in the Nineteenth Century: A Preliminary Investigation into the Issue of Gender Work Roles," in *German Women in the Eighteenth and Nineteenth Centuries*, ed. Ruth-Ellen B. Joeres and Mary Jo Maynes (Bloomington, Ind., 1986).

4. One estimation of the ratio is one braker to six to eight scutchers. N. E. McClain, "Scottish Lintmills, 1729-1770," *Textile History* 1, no. 3 (1968-70).

5. Beside the works listed in note 1, see also, for example, Joan W. Scott, "The Mechanization of Women's Work," *Scientific American* 247, no. 3 (1982): 137-51; Lena Sommestad, *Fran mejerska till mejerist* (with English summary: "From Dairymaids to Dairyman") (Lund, 1992); Ulla Wikander, *Kvinnors och mäns arbeten: Gustavsberg 1880-1980* (Lund, 1988).

6. For an introduction to the research on protoindustrialization and the debate, see, for example, L. A. Clarksson, *Proto-industrialization: The First Phase of Industrialization?* (London, 1985); D. C. Coleman, "Proto-industrialization: A Concept Too Many," *Journal of Economic History* 36 (1983); A. Florén and G. Rydén, *Arbete, hushall och region: Tankar om industrialiseringsprocessor och den svenska järnhanteringen*, Uppsala Papers in Economic History, Research Report no. 29 (with English summary: "Work, Household and Region: The Process of Industrialization and the Swedish Iron Industry") (1992); P. Kriedte, H. Medick, and J. Schlumbomh, *Industrialization before Industrialization* (Cambridge, 1981); P. Kriedte, H. Medick, and J. Schlumbomh, "Proto-industrialization on the Test with the Guild of Historians," *Economy and Society* 15 (1986); M. Berg, P. Hudson, and M. Sonenscher, eds., *Manufacture in*

Town and Country before the Factory (Cambridge, 1983); F. Mendels, "Proto-industrialization: The First Phase of the Industrialization Process," *Journal of Economic History* 32 (1972).

7. While there were small local mills in Ireland and Scotland beside the larger ones, practically all mills in Sweden were operated on a much smaller scale.

8. Cohen, "Working Conditions and Experiences of Work in the Linen Industry," p. 4.

9. Compare W. A. McCutchen, *The Industrial Archaeology of Northern Ireland* (Rutherford, N.J., 1984), p. 241.

10. Gay Gullickson, *Spinners and Weavers of Auffay* (Cambridge, 1986), pp. 96-107, but mainly pp. 104-105; quotation from p. 104.

Walter Endrei and Rachel P. Maines *3*

On Two-Handed Spinning

$\mathbf{T}$he often-quoted chapter thirteen of Marx's *Capital*, "Machinery and Large-Scale Industry," contains a puzzling statement:

> In Germany they tried at first to make one spinner work two spinning-wheels, that is to work simultaneously with both hands and both feet. That proved to be too exhausting. Later, a treadle spinning-wheel with two spindles was invented, but adepts in spinning who could spin two yarns at once were almost as scarce as two-headed men.[1]

Marx mentions *Spinnvirtuosen*, which means masterly performing male spinners, but no doubt at least some of these rare virtuosi must have been women. This assumption is rooted in a long tradition of literary, linguistic, and cultural evidence identifying those who spin as women. In the Western tradition, artifactual and documentary evidence associates women with spinning in Egyptian times, and by the time Homer wrote of Helen spinning at the court of Menelaus at Sparta, the femininity of the craft was well established.[2] In the familiar King James translation of the New Testament, Jesus of Nazareth asks his listeners to "consider the lilies of the field, they toil not, neither do they spin." While gender is not mentioned, it is likely that the *ou . . . oude* construction of the Greek in which the text comes down to us was meant to suggest a distinction between two kinds of labor, one traditionally performed by men and the other by women.[3]

The origins of spinning as female-gendered work may in fact be Neolithic, as old as spinning itself; deities of spinning, where they exist, are nearly always female.[4] It is possible that spinning (and indeed the textile arts generally) developed from gathering activities, since the finding and/or making of a container is the first requirement of gathering. Leaves, skins, and similar natural container materials must be fastened together securely if foodstuffs are to be carried in them for any significant distance. Gathering, an activity more compatible with childcare than is hunting, is nearly always gendered female, both historically and in modern gathering-and-hunting cultures.[5] The association of spinning with women is evident in language as well. We speak in English of the "distaff side" of the family, in French of inheritances as "tomber en quenouille," and in German of relations "über die Spindel verwandt." Like food preparation and child-rearing, textile production is a traditionally feminine and undervalued activity with paradoxically dramatic implications for the survival of the species.

The significance of textiles to culture at its most basic level stems from the vulnerability of the human body to extremes of climate.[6] Tacit or explicit cultural knowledge of this role of spinning in survival probably accounts for its associations with feminine power, wisdom, and virtue. In ancient Greece, the fate of each human being was thought to be embodied in a strand of yarn worked on a drop spindle by three goddesses, known as the *Moirae* or Fates. These women stood outside the world of physical reality, controlling birth, life, and death by spinning, measuring, and cutting off the magical silver yarn. In this paranoid fantasy of the late Mesolithic, textile producers stand between life and death for each individual. Like most such tales, it contains a germ of truth: textiles do often stand between life and death in potentially hostile environments.

Not only the Mediterranean has spawned such myths. The Hopi of North America believe that Spider Woman and her twin sons created the world and shaped its inhabitants by spinning and weaving a magical yarn. The Dogon of Africa assert that their messiah, the Nommo, taught humanity to speak (another survival adaptation) by spitting cotton threads from between his teeth.[7]

Without body coverings, human beings could inhabit less than 5 percent of the earth's land area. A development of the late Paleolithic, textiles have enabled the species to take up residence at every latitude from the equator to the polar circles, carrying on our backs the intimate shelter of our apparel. Textiles are sufficiently important to survival in the Quaternary that they may usefully be regarded as a kind of removable organ, an adaptive second skin that permits much greater flexibility than the fixed fur, feathers, and fat layers of our fellow vertebrates.[8]

Time and technology have only slightly modified our dependence on textiles. Buildings provide shelter from wind and precipitation, but not until the twentieth century could they be heated uniformly enough to obviate the need for warm indoor clothing in winter in subtropical, temperate, and cold regions. The products of spinning and weaving satisfied this fundamental need of humanity for warmth in a range of conditions, while spinners and weavers occupied the lowest rungs of the artisanal and, later, industrial hierarchy.

Spinning for family use is typically portrayed in literature and art as a virtuous and commendable feminine pursuit. As market activities, however, women's spinning and, later, apparel production have the dubious distinction of a consistent claim to the nadir of manufacturing wages throughout all of Western history, including the present. In the fourteenth century, for example, Piers the Ploughman met women who "whatever they save by spinning they spent on rent, or on milk and oatmeal to make gruel and fill the bellies of their children. . . . The miseries of these women who dwell in hovels are too pitiful to read or describe in verse."[9]

In this economic environment, improvements in productivity could mean the difference between survival and starvation. While great dexterity was required, some spinners apparently learned to spin two yarns at the same time even during the millennia of drop spindles, as G. M. Crowfoot asserts of Egyptian tomb representations of spinning:

> Many of these scenes show rows of women preparing flax fibres by hand. This may be regarded as hand spinning, and the final product as a partly spun thread [i.e., yarn] or rove for use of the spinners. This careful preparation no doubt contributed to the excellent quality of the linen. The same scenes often show spinning with two spindles at a time. Though this is an intricate way of spinning which requires great skill, it has been proved possible and modern instances are quoted. It goes to show what expert spinners the ancient Egyptians must have been.[10]

It may also go to show the economic pressures on the women artisans of Egypt. In Coptic times, a later text cited by Crowfoot speaks of a male spinner achieving similar ambidexterity: "forty-eight threads . . . which David has spun from each pair [of spindles]."

Like many writers, Crowfoot fails to recognize the distinction between thread and yarn. Yarn is the product of the spinning process, which imparts a twist in either the "s" or "z" direction to fiber prepared as roving or rolag. Thread is the hard-twisted product of plied yarns of linen, silk, or cotton.[11] Yarn can be produced from almost any fiber, the method of preparation depending on the fiber source. Wool, for example, must be carded after shearing to straighten and align the fibers. Pre-industrial carding was performed on two rectangular, slightly dished paddles to which leather card clothing was attached to the interior (convex) surfaces. Through this leather clothing, sturdy bent wires were punched to create a pair of working surfaces much like those of the modern brushes used for grooming pets. The carder worked the fiber between the paddles, pulling the wool back and forth across them until a smooth, relatively straight mass was formed. This was removed in a small bundle called a rolag and stored, usually in a basket, for spinning. Air circulation in storage was necessary, as wool is hygroscopic and will absorb up to three times its weight in water before it feels wet to the touch. While wool can be spun very fine, it could not until the eighteenth century be spun fine enough or plied tightly enough to produce the very strong and smooth products required for carpet warps, the longitudinal yarns in the loom. It is too rough and soft for use as a raw material for thread.

Linen is a plant fiber, the bast or longitudinal stalk fibers of the flax plant. Good linen is produced by pulling the stalks out of the ground whole, with the roots, and submerging bundles of them in water, a procedure called retting, until the plant pulp rots away from the bast fibers. The trash is removed from the bundles by pounding with a narrow wooden paddle, called scutching. The fibers are straightened in a process analogous to wool carding by drawing them through hackles, rectangular blocks of wood from which long iron spikes protrude. This separates the long fibers, called line linen, from the short fibers or tow. Line linen is sturdy and easy to spin; for centuries it was the only practical choice in Europe for the making of carpet and blanket warps. For this purpose the yarn was spun on the wheel more than once. The single-spun yarn was plied and hard-twisted with one or more additional yarns in the opposite direction from that in which it had been originally spun, either "s" or "z." The tow linen was the fiber of choice for making soft yarns for such end uses as undergarments, and for the making of thread. For this latter purpose, it was spun on small table wheels and then plied and twisted on the wheel a second time with other strands in much the same way carpet warp was made from line linen. This process was time-consuming, of course, and could not have been performed two-handed, as table wheels were hand-operated.[12] When cotton is spun by hand, a difficult procedure because of the shortness of the fibers, it is typically treated like tow linen, with an intermediate step of consolidating the combed fibers into roving, a soft, loose rope or elongated bundle.

Silk yarn was produced by two methods, neat silk by the traditional Asian method of reeling the 120-yard-long silk filaments from the cocoons and twisting them together, and spun silk by cutting the cocoons and spinning the noil or short fibers on a wheel, much like the process used for tow linen.[13] An expensive but very high quality sewing thread is produced by plying neat silk yarns.

From Neolithic times to the Middle Ages, the production of yarn in Western cultures was accomplished by twisting fibers together on a spindle suspended usually (but not always) from the spinner's dominant hand, rarely one from each hand, weighted with a whorl that served as a flywheel, regulating the rotary motion of the spindle. Fibers were fed to the yarn as it formed from a loose bundle on a forked stick or similar device, called a distaff. Whether spinning was performed standing or sitting, the spindle suspended from the attenuated fibers, twisted from the end of the spindle into yarn, eventually reached the floor. At this point the spinner paused to wind the yarn onto the shaft of the spindle, and to bring the spindle and its whorl or weight back up to shoulder or elbow height. This technique is called "drop" spinning, as the spindle is "dropped" as it rotates.[14]

Spinning techniques, whether hand or mechanized, vary considerably in accordance with the fiber being spun. Wool spins easily because the fibers are covered with scales that interlock readily when twisted and pulled. Although the cellulosic fibers of cotton and linen are smooth, the long fibers of line linen have considerable tensile strength, and their lengths, averaging from 30 centimeters to a meter, allow them to be joined by twisting. The shorter fibers of tow linen and of cotton are more difficult to spin, as more torque must be introduced per centimeter of spun yarn to make the fibers hold together in tension. It is difficult to imagine double hand spinning of cotton or tow linen.[15]

The spinning wheel translated the yarn attenuation, stretching, and twisting procedures from the vertical to the horizontal plane. The device is thought by some to have originated in ancient India, where it is in fact still in use. The primary fabric of India is, of course, cotton; the plant is indigenous there. Herodotus wrote of cotton being spun east of Persia in the fifth century B.C. Early Indian wheels had small knobs attached to a spoke; later and modern models were operated with a crank.

The wheel appeared in the Middle Ages first in Flanders and northern Europe, and was used in Austria in the fourteenth century. Changes and improvements were continuously made in the arrangement and dimensions of the wheel, distaff, and spindle. Although we have little documentary evidence, it seems likely that many of these innovations were made by women.[16]

Until the introduction of the flyer bobbin in the fourteenth and fifteenth centuries, the wheel spinner fed the fiber from the distaff and put tension on the yarn, into which she introduced torque by turning the spindle with one hand, drawing it back until she reached the limit of her arm's length. The rotation of the spindle was then reversed to wind the yarn onto it, and the cycle began again. The other hand was required to rotate the wheel, either with a crank or directly, as in the case of the great or walking wheel.

The flyer bobbin eliminated the winding step, as it wound the yarn during spinning, greatly enhancing the spinner's productive capacity. But both hands were still required to spin a single yarn, one to serve as the power source and the other for feeding fiber and drawing the yarn. Drop spinning with two hands required the use of both halves of the brain at an almost superhuman level of ambidexterity; wheel spinning with both hands added to this the requirement of a power source—the feet—to replace that of the spinner's subordinate hand.

Productivity gains in spinning and weaving have always been economically significant, as labor is the most costly input into textile production. In the Neolithic era, when textiles began to be traded over long distances, opportunities for saving and investment were, as one might expect, quite limited. Agriculture rewarded the worker with food for the family, and perhaps a surplus for trade, but few of its products kept well, and most were cumbersome to transport. Toolmaking was an honored and remunerative skill, but it required, both for education and for production, exemption from at least some of the endless labor of subsistence farming. Textile production, on the other hand, was highly compatible with agriculture, since its raw materials could be raised as part of the farming enterprise, and the labor of spinning and weaving could be carried out during the winter, when crops did not demand attention. Significantly, in the case of women, textile production was more compatible with childcare than such activities as hunting and warfare. As a trade good, cloth could be transported easily, did not spoil as grain, fruit, and vegetables did, was available at all seasons, and even a small family could produce a surplus over immediate needs. The market outside the community for such products consisted of two main groups: those from distant areas whose textiles were different and who wanted to trade for variety, and those whose specialized function in Neolithic society, such as warrior, hunter, or toolmaker, prevented their engaging in textile production themselves.

By 2000 B.C. cloth had become an important medium of trade, carrying with it not so much the value of its raw materials as of the labor invested in it. Textiles' position as the cornerstone of the trading economy had been elevated to symbolism of almost mystical significance as the embodiment of group identity. In the twelfth century B.C., flags were already well established as symbols of *esprit de corps*. Loss of the symbolic scrap of fabric held aloft in battle, then as now, meant demoralization, often followed by defeat. Costume, too, had already become a means of demonstrating economic power and personal rank.

Throughout antiquity, textiles were an important component of intercontinental trade. Linen traveled from Egypt as far north as Britain, cotton and silk came to the Mediterranean overland from India and China, and wool was traded everywhere along the coastal areas of Europe and Britain.

By the eighth century A.D., patterns of textile economics had begun to emerge that were to persist, in modified form, well into the modern era. Britain, for example, had begun exporting wool to continental Europe. Five centuries later, wool had become so significant to the economy of the British Isles that a red sack of it became, as it still is, the permanent seat of judges' court and of the Lord Chancellor in Parliament, lest these officials forget the source of Britain's power.

International rivalries inevitably arose, made especially bitter when competing nations were at war. France and Italy struggled for control of the international silk market from the fourteenth century until well into the nineteenth. Britain held its leading position in wool textiles with difficultly against stiff competition from nearly every European nation. Then as now, systems of tariffs and restrictions were imposed to protect domestic industries; few of these are thought to have been successful. Prohibitions of certain fabrics, such as the ban on Belgian lace in France and that on imported cotton in Britain in the seventeenth century, simply made these commodities more expensive and fashionable on the black market.

In this environment, an innovation that could double productivity in spinning would have created a considerable competitive advantage, and indeed did so when the spinning jenny and spinning mule were invented in the eighteenth century. Spinning two yarns at once on human-powered machinery proved so difficult that it was never implemented on a large scale. Our sources are silent for a millennium or so after David's achievement, but the idea was taken up again at some point in the seventeenth century. Sometime after 1600 in Europe, foot-powered spinning was introduced. The pedal had long been known for driving emery wheels and lathes; in the seventeenth century it was attached to a drive band on the spinning wheel. The speed of spindle rotation could be increased considerably with foot power, and it was thus necessary to deliver fibers and impart tension to the yarn at an accelerated rate. According to Mokyr's discussion of the industrial revolution in textiles,

> The central technical problem in textiles was that of spinning. Since time immemorial, the crucial operating part in the spinning process had been the human finger, the thumbs and index fingers of millions of women who gave the raw materials in the rovings the "twist" that made it into yarn. The spinning wheel increased the efficiency of the spinner's work, but did not replace the human finger as the tool that transformed the material.[17]

The release of one of the spinner's hands from turning the wheel might have given the impetus to new efforts to employ this anatomical resource in two-handed spinning, but it seems likely that other technological and economic factors played a role as well. Weaving productivity began to accelerate in England and elsewhere in the 1730s, putting pressure on spinners to produce more yarn. Later in the century, developments in spinning machinery were to reverse the situation, producing "demand pull" innovations in looms and their power sources. Clothiers, some of whom operated integrated protoindustrial factories employing hundreds of textile artisans, were especially concerned about maintaining workflow from spinners to weavers.[18] After the middle of the eighteenth century, hand spinners, especially those in worsted yarn, faced competition from power machinery that drove piece rates down. The spinning jenny and spinning mule both employed the principle of the great or walking wool wheel, in which the spinner attenuated the yarn by simultaneously stretching the yarn from the spindle, turning the wheel, and walking away from it. The machinery placed the spindles on a moving rack that "walked," or rather rolled, away from the distaffs that held the roving. These were, of course, multiple-headed so that a number of yarns were spun at once. Not only could these machines spin more yarn faster than even the most ambitious and ambidextrous hand spinner, but the mule could spin and ply a woolen yarn strong and smooth enough for carpet warp.

The double-headed wheel's place of origin is difficult to determine, but a case can be made for its emergence in England or France in the seventeenth century. The English origin is supported by the fact that its earliest representation is found in a letter of the philanthropist Thomas Firmin in 1681. It had already become well established in England by the eighteenth century. W. Bailey describes three different wheels of this type in the 1760s, and Macquoid's work on English furniture mentions a late seventeenth-century double spinning wheel.[19] Alastair Durie cites evidence that two-handed spinning wheels were being introduced into the Scottish linen industry in 1757, as part of a larger program to improve spinning productivity.[20]

There is evidence from the middle of the eighteenth century about technological transfer of the process to the northern countries and to France in the form of schools where the two-handed spinning was taught to girls and women. The first data came from Scandinavia, where an inventor, Abraham Hedman, is mentioned in 1738. A teacher of the technique, Elisabeth Forsellt, was sent to Finland, which had several spinning schools about 1750.[21]

A spinning school is depicted in a drawing by G. de Saint-Aubin (1724-80), now in the École des Beaux Arts, Paris. It shows at least forty young women spinning in a large room. The equipment, shown separately in the right corner, has one wheel in the middle driving two spindles with flyer bobbins. The fibers are spent from a single distaff, drawn with both hands.[22] The inventor of this wheel, de Bernière, had in mind training children to take advantage of what he took to be their natural ambidexterity. In Germany, the first evidence of double-spindle spinning is given by Krunitz, according to whom a certain Herr von Wullen improved a French prototype in 1760.[23]

In Austria, Josepha Sedlmayer is credited with having invented the double-spindle wheel in 1782, although her device clearly postdated similar inventions elsewhere. She developed her machine in Bruun (Brno), and her method was subsequently transferred to Klagenfurt in 1785, and then to Pozsony (Bratislava), then the capital of Hungary.[24] The Klagenfurt school still existed in 1793, when a Hungarian woman, Erzsébet Martini, applied for a *privilegium exclusivum* (patent) for her "spinning-machine," which she used in her "spinning school for two hands."[25] She claimed that this school trained fifty women in the skill. Some of the artifacts of this technolgocial movement have survived at the Technisches Museum in Vienna, which has several double-spindle wheels from the period of the Austro-Hungarian monarchy.[26]

The double-spindle wheel lost ground in these countries when spinning jennies escaped governmental efforts to control their spread and appeared in Vienna and Pozsony between 1787 and 1789. By 1811, a blueprint for Arkwright's water frame had been published in Pest. It seems doubtful that Arkwright's invention had much immediate effect on spinners of wool and flax, but as the harbinger of a trend it must certainly have suggested that the pace of spinning generally was undergoing irreversible acceleration.

The perception of actual or potential competition from other multiple-spindle machinery such as jennies may account for the double-spindle wheel's persistence in some German countries, where it survived tenaciously into the nineteenth century. Spinners may have felt a need to increase productivity in order to survive. Rettich mentions the invention of a certain Roemer in 1821, and gives a precise picture of Walter's wheel.[27] Vallinheimo writes about one Alois Mager of Würtemberg, whose wheel had been introduced in Sweden in the 1840s, but which cannot have represented much of an improvement in efficiency, as it required two women to spin on it.[28] In a German weaver's sampler of 1841, the introduction enumerates five different wheels of this kind, two of which are pictured.[29] The author describes the difficulties of spinning with both hands:

> It takes a lot of practice to pull the two strands out of the distaff using both hands simultaneously. In particular this requires agility because one hand must help the other separate the bundles into their constituent fibers so that a homogeneous yarn is spun. In order that this can be made easier, it is necessary to have not only a very well hackled flax, but also the flax must not be wound tightly around the distaff.[30]

This description shows that the device could be used only with excellently prepared flax; a part of the time saved had to be invested in the hackling process. Hackling is not, however, as skilled an activity as spinning, and good hacklers must have been far more plentiful than ambidextrous spinners. In addition, hackling is typically performed at a different time of year than is spinning, so the additional time burden required to prepare it for this type of spinning might not have been apparent to spinners.

The German inventors of this equipment made productivity studies which claimed that yarn output per unit of time could be doubled with their device. Müller, however, states that the double-spindle wheels "are not fit for fine yarns, as these require the undivided attention and the cooperation of both hands of the spinner." He then gives measurements of productivity showing that in a workday of thirteen hours, coarse numbers [Nm 13-17] ought to be spun in a relation of 2:1, i.e., 3,940 meters on the single- and 7,880 on the double-spindle wheel.[31] This diminishes with somewhat finer numbers [Nm 30-34] to the proportion 1.5:1, and becomes equal with the finest linen yarn [Nm 47-50]. That would mean that over a fineness of about Nm 40, the double-spindle wheel had no advantage. Rettich does not mention the fineness of yarn, but indicates 498 meters per hour for the double and 350 m/h for the single wheel, corresponding to the Müller data for about Nm 30 yarns. However, it seems doubtful whether anyone had the capacity to spin with both hands for thirteen hours a day. Jeremy provides figures of "340 yards of low-count (2-run) woolen yarn an hour on the [single] wool or spindle wheel (not including fiber preparation, chiefly carding)—some 4,080 yards in twelve hours" in eighteenth-century New England.[32]

Between 1880 and 1920, this spinning wheel for virtuosi was still used in remote places before finding its way into museums.[33] There is an analog in the brief fashion in the United States during World War I for knitting two socks at once on the same pair of needles; the technique was too demanding to remain popular after the war.[34] It is possible that the eighteenth-century double-spindle wheel was used for special occasions such as spinning contests in some places longer than it was used as a production mechanism; this may have been how Marx came to hear of it. We cannot call the appearance of two-handed spinning anything but an intermezzo in the preindustrial development of European countries, which brought additional burden and stress to the mainly rural working women whose economic condition in difficult times required productivity almost beyond human capacity. Had not Marx thought two-handed spinning to be a rare exception, he would have denounced it as an example of the total exploitation of the body.

Notes

1. Karl Marx, *Capital: A Critique of Political Economy*, introduction by Ernest Mandel, trans. Ben Fowkes (rpt., Harmondsworth, Middlesex, England: Penguin Books, 1976), vol. 1, p. 495.

2. R. J. Forbes, *Studies in Ancient Technology* (Leiden: Brill, 1956), vol. 4, p. 159; Homer, *Odyssey*, Book 4, lines 129-37. See also G. M. Crowfoot, "Methods of Handspinning in Egypt and the Sudan," *Bankfield Museum Notes*, 2nd ser., no. 12 (1931): 9-32.

3. Matthew 6:28 and Luke 12:27.

4. James George Fraser, *The Golden Bough* (New York: Macmillan, 1951), p. 23; Verla Birrell, *The Textile Arts* (New York: Schocken, 1973), pp. 14-15. In Egypt the goddesses Iris and Nephtys are called the "two spinstresses." We may call to mind, in addition, the Chinese Si Ling, Indian Ila, and Greek Pallas Athene (significantly, also the goddess of wisdom).

5. We reverse the normal word order here as the vast majority of all food consumed by gathering-and-hunting societies is gathered, not hunted. For the role of textiles in such cultures, see Elizabeth C. Baity, *Man Is a Weaver* (London: Harrap, 1947), and Horace Miner, "The Importance of Textiles in Archaeology," *American Antiquity* 1 (1935-36). The compatibility of commercial spinning with other home-based activities in medieval times is men-

tioned by A. R. Bridbury, *Medieval English Clothmaking: An Economic Survey* (London: Heinemann Educational Book for the Pasold Research Fund, 1982), p. 11.

6. Thus Thomas Carlyle's remark in *Sartor Resartus* that "Society is founded upon Cloth."

7. Evelyn Hively, "Weaving Myths," *Handwoven* (March 1982): 10-13.

8. There is a voluminous scientific literature on clothing and survival, most of it produced by the military of various nations, especially the United States, Germany, Russia, Canada, Switzerland, and Great Britain. For readily accessible examples, see A. P. Gagge et al., "The Influence of Clothing on the Physiological Reactions of the Human Body to Varying Environmental Temperatures," *American Journal of Physiology* 124 (1938): 30-50; W. H. Hall, "Medical Problems of Military Operations in Extremes of Heat and Cold," *Military Medicine* (July 1964): 641-51; C. S. Leithead and A. R. Lind, *Heat Stress and Heat Disorders* (Philadelphia: Davis, 1964), p. 71; and Col. Tom F. Whayne and Michael DeBakey, *Cold Injury, Ground Type* (Washington, D.C.: Department of the Army, 1958), p. 1-30.

9. William Langland, *Piers the Ploughman* (Harmondsworth: Penguin Books, 1982), p. 260.

10. Crowfoot, "Methods."

11. This subject is explored in greater detail in two articles by Rachel Maines: "Paradigms of Scarcity and Abundance: The Quilt as an Artifact of the Industrial Revolution," in *In the Heart of Pennsylvania: Symposium Papers*, ed. Jeannette Lasansky (Lewisburg, Penn.: Oral Traditions Project, 1986), pp. 85-89; and "The Tools of the Workbasket: Needlework Technology in the Industrial Era," in *Bits and Pieces: Textile Traditions* (Lewisburg, Penn.: Oral Traditions Project, 1991), pp. 110-19.

12. This process is illustrated in Sylvia Groves, *History of Needlework Tools and Accessories* (England: Country Life Books, 1966).

13. This procedure is illustrated in Mario Bussaglia's *Cotton and Silk Making in Manchu China* (New York: Rizzoli, 1980, second series of plates [unpaginated]). The captions to the illustrations should be disregarded, as the author, who seems to be an art historian, clearly does not understand the technology depicted.

14. One of the best practical descriptions of hand spinning is Marion L. Channing's *The Magic of Spinning* (Marion, Mass.: Reynolds-Dewalt, 1967).

15. Line linen is the long bast fiber of the flax plant, after hackling to remove the short fibers. Tow are the short fibers left in the hackles, which make a softer but less durable yarn.

16. See Daryl M. Hafter, "Agents of Technological Change: Women in the Pre- and Postindustrial Workplace," in *Women's Lives: New Theory, Research and Policy*, ed. Dorothy G. McGuigan (Ann Arbor: University of Michigan, 1980), pp. 163-64. See also Walter Endrei's "Changements dans la productivité, l'industrie au Moyen Age," *Annales: Economie, Sociétés, Civilisations*, 26 (September–December 1971): 1292-93 and 1299.

17. Joel Mokyr, *The Lever of Riches: Technological Creativity and Economic Progress* (New York and Oxford: Oxford University Press, 1990), p. 96.

18. E. Lipson, *The History of the Woollen and Worsted Industries* (London: A. and C. Black, 1921), pp. 50-53, 134-36, and 182-84. Lipson observes on p. 134 that "in 1750 a wheel was invented to spin with both hands, turned with the feet."

19. Thomas Firmin's letter is cited in P. Baines, *Flax and Linen* (Haverfordwest, 1985), pp. 11, 13, which also gives his illustration of a woman using a two-handed spinning wheel. See also W. Bailey, *The Advancement of Arts, Manufacture and Commerce* (London, 1772); and Edward Macquoid, *The Dictionary of English Furniture* (Edinburgh: John Donald Publishers Ltd., 1979), p. 75.

20. Alastair Durie, *The Scottish Linen Industry in the Eighteenth Century* (Edinburgh: John Donald Publishers Ltd., 1979), p. 75.

21. V. Vallinheimo, *Das Spinnen in Finnland* (Helsinki, 1956), p. 200.

22. Reproduced in *CIBA Rundschau*, no. 30, p. 1122. This appears to be a sort of missing link between the double-spindle wheel and the jenny depicted in the *Encyclopédie Méthod-*

ique. The invention of one "sieur Price" had the following appearance: "vingt-cinq fileuses autour d'un cinconférence de dix pieds de diametre, chaque ouvrière filant deux fils à la fois; un enfant de dix à douze ans, d'une seule main peut, la machine, faire mouvoir. . . . "

23. J. G. Krünitz, *Ökonomische-technologische Encyklopädie* (Berlin, Tiel, 1833), p. 93.

24. State Archives, H.t.t., Dep. Commerc., fons 44 (Budapest, 1793).

25. State Archives, M. Kir. Kanc., *Acta generalia,* 1793/8244 (Budapest).

26. Museum inv. nos. 12,447, 12,451, and 21,729.

27. Rettich, *Spinnradtypen Wien* (1985).

28. Vallinheimo, *Das Spinnen in Finland,* p. 201.

29. *Neuestes Weber- und Muster-Buch* (Ulm, 1841), pp. 36-37.

30. Ernst Müller, *Handbuch der Spinnerei* (Berlin, 1891), pp. 14-16.

31. Nm, the metrical number of a yarn, indicates how many meters of it weigh one gram.

32. David Jeremy, *Transatlantic Industrial Revolution: The Diffusion of Textile Technologies between Britain and America, 1790-1830s* (Cambridge, Mass.: MIT Press, 1981), p. 219.

33. Slavic people (Polabs) between the Elbe and Oder rivers in Germany. Tetzner, *Die Slaven in Deutschland* (Braunschweig, 1902), p. 363, provides the only known photograph of such a spinner. Swedish spinners in Shonen (Vallinheimo, p. 201) might have been the last.

34. Mrs. A. Reeder, "How to Knit Two Socks at Once," *Needlecraft* (August 1918). Errors in this technique would result in the two socks being joined, one inside the other. See also Ann L. MacDonald, *No Idle Hands: The Social History of American Knitting* (New York: Ballantine, 1988), pp. 199-238.

Women Who Wove in the Eighteenth-Century Silk Industry of Lyon

$\mathbf{A}$s historians have turned their attention to women's work in the preindustrial era, we now have a far more comprehensive understanding of the contributions women have made to the economy. The importance of women's dowries in starting the family farm, workshop, or business has been documented by Olwen Hufton, Maurice Garden, Sarah Maza, and Theresa McBride.[1] Other scholars have called our attention to the family economy in both cottage industry and urban trades.[2] We have been alerted to the preindustrial practice by which most craftsmen married in order to start a workshop. Laura Strumingher has demonstrated for the silk industry of Lyon that this tradition was carried on into the nineteenth century.[3]

Despite the wealth of new information, however, we are still in the dark about many aspects of wives' actual contribution to the regulated urban craft industry. Did guildmasters' wives perform solely managerial functions, or did they also work in the family trade? What happened after the bride contributed her hard-won dowry to create a family business? Did the guild value wives' and daughters' productivity? Were the masters' wives in competition with women workers who had no guild family ties? Did guild journeymen resent working with masters' wives?

This chapter will show why women's "shadow labor" was crucial for silk production in Lyon and how the terms of female employment became a subject of contention between factions within the guild. The major controversy between the master weavers and the merchants within the *Grande Fabrique*, as the silk guild was called, came to a climax during the eighteenth century. This struggle pitted master weavers, eager to retain the right to accept commissions on their own right, with the merchants, who wanted to gain exclusive control of the connection between the market and workers. When masters' wives could weave for employers outside the home, they contributed to the independence of guild families.

After many political conflicts within the guild, the merchants succeeded in reducing the master weavers to the level of virtual wage workers. Although nominally still masters, they had to accept contracts on the merchants' terms, since it was illegal for them to undertake work on their own behalf or to profit from the manipulation that direct contact with the market would afford. The 1744 statute that forbade master weavers' wives from legally working outside the home ateliers was a means of reducing the weavers' economic independence; it was also a sign of the master weavers' political defeat within the guild.

Enlightened administrative reformers who entered the intraguild struggle by midcentury appreciated the economic and symbolic role that women workers played. By fostering legislation permitting drawgirls to weave, the officials lent weight to the merchants' cause. They suggested that drawgirls, unrelated to guild families, could be used as cheap substitutes for master weavers. Thus royal officials consciously promoted the freedom of women's work as a means of curtailing the guild monopoly.

After the Revolution had suppressed the guilds, the family workshop found itself under pressure from the proliferation of Jacquard looms and the competition of innumerable workers in countryside and town. Ironically, it was the work of unrelated female weavers, willing to accept low wages and household board, that allowed urban family workshops to persist through the early years of the Industrial Revolution.

The Elusive Women Workers

For a number of reasons, ascertaining the contribution married women made to urban trades before the French Revolution is one of the most difficult fields of inquiry. Even when women retained their maiden names, as they generally did in the eighteenth century, their "covered" legal status as wives obscured their economic activities. In the family workshop, particularly the guild workshop, production was considered to be in the hands of the men. Unless the guild was open to female masters, the men alone were part of the prestigious group of sworn licensees. By virtue of their accepted "citizenship" in the guild, they provided management for the family business and political direction for the guild. The wife, children, and hired girls, meanwhile, were supposed to perform auxiliary, unskilled work.[4]

How could it be any other way, when females were generally deprived of formal training as apprentices? This is the view that has begun to emerge from recent scholarship. Earning their keep before marriage in the least desirable jobs, most females hired on as servants, industrial drudges, and day workers in any number of unskilled and semiskilled jobs. After marriage, women picked up the unskilled tasks that flowed from their husbands' trade. Frequently, the skills they had already developed were of no use in their new circumstances—if the bride moved from town to farm after marriage, for example, or if her husband's craft was different from what she did before marrying. While men's trades provided them with formal classification in official records and nicknames characterizing their trades, women's work identity was frequently undocumented. In sum, researchers have characterized married women as having an ephemeral work identity, which enabled them to turn their flexibility to their family's advantage.[5]

From a theoretical viewpoint, there are two problems with this conception. First, as historians repeat the judgment that women's work was not skilled and that women did not have a strong work identity, we come to associate women's work in a prescriptive way with unskilled work. It becomes almost automatic, then, to use the term "women's work" as a tag for unskilled labor. We then confirm the assumption that whether women were well paid or poorly paid, their employment was to perform rudimentary tasks, which were auxiliary to the main functions of the craftworker.

This definition leads to a second theoretical problem: we misunderstand the preindustrial era's conception of "skill." Before the Industrial Revolution, most techniques used in a particular craft were similar throughout Europe. As Michael Sonenscher suggested, in the preindustrial world, skill was found wherever people worked. Workers did not require drastically specialized training to use the tools of that era proficiently. Most techniques required practice rather than abstract schooling to be performed well. Therefore, to give skill the cachet of a special quality that could be monopolized, guilds clung to the idea that craftwork involved "secrets" that could be learned only from guildmasters.[6] In fact, skill was often an artificial label that shed more light on the sex and status of the worker than what was produced. Given the standards of gender-based work, the employment of males was readily designated as "skilled." This is in part because males were automatically paid more, and calling their activities skilled justified the higher salary, a reason that seemed to inhere in an unassailable rationale. This rationale was challenged when women workers entered industries and took over men's jobs either spontaneously or because management was purposely trying to undermine the male workers. Because society was unwilling to admit that work done by a skilled male worker could also be done by a skilled female worker, entrepreneurs changed the name of the task or altered it so that it could be reclassified. Thus reeling silk, the highly skilled technique of unwinding the cocoon and cleaning and winding the raw silk, was classed as low-paid "women's work" in both the eighteenth-century preindustrial workshop and the nineteenth-century factory. The fact that this task was crucial to the silk industry was irrelevant to its payment. It was the worker who set the standard for pay, not the work.

In the early period, nonguild workers who were not apprenticed or formally examined and licensed were known as unskilled, cheap workers. Women too, no matter what their actual capacity, usually fell into the nominal category of the unprofessional, the untrained. Thus the gender system contributed to the social structure of work and made for a segmented system of economic activity. Since many skills could be acquired by informal training, however, women in some guild families became adept at the family manufacture.

These unofficial workers contributed to the family economy without challenging the guild framework. In this way, gender was used to designate a group of workers whose access to skilled work would not require them to be given privileged status.

The unit of the family workshop blended into the guild structure: skill was taught in the family unit, which was also the guild unit. Thus the hands-on nature of acquiring techniques could not be generalized to the outside world. Those with familiarity and experience with the trade—sons and daughters, and sometimes wives of masters—were acknowledged to gain proficiency by hands-on experience. Others brought into the family setting to get the same training received the designation of apprentices.[7]

While the family workshop accorded well with the social structure of the precapitalist or protocapitalist era, it contained problems of definition that would become irritants in difficult times. This was mainly because the artisanal system conflated the economic hierarchy of work skills with the social structure of the family relationships. As master of the trade, the father set the standards for training and acted as business manager at the same time that he provided the legal and moral focus of family life. The state expected that in his person he would combine the dual qualities of technical and moral authority. This gave the guild system its niche within traditional society and made it appear to be a quintessentially patriarchal institution.[8]

Women's place in this system adds to our difficulty in gaining concrete evidence which can help us understand what women workers did and how their employment was perceived. Three factors have contributed to this lack: (1) We have found it difficult to discover the importance of married women to guild manufacture because they were so infrequently listed as bona fide workers. (2) Our present preconception of women as domestic workers, or at the most managers, led us astray. (3) The guildmasters of the past also had a hand in misleading us by their disingenous treatment of women's work, an attitude that had everything to do with their own material interests. Guild families used a variety of strategies to apply women's work to current needs. By alternately revealing and concealing women's activities, depending on how the political climate shaped guild regulations, guild families took advantage of women's work capacity without necessarily crediting them with the skills so automatically pressed into service. Because contemporaries in the crafts were perfectly conversant with this shadow economy, these practices were not necessarily recorded. Thus documentation is difficult to find and must be pieced together from such indirect sources as laws and guild tracts.

Even current scholarship may have obscured the women workers' perspective about their work. While much crucial investigation has informed us about the importance of dowries in beginning a family farm, workshop, or business, we invariably perceive them as a donation to found a family, resources that enabled the husband to work. To be sure, with men's salaries twice those of women, providing a vehicle for men to work made rational economic sense. But the new economic unit also provided a means for the wife to maximize her work efforts, not only by assisting the husband but by contributing to the pool of production that was subsumed under the mantle of the husband's privilege. In the family workshops of Lyon's silk industry, wives participated in the work, which included the prestigious task of weaving, and formed a sizable part of the labor force.

Lyon: Capital of Industry

Lyon's role as a large, centralized, industrial city ironically encouraged this use of corporate privilege, whereby the guildmasters' wives provided work in the home atelier. Located in what was then France's second-largest city, with its population rising to 143,000 inhabitants by 1789, Lyon's silk industry presented a striking example of merchant capitalism. Approximately 25 percent of the working population was employed in some aspect of silk manufacture. As a luxury industry, tightly controlled by guild officials who were under the influence of the wealthy entrepreneurs, the silk manufacture was a natural setting for a large capitalist export industry. Its labor history focused on the struggle between the large-scale merchants' campaign to control the industry and the master weavers' unsuccessful efforts to keep from becoming proletarianzed laborers. In such a setting we should expect female workers to be in the lowest echelon of the labor force, at the mercy of their employers, and lacking in status or training.[9]

Recent scrutiny of the late medieval economy by Martha Howell,[10] however, has suggested that merchant capitalism had a more nuanced and varied development than we have thought, and that female workers played a more important and disparate role than has been revealed. By reappraising the nature of the work structure, we learn that more gradations existed in the eighteenth-century productive process as well. Arguments over the terms of women's employment recurred as a constant theme, as the silk guild debated the hegemony of merchants vs. workers, urged the central government to lift the duty on imported silk, and debated the wisdom of permitting non-Lyonnaise apprentices.

Historians since the late nineteenth century have demonstrated that women's work played an important role in silk manufacture. In the first major histories of Lyon's silk guild, Justin Godart and Ernest Pariset signaled that female labor was extensive in Lyon. Maurice Garden's demographic research indicated that females provided at least 60 percent of the labor force, and that all our statistics about eighteenth-century employment in Lyon are skewed by the deficiencies in our knowledge of women's production and wages. Jean-Pierre Gutton's study of the poor showed that women's work was "widespread in the Lyon of the Old Regime." Pierre Cayez's estimate was that 69 percent of the silkworkers were female. He emphasized that their numerical dominance was eclipsed by their economic dependence. It was not just the size of the female workforce which marked their importance but their function within the guild industry.[11]

Of the approximately 35,000 persons working directly to manufacture articles of silk in 1788, Maurice Garden counted 5,575 master weavers, 1,796 journeymen, and 507 apprentices. Along with these workers, who were all male, the women weaving numbered 3,924 wives, an estimated 5,575 children, and 1,015 females weaving illegally.[12] The wives were already accustomed to work in the silk *fabrique*, and many had earned dowries unwinding silk cocoons (*dévideuses*), pulling cords (*tireuses*), reeling warps (*ourdisseuses*), or doing other tasks. Garden's analysis of marriage contracts shows that two-thirds of the silkworkers' wives had immigrated to Lyon. The other third comprised many daughters of silk masters who contributed their skill rather than a dowry to the new household.[13]

Although the silk industry seemed like a monolith from the exterior, it was divided into separate guilds which handled different types of manufacture. The part with most prestige consisted of the silk weavers. Like all such organizations, the guild included master merchants, master weavers, journeymen, and apprentices. But the internal composition of the silk fabric makers was more complex, having experienced within its own unit some of the struggles between artisanal and capitalist ways of organizing work. Long and acrimonious disputes between the merchants and the weavers had resulted, by the mid-eighteenth century, in the merchants' exclusive control of sales. The early eighteenth century saw the establishment of between 120 and 180 large-scale merchants. They hired hundreds of master weavers and determined both the contracts with consumers and the weavers' wages. At their side were some 700 *petits marchands*, struggling to maintain the legal right to sell their woven goods directly to consumers.

The capitalist nature of the business, the large sums needed to purchase raw silk, and other exigencies of a far-flung luxury trade had gradually allowed the large-scale merchants to gain the upper hand in their disputes with the master weavers. By 1737 the master weavers lost their right to market their goods and had to accept the increasingly less advantageous contracts the merchants forced on them. Economic cycles buffeted the industry. War created a demand for the plain black textiles required by royalty's mourning, and silk cocoon shortages further shook the economic independence of the weavers.

In this situation, women's labor became a resource that had decisive ramifications for the factions involved. Before the industrial era, power was an inelastic resource, laying heavy emphasis on workers as the key to increased production. As the most prevalent workers in the silk *fabrique*, women determined whether more or fewer goods would be produced, both for capitalistic merchant masters and for artisanal master weavers. The future structure of Lyon's silk industry depended on the access of either group to cheap female labor. To understand what was involved, we must analyze the status of the women workers in Lyon.

Female workers in the *Grand Fabrique* comprised two groups: the daughters and wives of masters on the one hand, and the crowd of auxiliary workers on the other. The silk industry needed thousands of auxiliary workers to unwind the cocoons, warp the looms, and advance the brocade patterns. These jobs were filled in Lyon by young female workers from the surrounding regions of Bugey, Beaujolais, and Savoy. Recruited by entrepreneurs or brought by relatives already in the metropolis, these young workers started their employment as servants and industrial assistants as young as age ten or twelve. Guild statutes insisted that they be hired for the year, and that they be given contracts they might read and sign. In the course of events, their masters declined to pay them when business was bad. Their illiteracy kept them from effectively protesting the broken contracts. Competition from other female immigrants kept their salaries low. No matter how minimal the salaries of these auxiliary workers were, master weavers complained about them bitterly as a drag on their slim resources. These unlicensed workers were legally forbidden to perform the prestigious art of weaving.[14]

Masters' Wives

The most controversial and problematic workers in the privileged group were the wives of masters. They received their training and status from their husbands; their most gainful employment was in weaving, alongside husband, journeymen, and apprentices; and their products were sold without prejudice or differentiation among the other products of the workshop. Through the successive rules that permitted household ateliers to have two, three, four, or five looms, the contribution of weaving wives could constitute a half, a third, a quarter, or a fifth of the family's income. Pierre Cayez has estimated that the average family workshop consisted of 2.4 looms in 1788. Thus the authorization permitting wives to "sit at the loom" can be seen as an important resource. Particularly in guild families without the means to employ journeymen, the weaving wives' efforts were crucial in maintaining the workshop's independence. This category of work was a prize in the struggle between merchants and master workers in the corporation.[15]

As in other crafts, women found their least restrictive opportunities when the manufacture was in its early days. When Louis XI installed the silk industry at Lyon in 1466, the edict offered work to males and females without discriminating among the tasks. As a result, women became apprentices and journeyworkers. In the next century the regulations of 1561, which converted the industry into a guild, restricted their access to silkwork. From then on, successive regulations defined new categories of workers whose access to technology was determined by their relationship to the masters. Instead of the "free crafts" which were a Lyonnaise tradition, silkmaking evolved into a centralized industry that was composed of hundreds of family workshop units. In these family cells, economic function coincided with social discipline. The necessity to control the size of the workforce, as well as the process of technical training, found expression within the master's family.[16]

While the transition from free trade to guild industry was in progress, guild statutes affirmed that as a wife's legal person was subsumed in that of her husband, his license to work inhered to her. Accordingly, the statutes of 1561 assumed that wives would work alongside their husbands at the loom, and private contracts made this specification explicit. Moreover, in this flexible business community, the work of husband, wife, or both might take place in their own workshop or in that of another master. As Natalie Zemon Davis has written, "Indeed in 1561, the master silk weavers were still talking about *compaignonnes*, as well as *compaignons*, in their shops, which means that some trained females were weaving for wages."[17]

As time went on, the industry moved toward using restrictive regulations as a response to its problems. Economic difficulties through the religious wars of the sixteenth century stimulated the journeymen themselves to request that masters restrict access to the industry. The regulations of 1569 imposed a five-year term for apprentices and a term of two years for journeymen, stipulated a limit of two apprentices per master, and forbade women in guild families to work at the loom.[18]

Although regulations may have put restrictions on women's legal access to weaving, the idea that they had the skill and obligation to contribute to this aspect of the family business was deeply rooted. It persisted even when the pressure to limit new members of the silk *fabrique* canceled the automatic awarding of masterships to journeymen marrying widows or daughters of masters, if the men originated from outside Lyon. While the "foreign" journeymen would not automatically succeed to the mastership through their wives' connections, they received an economic bonus as their wives were permitted to weave.

The regulations of 1686 stipulated that "the journeymen born outside the vicinity of Lyon or in a foreign country, who marry a widow or a daughter of a master, acquire through this act the license needed for both himself and for his wife, to occupy two looms, and work at them." The rule's wording underscores the equal contribution of wife and husband, authorizing "la franchise nécessaire pour occuper deux métiers, et y travailler *tant le mari que la femme*" (italics added). With this formula, the guild was able to modify its draconian restrictions on the nonnative workers: workers from other regions had to pay 200 livres, and those from outside France 300 livres, for the privilege of working ten years without the aid of apprentices or other journeymen. During this period, the household workshop would be limited to subsistence productivity. Since it was always considered legitimate for a woman to work to support herself at a subsistence level, and by extension to do her part in contributing to her household, it was appropriate for these journeymen's wives to weave at home.[19]

That rationale continued to operate into the eighteenth century, permitting daughters, as well as wives or widows of masters, to weave, provided they were able to demonstrate their ties with the masters. Thus the regulations of 1703 required these female weavers to show documents to the guild officers on their periodic visits.[20]

We can interpret the new regulations to mean that women's employment in weaving had proliferated by the early eighteenth century. It was not unusual for poor masters or their wives to be found weaving for others. Large-scale workshops run by master merchants, who did no weaving themselves, competed with family workshops of master weavers employing their own female relatives, their journeymen, apprentices, and perhaps hired workers. Evidence suggests that journeymen and their wives also sought work at busy ateliers, whether run by the originally contracted master or not.

Economic pressure on journeymen's families and the necessity for weavers to complete rush orders inevitably drew "foreign" journeymen's wives and daughters into workshops outside their home. Thus a metamorphosis occurred in which the skill the wife was permitted to acquire because of her legal indivisibility from her husband enabled her to function as a wage earner in her own right. Acknowledging this reality, the 1703 statute forbade the hiring of nonlocal and foreign journeymen or their daughters and wives, "*unless they had been registered in the guild's book of workers*" (emphasis added). Both master merchants and master weavers who worked on their own account were liable for fines for the first offense and loss of mastership for subsequent ones. Not only do these rules validate the work of journeymen's female relatives, they also suggest that women without family ties to guildsmen frequently infiltrated the workshops.[21]

Who benefited from the work of women in guild families and from the employment of females without guild ties? For entrepreneurs with resources to pay wages, hiring additional labor was a rational economic strategy. Thus the master merchants found ready use for any weaver available to undertake particular jobs as they came along. Except for being concerned over a possible fine imposed by guild officers, it did not matter to the master merchants whether the female workers belonged to guild families or not. Master weavers, on the other hand, had a vested interest in closing off work to nonrelatives, so they caused the statutes to exclude female auxiliary workers from weaving.

The sanctity of guild tradition extended to daughters and sons of masters the freedom to weave at home or in outside workshops. Under the cloak of guild solidarity, journeymen also retained the freedom to employ their own wives and children. This privilege may have been one factor influencing journeymen to throw in their lot with the master workers in their struggle against the master merchants. Throughout the century, journeymen were able to rise to the rank of master weaver, and this must have cemented their loyalty to their own guildmasters.[22]

The changes in guild regulations which we have examined were produced in stages as part of the ongoing struggle of factions within the guild dealing with outside economic pressures. The early eighteenth century saw a surge of influence by the large merchants and increasing discomfort on the part of all the other classes within the guild. Small-scale merchants were in an intermediate category between the merchants and the weavers. They were increasingly unable to maintain their position as merchants and began falling into the ranks of master weavers, living by their labor alone rather than by sales. With their ranks thus increased, the master weavers raised a crescendo of complaints to Paris. The royal government responded by ordering the redaction of new statutes designed to assuage the master weavers' cries of injustice. The statutes of 1737 were an unabashed instrument for master weavers and the former *petits marchands* to recover their position of equality with merchants in the guild. These rules reinstated the possibility that master weavers could enter commerce, giving them the freedom to "produce or to be responsible for production for all sorts of persons, merchants and others, who wish to place orders, whether for their own use, or even to sell," provided that these individuals belonged to the guilds.[23]

The guild's governing body was redrawn to create a balance between master weavers and merchants (four master guards were to come from each segment). The statutes acknowledged the harsh economic conditions that kept many master weavers from maintaining independent workshops. For the first time, regulations explicitly permitted the master weavers' wives to work outside the home ateliers. The new rules stated: "Masters who work at the houses of other masters, in the status of journeymen, just like their wives or widows, are held to conform to that which has already been prescribed for journeymen."[24]

As master weavers were falling into the dependent economic situation of hired hands, they grasped at the idea of extending the guild family ethos to what was actually a wage-work situation. In this formulation, wives and widows would retain the status that they had gained from their master weaver husbands, the "property of skill" acquired by hands-on training and consecrated by the guild's moral authority. Extending the right of wives to work as independent artisans was not a step toward promoting women's independence; it was a desperate means of stretching the family-based traditional mode of production to gain a vital advantage in an increasingly rationalized economy. The fact that the statutes recognized that this enabled the masters' wives to follow the path already taken by the journeymen's wives shows that the masters were conscious that they were now in the same economic condition as their former subordinates. Here a clear example of John Rule's "age of manufacture" presents itself, with its first characteristic of an artisanal system under siege, trying to defend itself by means of the ideology of tradition.[25]

In the aftermath of the propaganda war of tracts from various factions of the guild, the statutes had linked the rights of masters' wives to "sit at the loom" with that of their children. Masters' daughters and sons had long been legally privileged to work either in their fathers' workshops or for wages at the homes of other masters. So deeply rooted was this tradition in Lyon that the right of *fille de maître* (daughter of a master) belonged to a woman all her life, regardless of whether her eventual husband was in the guild. The advantage of this entry into high-status work can be seen in estimates that daughters of masters earned wages at least one-third higher than their brothers. Masters' families clearly regarded this privilege as an important economic contribution. The one extant book which registers work assignments of *filles de maîtres* records numerous requests on behalf of the masters' families that their daughters should be entitled to work for a certain period to support aging or needy parents.[26]

Whether masters' wives and daughters might work for wages continued to be part of the complex struggle which the elements of the silk *fabrique* conducted over their internal destinies. As the merchants reasserted their dominance in guild politics, they agitated against the master weavers' economic independence. By 1744 the three hundred or so merchants had successfully lobbied Paris to rewrite the regulations prohibiting master's wives from weaving outside the home workshop. The beleaguered master weavers' families lost the benefit of salaries their wives might have brought into the guild families. The statutes that were registered in June of that year also put a definitive end to the master weavers' hopes for access to the advantaged position of merchant. In the future, a fee of 800 livres had to be paid to the bureau of the guild by any master who wanted to have weaving done by another weaver. Only the large-scale wealthy merchants could afford such a price. To keep the master weavers from giving them even minor competition, the merchants inserted a clause requiring a fee of 200 livres for any master wishing to change his status from weaver to merchant or vice versa.[27]

That is not to say that the merchants had gained unchallenged control of the silk industry, or that the master weavers had lost all rights. The guild remained a forum for mediating the tension between merchants, weavers, and journeymen. The master weavers received a concession in the form of a traditional repetition of the requirement that "no one may have an open workshop to manufacture, nor to put out work, neither for piece wages, nor for his account or for himself, if he has not been received master in the guild." Although the guild still ensured master weavers their place in the workshop, the economic struggle was over. Defeat led to the shrinkage of the legal rights of women in the families of master weavers to work independently. An *ordonnance consulaire*, set forth by Lyon's city authorities on 2 October 1744, "revoked all permissions given to the daughters of masters or to the wives authorizing their working."[28]

Productivity of Masters' Wives in the Family Workshops

The 1744 laws set the legal standards for masters' wives until the eve of the Revolution. Provisions outlawing daughters' weaving outside the home were soon eliminated, but the prohibition against wives' work remained on the books until 1786. Nevertheless, it was an open secret in Lyon that masters' wives were continually at work weaving. Justin Godart asserted that after 1744, "almost none of the masters or wives of masters differentiated among the privileges which bound the guild together as a unit."[29] Within the intimacy of the household atelier, the guild's careful provisions for work were modified so that the home-workshop was treated as a seamless whole, a continuous process, rather than a rigidly hierarchical work station.

While they could not legally hire themselves out as weavers, wives found it was an accepted part of work culture to be occupied with the loom in guild families. In calculating the number of family members dependent on each workshop, respondents to the Lyon Academy's 1777 prize question, "How to occupy silkworkers in time of crisis?" demonstrated contemporary standards for normal years. Estimating the needs of a master who wove only plain silk (*étoffe unie*), one author wrote:

Given:

1. That the worker has three looms;
2. That his wife or an apprentice occupies a loom;
3. That he has a journeyman;
4. That he has only three children, one still nursing;
5. That he has only one servant who takes care of things outside the house and in the atelier, winding silk cocoons and making the bobbins.

The author estimated that food and shelter would be needed for seven persons. Taking for granted that the nursing baby would be farmed out to a wet-nurse, he included as normal expense the 72 livres annual fee for the infant's feeding and care. This, of course, would free the wife for industrial as well as household tasks.[30]

A similar scheme obtained for those who wove brocaded silk, either with colored silk and gold thread or with velour. The author's list of workers was identical except for the additional workers needed for the brocading techniques. Thus he assumed three looms, with "the wife or an apprentice occupying one loom," one journeyman, three children, of whom one is with a wet-nurse, and one domestic servant working at household and industrial tasks for the looms. In addition, five workers, needed specifically to service the brocade looms, would be used on a part-time basis. The wet-nurse's fee of 72 livres for care and feeding of the infant was again listed as a normal expense.[31]

As Olwen Hufton has indicated, the choice of keeping infants at home and caring for them within the crowded loom-filled household workshops was not possible for master weavers' families. "The wife of a weaver of Lyons, working fulltime, and perhaps organizing the labor of three girls, however slender the apparent profits of her work offset against the costs of keeping a child *en nourrice*, parted with her children until they reached the age of seven rather than have them dislocate the family's industrial activities, most of which took place within a single room." Even if half the mother's wages went to pay for the childcare, her role in maintaining the continuity of the family business made it worth the loss of money. The sacrifice in terms of children's lives was high: Maurice Garden estimated that almost 60 percent of the children placed with wet-nurses in the country around Lyon died by the age of six and a half years. The prevalence of this practice suggests that urban families may have used it as a form of population control, as well as a means to enable wives to continue working.[32]

In later years, wives continued to be mentioned as weavers, but increasingly with apologies that reflected society's changing ideological perspectives. The silk weavers' rhetoric began to become a subtle part of a local acceptance of wives' work and new standards of feminine domesticity that were becoming generalized. Their request in 1779 that the city government increase the minimum wage may also have influenced the master weavers to describe their wives' work as sporadic. Referring to a typical workshop with three looms making taffeta, the masters enumerated the workers as the master, a servant, and the wife. The wife, they wrote, "continuously occupies the loom, which is not usual in view of the need to care for the household, the workshop, and other domestic details." This hypothetical household consisted of three children, one of whom lodged at the wet-nurse's. Again, the expense of boarding out the infant, this time at 79 livres, was listed among the other regular fees.[33]

The continuing necessity for wives to work at the loom was expressed near the end of the century, when master weavers were marshaling their efforts to obtain a tariff from the city officials. In a handwritten document that Godart judged a good representation of workers' views, one Antoine Celle, *maître fabricant d'étoffes*, described a typical workshop in May 1786. Included in his description was a disclaimer paying lip service to the new notion of female frailty and the ideal of fulltime housekeeping:

Our example assumes that a master fabricant has three looms mounted with taffeta d'Angleterre. He occupies one; his wife, *contrary to the custom and difference owing to the weakness of her sex* [*sa femme, contre à l'usage* [sic] *et la différence due à la faiblesse de son sexe*], occupies another. The third loom is occupied by a journeyman and there are two persons for the unreeling of cocoons and the necessary canettes, and to do all the other tasks.[34]

Celle's close description of the workshop production puts the lie to any protestation of wifely idleness, as it shows just how necessary her work was to the enterprise.

Let us say further that seven hundred fifty *aunes* of cloth can be woven on each loom per year; this constitutes the output of a good worker without contradiction. In sharing these estimates, it is clear that the looms of the husband and the wife produce fifteen hundred *aunes* per year at 16 sous . . . and that the sum of their work will be 1,200 *livres*.[35]

By contrast, the product of the 750 *aunes* of the journeyman, at a rate of only 6 sous 8 deniers per *aune*, is worth only 249 livres.

Even the optimum number of brocade looms was calculated on the assumption that the wife would provide one-third of the labor. Hence the following curious testimony from the period: "The merchants say that a master worker can have four looms. We reply to them that you can calculate the most lucrative proportion of looms as three, because with four it is virtually impossible that the wife can occupy one, which diminishes by a great deal their daily gain. . . ."[36] The problem in using all four looms to which the guildmaster was legally entitled was the number of auxiliary workers needed for each loom. Celle estimated that to fetch the material, to weigh, measure, and finish the cloth by cleaning it, seven workers would be required for four looms. It was more profitable, he asserted, to use only five workers for three looms. And even if only six persons were employed for four looms, "the wife could not work" because she would have to help the other weavers. Given the demand for auxiliary workers and weavers during this period, guild families found it very difficult to maintain productivity.

A New Source of Weavers

Productivity was a preoccupation not only for the master weavers' families but for the merchants as well. While the use of unpaid wives' labor and their clandestine work outside the home helped to maintain the guild families' slim margin of survival, the merchants' orientation to the market caused them to seek cheap workers regardless of their origin. The 1789 survey showed over one thousand females employed in this way. The drawgirls, who were so much in evidence in the workshops, provided an irresistible pool of workers to entrepreneurs with the means to activate numerous looms. Strictly forbidden from weaving, these female workers, and probably others involved in the arduous and low-paid tasks of unwinding cocoons, reeling, and cleaning, viewed clandestine stints at the loom as worth the risk. Because their work put drawgirls-turned-weavers into direct competition with weavers, the master weavers had been fiercely opposed to their training as weavers.

Thus guild conflict aroused controversy not only over wives and daughters of masters, but also over drawgirls. These two groups of women workers found themselves pitted against each other. The families of master weavers and journeymen viewed their wives' work outside the home as central to their economic independence. The merchants preferred to draft drawgirls or other nonguild female workers into their shops. With this practice, the merchants could deal a double blow to the master weavers' pretensions. They could cause the master weavers to become more economically dependent, and they could increase their own profits through large workshops staffed by cheap and pliant workers.

Since the silk industry employed hundreds more girls than masters' wives, any ruling that categorically permitted females to weave—without specifying that they must be related to guild families—would have flooded the weavers' desks with applications from drawgirls. This was precisely the aim of the merchants in legitimizing all female weaving when they caused yet another revision and rewrote the 1744 statutes in their own favor.

Although the weavers and journeymen were not strong enough in the guild to overturn the entire code of new rules, they launched a general uprising that protested opening the workshops to women. A contemporary account vividly portrays the workers' mood. Silk weavers had congregated at an inn called the Moulin-à-Vent, dancing and chatting. At three o'clock in the afternoon, when an officer appeared and tried to disperse them, the workers talked with him and "complained about the new regulation . . . and of the abuse that certain masters were committing by having 'women' work at the loom." The weavers' unrest caused the royal government to overturn that portion of the new law that applied to women workers. By phrasing the revision in general terms, however, the officials caused the work of guild wives outside the home to be illegal as well.[37]

The significance of this description—that it represents a protest against the acceptance of drawgirls and other nonguild female workers—is found in a later tract that was written to protect the decorative braidmakers against closer amalgamation with the silk weavers. In an undated memorandum addressed to Vergennes, the officers of the Decorative Braid guild (*Passementiers-Guimpiers*) stated that incorporating their craft with that of the silk weavers would require changing the regulations to permit the employment of girls. This, they warned, "will cause a rebellion among the workers of this guild as in 1744."[38]

The Imposition of Enlightened Reform

The guildmasters inadvertently gave an opening to the very situation they opposed when an unusual scarcity of drawgirls in 1759 aroused the masters' complaints about the difficulty of attracting auxiliary workers from the regions around Lyon and Savoy. To the silk masters' dismay, the controller general, Bertin, advised them to create a market for the labor by admitting young women to the weavers' trade after a stint of drawing cords. This signaled the beginning of a full-fledged campaign on the part of royal officials to insert laissez faire reforms into the economic life of Lyon. As a major industrial city rent by acrimonious guild disputes, Lyon had already attracted the censure of enlightened critics. In 1751, the early proponent of reform Vincent de Gournay used his position as intendant of Lyon to write the first tract advocating the suppression of guilds.[39]

Based on natural rights principles, the reformist position chastised guilds for hampering the natural flow of economic activity, preventing the poor from sustaining themselves, and retarding the progress of inventions. According to this theoretical framework, God had given human beings needs that could be satisfied only by employment; therefore the system of rules which constrained access to work must be overturned. The reformers noted the guilds' prohibition of female access to the guild hierarchy and asserted that the right to work should be open to all. As Intendant Terray wrote of guilds later in the century: "The exclusion of women is a practice contrary to natural law."[40]

In 1759, Bertin had proposed the idea of admitting female auxiliary workers to the weaving trade as a practical move. He suggested "that the anticipation [of weaving] would influence the drawgirls to withstand the exigencies and inconveniences of their condition more patiently, and would attract more to the work."[41] In their reply, the officers of the *Grande Fabrique* set the lines of argument that they were to use for the next thirty years. They reasoned that if the drawgirls could leave their ill-paid drudgery for better work, they would flee the auxiliary jobs and the silk industry would come to a standstill. All the women's tasks of preparing the silk— unwinding the cocoons, twisting and preparing thread, making bobbins, fashioning the cords for brocading—would be abandoned. The *Grande Fabrique*'s solution to the shortage of auxiliary workers was to send out "intelligent persons" as recruiters, who would assure the girls that the masters would never again repeat their bad faith of 1750 and default on salaries.[42]

At the heart of the guild's objection lay the fear that since the former drawgirls' salaries would be lower, females would come to supplant males in the trade. This would harm the journeymen directly, since "in hard times especially, the masters would given them [the drawgirls] preference. They alone would be hired, and the men would have no other choice but to leave the country." The girls would "take the work away from our men and discourage our aspirants." Indeed, the guild officers suggested, since "the masters' interest is to reduce their ranks to the smallest possible number, there is no doubt that they would form a preference for these girls who could never claim a higher status than that of journeywomen."[43]

Journeymen were not alone in opposing this proposition. The master weavers also viewed work expansion for drawgirls as a threat, because by using them the merchants could sidestep the family workshops. For the merchants, the new scheme offered several attractions: lower salaries, the chance to fire workers at will, and a way to avoid tortuous disputes with master weavers intent on following the regulations literally in disregard of market demands.

Despite the many well-founded arguments against the "Bourgeois Revolution," the documents show that with respect to Lyon's silk industry, the merchants found allies in the reforming ministers' campaign to overturn the guild system. Although Turgot's rulings to outlaw guilds failed, subsequent royal administrators kept up the pressure to weaken guild control of the industry. A rationalized system putting all workers on an equal footing would satisfy the freedom-to-work ideals of natural rights advocates. In national economic terms, it was expected to increase employment and production. This atomizing of the labor force was designed to annihilate guild privilege, as it invalidated the work monopoly of the masters and the special access of guild families to trade secrets. As Maurice Garden wrote, the liberty to increase the number of looms and the freedom to hire girls as weavers was "in fact, a formal and definitive attack against the guild itself and its regulations."[44]

In support of these enlightened ideas, in 1781 the intendant of Lyon drafted a bill to reorganize silkmaking into five categories. Wives and unmarried females would receive explicit permission to become apprentices, journeywomen, and masters in all aspects of the manufacture, in accord with the special regulations of each guild. For access to silk weaving, an old scheme requiring four years of work pulling the cords of a drawloom or a button loom was revived. Four years of work as a cocoon unwinder would also entitle a *dévideuse* to enter the new craft. The girls who wished to learn weaving could then spend two years as apprentices and four as *compagnonnes*. "And so after ten years of work and formation, girls and wives could become *maîtresses ouvrières*."[45]

While the master weavers were able to resist the intendant's 1781 formula to open their ranks to young women, they were only postponing this step. Pressure to incorporate hired girls into weaving became irresistible as the economic crisis of the 1780s caused masters to shrink their expenses by any means. This time, impoverished masters themselves broke the rules and hired drawgirls for weaving. The maintenance of guild regulations was now undertaken by the city administration. But no amount of threats by the local officials could succeed in chasing the drawgirls and other auxiliary workers away from the weaving benches. Finally the matter was settled by the king's jurisdiction. An *Arrêt du Conseil* on September 3, 1786, made weaving legal for hired female workers who had no family ties to silk masters (*filles, sans distinction*).[46] Royal officials finally succeeded in imposing their standards of enlightened reform on the *Grande Fabrique*.

What effect did the legal entry of female wage weavers have on the silk industry? Many factors hinder our ability to draw neat conclusions. The economic downturn associated with the lowered tariffs of the treaty of 1786 exacerbated problems in the silk trade. While cheap female wage labor may have taken employment from male master weavers, it also displaced the masters' wives and daughters symbolically as the privileged female workers. The turbulent events of the Revolution threw production and markets into disarray. Moreover, in 1791, Revolutionary legislation suppressed the entire guild system, rendering moot the issue of female prestige within the silk weavers' household.

The Revolution and Beyond

The silk masters, however, blamed their misery in 1789 on the entrance into the trade of untrained girls from the countryside who undercut the male weavers' wages and turned out faulty cloth. It was the merchants who had turned one sex against the other and succeeded in enslaving both, they argued. The silk masters' complaints were instructive to our analysis of women's work. They recommended that weaving be "reserved to men, stronger and therefore more capable of making all sorts of textiles, [and] to the daughters of masters who by their experience have the right to this favor." In this reassertion of moral principles in the guild economy, women workers were not discredited as a category but were differentiated according to their ties to the association.[47]

According to the former masters, it was the new female weavers, unqualified either by training or by breeding, who were responsible for subverting the families of the honest silkworkers by causing their salaries to be cut in half. This wage squeeze forced "the fathers of families, them, their wives and their children, to work seventeen to eighteen hours a day, unable to earn enough without public charity."[48] The irony of this situation would become felt when the girls themselves wanted to marry, the guildmasters warned. If the girls managed to rise above the "corruption of their habits" to find husbands, their economic situation would immediately throw them into "the most frightful misery."[49]

Silkmaking in the Nineteenth Century

Prophecies that the workshop economy would collapse on the altar of unregulated work did not prove accurate. The family structure of the industry conformed to the demands of silkmaking into the nineteenth century, and so it persisted. Even as the manufacture of plain silks spread to rural areas, fancy silks and brocades required the high level of skill that only urban workshops could provide. While this was so, Lyon's silk industry continued to follow the structure it had developed in pre-Revolutionary times. Even though the guild system was dead, the master weaver and his wife continued as partners in managing family life and production within the home.[50] This pattern was neither a novelty of the new industrial age nor an example of post-Revolutionary freedom for women workers; it was rather a time-tested practice of the guild system.

As they confronted the technological and economic problems of the nineteenth century, silkworkers continued to rely on traditional strategies and to use hand weaving rather than the power loom. Their problems were formidable. Suppression of the silk guild enabled the weaving of plain silks to proliferate in rural areas. Silkworm disease had increased the price of raw silk and made the lower rural salaries more attractive to manufacturers. With the invention and spread of the Jacquard weaving device, manufacture of brocaded textiles had become open to less-skilled workers. Finally, changes in fashion had shrunk the demand for fancy brocade silks. These factors created a crisis for urban silk manufacture. By 1861, the number of hand-loom cottage manufactures and factory power looms in the countryside surpassed that of looms within Lyon.[51]

George Sheridan's pioneering work has shown to what extent the urban silkworkers' response drew on preindustrial economic assumptions and repeated eighteenth-century behavior. Using censuses of 1847 and 1866, Sheridan reveals that a structural change in the formation of the family workshop emerged from a shift away from brocade weaving to the manufacture of plain silks. In addition, there was "a reduction in the numbers of looms and household residents, a reduction in the proportion of nonresident workers needed to weave the active looms ('familialization'), and a reduction in the proportion of males, both kinfolk of the head or spouse and non-kin, residing in the same household ('feminization')." This was particularly striking among the remaining brocade workshops, since the plain-weaving workshops already had these characteristics.[52]

Nineteenth-century weavers responded to crisis just as their forebears had, by calculating the relative gain for each loom and by shrinking the working household accordingly. As Antoine Celle had written a century earlier in 1786, even though the use of four looms with seven workers was legal, it was more profitable to use five workers for three looms. Sheridan's analysis shows a drop in average number of looms per household from 2.77 in 1847 to 2.53 in 1866. The nineteenth-century silk families had the same motive for this shift as their predecessors a hundred years earlier. A major source of profitability, in Celle's view, was the large proportion of weaving that might then be done by the wife. The debate over the Lyon Academy's 1777 appeal for advice in time of crisis also leaned heavily on the role that wives undertook in weaving. Diminishing the size of the workshop and "familializing" it were strategies already widely used by preindustrial craftworkers.[53]

What was new in the equation was how "feminization" worked in the later period. The women workers still provided most of the crucial auxiliary work for the silk looms, but the important difference was that, with the restrictions against them lifted, female workers provided an abundant source of cheap weavers. Faced with the alternative of even lower paid work in miserable conditions such as the crowded *dévidage* workshops, many of these girls and women preferred weaving in a silkmaking family workshop. Sheridan demonstrates that it was their willingness to work as resident weavers that enabled the hand-loom master weavers' businesses to survive in Lyon. It was the women's labor which made possible the "effective resistance" of traditional silk artisans both to factories and to rural cottage industry.[54]

Although the exploitation of women weavers enabled the urban silk industry to endure beyond rational expectation, the industry did not survive without changes. The dire prophecies of guildmasters and journeymen came true to some extent. Female labor did depress weavers' wages, and many male weavers left the industry.

Nevertheless, a significant number of skilled journeymen circulated among the workshops which still turned out fancy goods; this group of weavers helped to maintain the advantage of sophisticated technology belonging to Lyon. Nor was the trade without renewal, as some masters' sons found in the female workers a means to continue in the old way.[55]

What changed was the permeability of the industry and the ramifications of this change for women. As silkmaking households became less "entrepreneurial" by virtue of their smaller size and family orientation, the silk trade stopped recruiting weavers who would eventually become heads of businesses. Women were valuable because they could not compete with masters, and their status as low-wage workers was a double-edged sword for the industry. Their circumstance prevented the female weavers from becoming integrated on a managerial basis and maintaining the dignity of the trade. Moreover, just as the guild tracts had warned, their chances of becoming masters' wives diminished as the number of male weavers declined. It is not surprising that some displaced male weavers considered their female weavers unfair rivals and that they came to regard women workers in general as strikebreakers, wage depressers, and the tools of repressive bosses.

However, the use of women as low-paid workers in skilled jobs did not at first drive a wedge between the masters and journeymen. Surprisingly, the ties that had developed through the eighteenth century between the poor but privileged masters and the journeymen who made common cause with them lasted even when the prize of a mastership no longer existed. The separation of categories by privileged status, which had enabled wives to become associated as welcome helpmeets with their privileged guild husbands, had been changed into a struggle by all to maintain hand silk manufacture. Segmentation owing to legal category had given way to segmentation depending on sex as Lyon absorbed the lessons of the post-Revolutionary casteless society.[56]

Notes

The author gratefully acknowledges the generous support of the National Science Foundation, the American Philosophical Society, and the National Endowment for the Humanities in funding research for this project.

1. Olwen Hufton, "Women, Work, and Marriage in Eighteenth Century France," in R. B. Outhwaite, ed., *Marriage and Society* (London: Europa Pub. Ltd., 1983), p. 198; and Hufton, "Women and the Family Economy in Eighteenth-Century France, *French Historical Studies* 9 (Spring 1975): 9-10; Maurice Garden, *Lyon et les lyonnaises au XVIIIe siècle* (Paris: Société d'Edition "Les Belles-Lettres," [1970]), pp. 296-97; Sarah C. Maza, *Servants and Masters in Eighteenth-Century France* (Princeton, N.J.: Princeton University Press, 1983), pp. 61-63, 80-82; Theresa McBride, *The Domestic Revolution: The Modernisation of Household Service in England and France, 1820-1920* (London, 1976).

2. Louise A. Tilly and Joan W. Scott, *Women, Work, and Family* (New York: Holt, Rinehart and Winston, 1978), and Gay L. Gullickson, "The Sexual Division of Labor in Cottage

Industry and Agriculture in the Pays de Caux: Auffay, 1750-1850," *French Historical Studies* 12 (Fall 1981): 177-99.

3. Laura S. Strumingher, "The Artisan Family: Traditions and Transition in Nineteenth-Century Lyon," *Journal of Family History* (Fall 1977): 214-15.

4. An important source of information documenting the range of women's work in the early modern period is Merry E. Wiesner, *Working Women in Renaissance Germany* (New Brunswick, N.J.: Rutgers University Press, 1986); see pp. 152-57 for guild wives' work.

5. Natalie Zemon Davis, "Women in the Crafts in Sixteenth-Century Lyon," *Feminist Studies* 8 (Spring 1982): 49-53. For the variety of women's occupations and their lack of mention in records, see Kathryn L. Reyerson, "Women in Business in Medieval Montpellier," in *Women and Work in Preindustrial Europe*, ed. Barbara A. Hanawalt (Bloomington: Indiana University Press, 1986), p. 119.

6. Michael Sonenscher, *The Hatters of Eighteenth Century France* (Berkeley: University of California Press, 1987), pp. 35-36.

7. Sonenscher also asserted that the rituals of journeymen's organizations, the *compagnonnages*, evolved as a means of conferring mystery and distinction on work. "Their ceremonial was a commentary upon a world in which the work that people did was often very similar. The point, however, was to make it appear different." Citation from "Mythical Work: Workshop Production and the Compagnonnages of Eighteenth-Century France," in *The Historical Meanings of Work*, ed. Patrick Joyce (Cambridge: Cambridge University Press, 1987), p. 32.

8. William H. Sewell, Jr., *Work and Revolution in France: The Language of Labor from the Old Regime to 1848* (Cambridge: Cambridge University Press, 1980), p. 31, argues that law and custom disqualified women from full membership in guilds.

9. Garden, *Lyon*, pp. 34, 315-16.

10. Martha C. Howell, *Women, Production, and Patriarchy in Late Medieval Cities* (Chicago and London: University of Chicago Press, 1986).

11. E. Pariset, *Histoire de la fabrique lyonnaise: Etude sur le régime social et économique de l'industrie de la soie à Lyon depuis le XVIe siècle* (Lyon: Rey, n.d.). Justin Godart, *L'ouvrier en soie* (Paris: Bernoux et Cumin, 1898), p. 172; Jean-Pierre Gutton, *La Société et les pauvres: L'exemple de la généralité de Lyon 1534-1789* (Paris: Société d'Edition "Les Belles Lettres," [1969]), p. 35; Garden, *Lyon*, pp. 318-20;. Pierre Cayez, *Métiers Jacquard et hautes fournaux: Aux origines de l'industrie lyonnaise* (Lyon: Presses Universitaires de Lyon, [1978]), p. 44.

12. "Ouvriers et artisans au XVIIIe siècle: L'exemple lyonnais et les problèmes de classification," *Revue d'histoire économique et social* 48 (1970): 29-32, 53-54.

13. Garden, *Lyon*, pp. 296-97; and Hufton, "Women and the Family Economy," p. 10. For information on the auxiliary tasks performed by women in the silk industry, see Laura S. Strumingher, *Women and the Making of the Working Class: Lyon 1830-1870* (St. Alban's, Vt.: Eden Press, 1979), pp. 17-33, and Chapter 8 of this volume.

14. For information on drawgirls see Daryl M. Hafter, "The 'Programmed' Brocade Loom and the Decline of the Drawgirl," in *Dynamos and Virgins Revisited: Women and Technological Change in History*, ed. Martha Moore Trescott (Metuchen, N.J.: Scarecrow Press, 1979), pp. 49-66; Silkmasters' comments on the contract with drawgirls are discussed on pp. 58-59.

15. Godart, *L'ouvrier*, p. 358; Cayez, *Métiers Jacquard*, p. 44.

16. Henri Hauser, *Ouvriers du temps passé* (Paris: Felix Alcan, 1909), p. 48. The original edict encouraged workers of every condition to join the silk manufacture, even those who were in religious orders.

17. Davis documented this point with notarized contracts that specified husband and wife as *tissotiers* at this time. See "Women in the Crafts in Sixteenth-Century Lyon," in *Women and Work in Preindustrial Europe*, ed. Barbara A. Hanawalt (Bloomington: Indiana University Press, 1987), pp. 175, 177.

18. Jean Jacques, *Vie et mort des corporations: Grèves et luttes sociales sous l'ancien régime* (Paris: Spartacus, n.d.), p. 114.

19. "Les compagnons Forains ou Étrangers qui épouseront une Veuve ou fille de Maître en

ladite Ville acquerront, moyenant l'experience cy-dessus, la franchise nécessaire pour occuper deux métiers, et y travailler tant le mari que la femme." "Règlements de 1686," *Règlemens et Statutes* (Lyon: Andre Laurens, 1720), Art III, Archives Municipal Lyon 4.301, hereafter cited as AML.

20. "Les Filles, Femmes, ou Veuves de Maistres qui seront employées au travail de ladite Manufacture, seront tenues de justifier de la maîtrise de leurs Pères ou de leurs Maris, dans les visites des Maistres et Gardes." "Arrêt du conseil et lettres patentes portant règlement pour la manufacture des étoffes de soye, or, et argent de la ville de Lyon," 26 December 1702 and 2 January 1703. Registered in Parlement 27 January 1703, in *Règlemens et Statutes*, the phrase "employées au travail de ladite Manufacture" in this context refers to weaving, not to the auxiliary tasks commonly known as female work.

21. "Les maîtres-marchands qui feront travailer chez-eux, et les Maîtres-Ouvriers travaillans à facon, ne pourront à l'avenir employer aucun Compagnon forain ou étranger, ni des Filles et des Femmes foraines ou étrangères, qui n'auront pas été reçues par les Maistres et Gardes, et enregistrée sur le Livre de la Communauté, à peine de cent cinquante livres d'amende, applicable comme dessus pour la première fois; et en cas residive d'être déchus de la maîtrise." "Arrest du conseil . . . ," Registered in Parlement 27 January 1703, *Règlemens et Statutes*, Title XXIV.

22. The one remaining book recording requests of masters' daughters to weave for their own wages (1773-1786) is Register, "Permissions Acordées aux Filles de Maîtres," AML HH 586. See also Pariset, *Fabrique lyonnaise*, pp. 132ff., and Garden, *Lyon*, pp. 572-82, who described the keen interest of masters and journeymen to employ their own wives and children at weaving.

23. "Lettres patentes du Roy, Pour l'execution du règlement conçernant les Manufactures des étoffes de soye, or, et argent, de la ville de Lyon, et la communauté des maistres marchands et fabriquans desdites étoffes." Fontainbleau, 1 October 1737, Title LX.

24. "Les maistres qui travailleront chez d'autres maistres, en qualité de compagnons, de mesme que leurs femmes ou veuves, seront tenus de se conformer à ce qui est cy-devant prescrit pour les compagnons." "Lettres patentes," Title CLXXVIII.

25. John Rule, "The Property of Skill in the Period of Manufacture," in *The Historical Meanings of Work*, ed. Patrick Joyce (Cambridge: Cambridge University Press, 1987), p. 105. Joan Wallach Scott discusses the larger framework of such use of gender in "Gender: A Useful Category of Historical Analysis," in Scott, *Gender and the Politics of History* (New York: Columbia University Press, 1988).

26. Godart discusses the advantageous salaries earned by daughters of masters in *L'ouvrier*, pp. 169-72. Documentation of their work is found in Register, "Permissions Acordés," AML HH 586.

27. "Arrest du Conseil d'Etat du Roy." "Qui ordonne l'exécution des Statutes et Règlements pour les fabriques de Lyon." 19 June 1744, AML 704.603. The merchants were also given express permission to have spinning wheels with which to twist, prepare, and dress silk thread destined either to be used in their manufactures or to sell. They might also have tools ("des moulins et des rouets") to prepare and spin gold and silver; in addition they were allowed instruments to prepare warps, to glaze, and to create moiré effects. Clearly the merchants were instituting in legal form the capitalist structure they were actually imposing on the industry, with vertically integrated production on their own premises. Title X.

28. The reiteration of the closed guild workshop is found in "Arrest du Conseil," 1744, Title VII, Article I. The city ordinance revoking women's work permits is cited by Godart, *L'ouvrier*, "Placard," G.F.30, p. 460. A riot protesting these provisions in 1744 caused the regulations of 1737 to be temporarily reinstated. The regulations of 1744 were permanently reimposed by troops under martial law the next year. See Robert J. Bezucha, *The Lyon Uprising of 1834: Social and Political Conflict in the Early July Monarchy* (Cambridge, Mass.: Harvard University Press, 1974), p. 6.

29. Godart, *L'ouvrier*, p. 172.

30. Godart, *L'ouvrier*, p. 172, "Devenus maîtres ou femmes de maîtres, plus rien ne différentiat ces privilegiés, qui rentraient des lors dans l'ensemble de la Communauté"; Citation of the Academy document, pp. 405-406.

31. So accepted was the practice of full-time working mothers that the Lyon bourgeoisie set up a charitable fund in 1779 to hire healthy countrywomen to perform this service for the babies of urban working women. The effort was aimed at curbing the high mortality rate of infants given out to village wet-nurses. See Louis Trenard, "La crise social lyonnaise à la veille de la Révolution," *Revue d'histoire moderne et contemporain* 2 (1955): 36. See also George Sussman, *Selling Mothers' Milk: The Wet-Nursing Business in France, 1715-1914* (Urbana: University of Illinois Press, 1982), for the extent of the practice in eighteenth-century France.

32. Hufton, "Women and the Family Economy in Eighteenth-Century France," p. 13. Garden, *Lyon*, pp. 114-40, analyzes the effects of wet-nursing on the population of Lyon; see esp. Tableau XX, p. 127.

33. The request was for an increase of one sou per *aune* in wages. Godart cites the master weavers' tract in *L'ouvrier*, pp. 408-409.

34. Godart, *L'ouvrier*, p. 412, italics added.

35. Godart, *L'ouvrier*, p. 412. "L'on suppose de plus qu'il ce peut fabriquer sept cent cinquante aunes d'étoffes par année sur chaque métier, ce qui fait le travail d'un bon ouvrier sans contredit; en partant de ces supositions, l'on verra que les métiers de l'homme et de la femme produiront quinze cents aunes par annee à 16 sols . . . et le produit de leur travail sera de 1,200 livres."

36. Godart, *L'ouvrier*, p. 413. "Les marchands diront qu'un maître fabriquant peut avoir quatre métiers. On leur repondra que l'on a pris la proportion la plus lucrative pour le maître en ne lui supposant que trois métiers, puisque avec quatre il est comme impossible que la femme puisse en occuper un, ce qui diminueroit de beaucoup leur gain journalier."

37. Expressed as "l'abus que comettaient certains maîtres en faissant travailler les femmes sur le métier," cited by Jacques, *Vie et mort des corporations*, p. 79.

38. "Mémoire," Passementiers-Guimpiers to the Bureau of M. de Vergennes, Archives Nationales F 12 762, No. 4977, hereafter cited as AN.

39. Vincent de Gournay and Clicquot de Blervache, *Considérations sur le commerce et en particulier sur les compagnies, sociétés et maîtrises* (Amsterdam, 1758), and François Véron de Forbonnais, "Observations sur l'examen," in *Examen des avantages et des désavantages de la prohibition des toiles peintes* (Marseille, 1755). For the influence of Vincent de Gournay on reforming ideology, see George Weulersse, *Le mouvement physiocratique en France (1656-1770)* (Paris, 1897), vol. II, pp. 723ff., and Gustave Schelle, *Vincent de Gournay* (Paris, 1897).

40. The intense link between the natural law ideology and the attack on the guilds is developed comprehensively by Michael Sonenscher, *Work and Wages: Natural Law, Politics and the Eighteenth-Century Trades* (Cambridge: Cambridge University Press, 1989), esp. pp. 49-66.

41. Extract, Registre Grande Fabrique, January 10, 1759, AML HH 572.

42. "Avis conçernant les tireuzes de cordes," "Livre de Déliberations de la Grande Fabrique," AML HH 572.

43. "Avis concernant les tireuzes de cordes."

44. Garden, *Lyon*, p. 578.

45. "Projet et Déclaration du Roi," addressed to M. de Villevault, 1781, AN F 12 763.

46. Godart, *L'ouvrier*, pp. 175, 361.

47. "Doléance au Roi et a la Nation Assemblée," cited by Godart, *L'ouvrier*, pp. 261-62, "aux filles de maîtres qui par leur expérience ont droit à cette grâce."

48. E. Levasseur quoted from the master workers' *cahier* in *Histoire des classes ouvrières* (Paris: Alcan, 1899), vol. 2, p. 855.

49. Godart, *L'ouvrier*, p. 362.

50. Struminger, "Artisan Family," p. 215.

51. George J. Sheridan, Jr., "Household and Craft in an Industrializing Economy: The Case of the Silk Weavers of Lyons," in *Consciousness and Class Experience in Nineteenth-Century Europe*, ed. John M. Merriman (New York and London: Holmes and Meier, Inc., 1979), pp. 109-10. The most comprehensive analysis of the industry for the nineteenth century was made by Yves Lequin, *Les ouvriers de la région lyonnaise (1848-1914)* (Lyon: Presses Universitaires de Lyon, 1977), vol. 1: *La formation de la classe ouvrière régionale*.

52. Sheridan, "Household and Craft," p. 111. Bezucha suggests that a male labor shortage accounted for the acceptance of women as weavers; see *Lyon Uprising*, p. 13.

53. The silk guild had also responded to economic downturns by tightening the accessibility of journeymen to privileges, by reducing the number of looms permitted in the family workshop, and by discouraging "foreign" (individuals born outside Lyon) apprentices.

54. Sheridan, "Household and Craft," pp. 113-25.

55. This is not to suggest that the women weavers were unskilled workers. Even the Jacquard device had to be managed with care and knowledge. See Bezucha, *Lyon Uprising*, p. 45, for evidence of skilled women weavers.

56. See Mary Lynn McDougal, "Consciousness and Community: The Workers of Lyon, 1830-1850," *Journal of Social History* 12 (1978): 135-36.

PART II

The Persistence of Handicraft in the Industrial Age

John F. Sweets 5

The Lacemakers of Le Puy in the Nineteenth Century

In February 1799, several months before the coup d'état that was to bring Napoleon Bonaparte to power in France, a government official touring the Haute-Loire wrote: "The two *arrondissements* of Le Puy and Yssingeaux and the mountainous part of Brioude form one vast lace workshop, occupying all of the young girls and all of the old or feeble women."[1] This description would remain valid for at least another century until changing fashions, the social and economic dislocation associated with the First World War, and competition from improved lacemaking machines dramatically reduced the demand for handmade lace.

Estimates of the number of lacemakers in the departmental capital, Le Puy, and its environs ranged from 30,000 early in the century to between 70,000 and 100,000 in the 1850s and 1870s. Given that the total population of the Haute-Loire in the second half of the century was little more than 300,000, a home without a lacemaker was obviously a rarity. At the end of the century three-fourths of all lacemakers active in France lived in the Haute-Loire.[2] Understandably, the prefects of the Haute-Loire consistently referred to lace as the mainstay and principal industry of the area. Oddly—or perhaps instructively—the same prefects frequently described the contribution of women who made lace in the region as a "supplement" to the family income, even though their husbands' wages in agriculture or as manual laborers often provided little more, and sometimes less, than was brought into their households by the lacemakers.

The nerve center of the lace trade at Le Puy in the nineteenth century was located in two streets, rue Chènebouterie and rue Raphaël, narrow passageways from the center of town, the Place du Plot, just behind City Hall and the Tribunal de Commerce, climbing up to the fountain on the rue des Tables, which offered the most direct access to the great cathedral overlooking the city from its heights. Almost every building on these streets housed one or more lace merchants. On Saturdays and fair days these streets were beehives of activity from earliest light until well into the evening. Contemporary observers witnessed what might have appeared to be two converging processions of lacemakers, the women arriving from the northwest through the Saint-Laurent toll gate (*octroi*) moving down the hill from the Place des Tables, and those entering the town from other directions climbing up from the Place du Plot.

Inside the small boutiques the lacemaker was greeted by the merchant seated behind a large counter, elevated by a couple of steps in his, or more frequently *her*,[3] cashier's booth. The merchant was separated from the client by a sliding glass window through which lace and money would be exchanged after the strips of lace were measured with a *demi-aune* (roughly sixty centimeters) or, more often, by a length marked by two nails driven into the side of the counter. A lacemaker who was unhappy with the first price offered her might try two or three shops along the rue Raphaël or return to the first merchant to haggle for a price acceptable to both buyer and seller. Strips of lace bought in the morning would be joined together as required, folded or wrapped around a *plioir*, a frame used to wind the lace into a bundle, and then prepared for shipping. In the afternoons the "Dames de Raphaël," as the merchant women of the district were called, would sell their packets of lace to agents of fashion houses in Paris or London, or perhaps to the representatives of the larger lace businesses in Le Puy.[4]

This commerce of the rue Raphaël handled a large part of the ordinary lace, "l'article de rue," made with patterns that every lacemaker knew, the classic patterns for trim on dresses, ruffles on shirts, edging on tablecloths, and so forth, that had been produced in the region for generations. The higher-quality lace and the new patterns introduced in hopes of capturing the attention of the trendsetters of Parisian fashion were channeled through the big lace merchants at Le Puy, who provided the lacemakers with thread and patterns for their lace and either picked up the finished lace directly or received it from agents, called *leveuses*, who selected it for them on fortnightly tours of the region.

This traditional practice of providing the raw materials (thread) and patterns for the lacemakers was the source of frequent disputes between lacemakers and merchants. The merchants who had created the patterns complained that lacemakers sold their lace to other merchants offering a better price or to unscrupulous agents of fashion houses who cut the merchants out of their just due for having created the original designs. In 1843 many of the leading merchants at Le Puy addressed a petition to the prefect asking him to stop itinerant buyers from approaching the lacemakers along the road to Le Puy on fair days. These individuals, who were unlicensed and paid no taxes, were buying the lace that had been commissioned by merchants in Le Puy who owned the patterns used by the lacemakers. Alleging their concern for the unwitting lacemakers who were being taken in by such rogues, the merchants noted that the lacemakers had no recourse when they were cheated by such characters because they had no local address.[5] One may assume, however, that the lacemakers knew what they were doing, and probably sold their lace to such men because they offered better prices than the merchants in Le Puy.

Various methods were tried to limit disputes between lacemakers and merchants, but apparently with little success. Under the first Napoleon, lacemakers were ordered to have *livrets* (workbooks) as were all other workers;[6] but there is no evidence that the system was enforced at that time. The idea of a *livret* that would

record the details of each transaction between lacemakers and merchants was revived under the Second Empire and tried by a few merchants,[7] but the experiment
was soon abandoned. In the absence of written contracts to record their agreements, complaints of bad faith on both sides continued throughout the century, and
when the government introduced the minimum wage and old-age pensions in the
twentieth century, merchants argued vociferously that they had no responsibility to
contribute to these, asserting that lacemakers were not "workers" but independent
artisans who made their own deals with anyone who would buy their lace.[8]

In the late nineteenth century, several of the leading merchants in Le Puy began
to alter traditional practices by selling the thread to individual lacemakers rather
than giving it to them, allowing them credit only for the amount that had been used
in the lace returned to the merchant when he made his rounds to pick up the finished product.[9] With the improvement of rural roads and the coming of the auto-
mobile, the merchants could also begin to dispense with the services of the intermediary *leveuses* (most of whom had been women) who in the past had collected
the lace for them from the isolated hamlets of the region. In a similar fashion the
coming of the railroad to the Haute-Loire in the 1860s[10] had reduced the influence
of the women in the Raphaël district as railroad stops closer to the lacemakers'
homes served as direct channels to the exterior for the lace business; and even in Le
Puy several important merchants moved their businesses to the southeastern side of
the city for easier access to the rail terminal.[11]

If certain traditional practices associated with the lace trade were altered over
time, one thing remained constant—an idyllic notion that lace was the best sort of
"women's work," a morally uplifting craft. Given the ideological bias of France's
Vichy regime, it was not surprising that a lace conservatory was created under its
auspices during the Second World War to try to revive the handmade lace industry
in the Haute-Loire. Vichy officials, arguing that lacemaking would foster social har-
mony, praised it because it would keep women in the home and contribute to the
regime's programs in favor of a "return to the land."[12] Sources from the period emphasized as well the idea that lacemaking was an ideal complement to agricultural
labor. Because of its poor soil and harsh climate, the land in the Haute-Loire was
inadequate in and of itself to sustain a substantial population; families required a
"supplementary activity." Without it the mountainous countryside would soon be
depopulated and the land would return to nature. According to the prefect of the
Haute-Loire, each crisis in the history of the lace industry corresponded to a period
of misery and social troubles, whereas when the lace industry was healthy, "the
women, while taking care of their housework and the farm, make lace, especially
during the winters, and thereby earn the indispensable supplement for their family's
livelihood."[13] If these two themes, that lacemaking was ideal "women's work" and
that wages from the lacemaker's efforts were a "supplement" to the family income,
were congenial to Vichy's paternalistic government, they were by no means an invention of that regime.

Writing in the middle of the nineteenth century, one author, with a peculiar view
of the potency of women's breath, observed: "Lacemaking is an industry that is at

once healthy, moral, and lucrative. It is healthy because it forces the worker to pay attention to cleanliness, without which she could not work. A lacemaker who does not have fresh breath could produce only a tarnished lace, lacking firmness and value. This industry is healthy also because the workers are not crammed into workshops; it is moral because it is done in the home, associated with work in the fields under the eyes of the mother, who is thus able to guard her daughter from all pernicious contacts; it is moral finally because it is lucrative, something which is very rare today when life is tough and at the same time so slippery for poor women."[14]

The police commissioner at Le Puy, writing a generation later during one of the periodic slumps to which the lace trade was subject, made the same connection between lacemaking and morality. With the shops overflowing with merchandise, the lacemakers were unable to find an outlet for their lace. This situation, combined with the recent arrival of two thousand troops in the city meant that many young girls, deprived of their livelihood, had turned to prostitution, "seeking in vice the resources that their work refuses them."[15] In a similar vein, when encouraging fashionable French women to insist on handmade lace rather than machine-made imitations, the coauthor of a law that required girls to take lacemaking classes in the schools of the Haute-Loire at the turn of the century pointed out that these women could have the comforting assurance that in buying handmade lace they were sponsoring "a little comfort and well-being in some faraway cottage, that they were helping stout peasants to overcome the difficulties of their life, and perhaps preventing some disadvantaged young girl from coming to ruin in the streets of a big city, ending up God knows how!"[16] All in all, lacemaking was "really the ideal sort of women's work, not tiring, almost recreational, distinguished, healthy, done in the home or, in good weather, outside in the fresh air, begun in infancy and continued until death."[17] Lacemaking kept the young girls in the house, "preserved them from the risk of dissipation, gave them an interest in housework, and attached them to their village."[18] Lace was the "good fairy"[19] who had kept her children in the mountains of the Velay.

We have seen that women gradually became less prominent, or at least less visible, in the commercial side of the lace industry at Le Puy in the second half of the nineteenth century. Were they affected by the "cult of domesticity" influencing middle-class Frenchwomen elsewhere to accept the idea that their place was in the home?[20] This is quite possible, although I have found no documentation to prove it. Certainly the changes in transportation and the Third Republic's removal of the *béates* from control over primary education in the rural parts of the Haute-Loire had an impact on the visibility of women in the commercial aspects of the trade.

The *béates*, members of a lay order, the Filles de l'Instruction de l'Enfant Jesus, founded at Le Puy in the seventeenth century, were women who had traditionally taught young girls at age four or five to make lace and often served the merchants as *leveuses* for the most isolated parts of the region. Residents of Le Puy at the turn of the century remembered that fifty years earlier women, as evidenced by their dominance of the commerce in the Raphaël district, had been more obviously prominent in the business side of the trade. Their husbands were "relegated" to occasional buying trips at commercial fairs in distant towns, to entertaining foreign clients in local cafés or restaurants, or to looking after their small vineyards which covered the hillsides surrounding Le Puy—and given the difficulty of cultivating grapes in the harsh climate of the area, they probably expended a good share of their wives' lace profits unfruitfully.[21] It was notable that when successive patronal syndicates were organized in the last decades of the nineteenth century in order to try to protect an ailing lace industry, almost all of the prominent spokespersons and most of the members were men.[22]

Aside from this progressive diminution of women in the commercial side of the lace business, there were several aspects of the trade that, despite the occasional exception to prove the rule, were always differentiated by sex.[23] Virtually all of the largest merchant houses, those that received commendations and awards throughout the century for the lace they displayed at the various government-sponsored, commercial expositions, were headed by men.[24] These men were usually merchant-fabricants or *fabricants-dessinateurs*, indicating that they played a direct role in the production of their lace. The chief role for which these men were distinguished, or failed to receive distinction, was as designers of patterns. For example, Theodore Falçon, by all accounts the most influential lace merchant-designer in the history of lacemaking at Le Puy, reinvigorated a slumping industry in the 1830s, 1840s, and 1850s with the introduction of silk threads and highly artistic designs drawn from his research on lace patterns in French and Italian archives. When classes were created at the lycée in Le Puy to train lace designers, the only students were males; and men or young boys were the ones who served as designers of patterns in the merchants' shops. In addition to creating new designs, they also frequently traced the designs onto *cartons*, the pasteboard patterns used on lacemakers' *carreaux* (lace pillows—the apparatus upon which handmade lace was produced) to guide their work. Then, using an instrument called a *piquaire*, they made holes in the *cartons* to indicate pin placement to the lacemaker. During the long winters, at *veillées*, traditional evening social gatherings in the homes of lacemakers, while the women worked at their *carreaux*, old men often made intricately carved *plioirs* around which the lace would be folded. Otherwise, lacemaking in the Haute-Loire was women's work.

In addition to their activities as merchants and *leveuses*, women had several important functions in the lace trade. In the lace merchant's shop the work of the *échantillonneuse* was crucial to the success of a new lace pattern. This highly skilled lacemaker was the person who tried out a new design to determine whether or not it could actually be made, whether the design could hold together and stand up as finished lace. Some of the designer's ideas might be very attractive on paper but impossible to reproduce as lace; and this critical determination was the responsibility of the *échantillonneuse*. Although some of the best male designers could themselves use a *carreau* and had a fairly good idea of what might work as a lace pattern, in effect all lace designs were the product of close collaboration between the designer and the *échantillonneuse*. This expert lacemaker would also produce samples of all of the sorts of lace marketed by the merchant for use by salespersons representing the company, and the time required by the lacemakers to produce a certain pattern would be estimated in relation to the work of the *échantillonneuse*.

In the lace merchant's workshop women acted as *crayonneuses*, marking with goose-quill pens in red and black ink the path that the lacemaker's threads were to follow on the *cartons* attached to the rollers on their *carreaux*. Others served as *apponceuses*, joining together strips of lace of various lengths purchased from the lacemakers and preparing them for shipment in standard lengths of thirty-three meters; or as *crocheteuses*, specializing at joining together different types of lace for a particular effect or attaching different parts of complicated patterns requiring several *cartons* to hold the complete design. These workers were so skilled that only the trained eye would be able to detect where the separate patterns or strips of lace had been joined. Finally, a *brodeuse* might sew embroidery or other types of handwork to the lace or attach the lace to cloth for objects such as tablecloths or fabric for upholstery. Some types of lace were soaked in beer and ironed with special irons to give them more body, and this finishing work would be done by women in the merchant's workshop. The smaller shop would employ one or two workers for all of these tasks associated with the lace trade, whereas the large merchants might need ten to fifteen workers.

The concept of "women's work" as applied to the lacemakers of the Haute-Loire seemed to imply that it was "cheap" labor in terms of employers' payrolls and that it was somehow less significant than the work of the lacemaker's husband, father, or brother. All sources concur that in normal times the lacemakers were paid very little. During the Second Empire, the prefect at Le Puy reported that lacemakers were earning between thirty centimes and one franc, a sum he considered to be the "normal level." Highly skilled workers might make a few centimes more than this. "This salary might seem very low in itself," he wrote, "but one must remember that the lace industry is entirely domestic, so to speak, it is exclusively in the hands of women and is interspersed seasonally with agricultural work."[25] Although acknowledging that there were some women in Le Puy who lived exclusively from their lacemaking, contemporary sources from the nineteenth century, as well as later histories and commentaries on lacemaking, suggest repeatedly that the lacemakers' work was "a supplemental earning, in effect a bonus."[26] Agriculture fed the lacemaker's family, while lacemaking allowed a bit of extra money for the home or the individual. Lace provided enough for a bit of white bread or warm clothes for the children: lacemaking meant "a little more well-being, a little comfort in the poor households of this region."[27] According to one observer, writing immediately after the Second World War, for nine-tenths of those involved, lace was "a supplementary trade to agriculture, made necessary by the mountainous character of the region and engaged in during *idle time*."[28]

It is possible that this last characterization of lacemaking was more valid for the mid-twentieth century, when there were fewer lacemakers and income from agriculture was substantially better, than it was for the nineteenth century. But overall, it would be wrong to imagine lacemakers sitting in their doorways or chatting with their neighbors as their busy fingers twisted threads and placed pins in the *carreaux* on their laps, or out in the field making lace as they watched the sheep or cattle, merely in order to bring in some extra income for "luxuries" or added comfort. The author of the best social and economic survey of the Haute-Loire in the nineteenth century, although adopting the common terminology of "supplemental" work, noted oxymoronically that industries such as lacemaking provided "an *essential* supplementary resource."[29]

In fact, the very notion of *supplementary* work for women in the Haute-Loire during the nineteenth century seems problematic. Virtually all of them had to make lace in order for their families to make ends meet; their wages from lace were as indispensable as the money brought in by the men. In response to arguments at the turn of the century that low wages were "good" for women because they kept them in the home, one perceptive writer commented: "One cannot repeat too often that women workers, whether peasants or not, as a general rule work in order to support their own needs or those of a family; those for whom a salary is truly supplementary, that is to say for buying uniquely superfluous goods, are the most rare exceptions."[30] Emphasizing the importance of lacemaking to the Haute-Loire, the author of a statistical survey published at the end of the Second Empire noted: "It gives to the woman a very large part in the work which ensures the upkeep and well-being of the family." Indicating clearly that lacemaking was more than a part-time hobby for the women of the region, this writer even complained: "However, in absorbing the greatest part of female activity in a large number of rural communes and in certain cities, notably the most important town [Le Puy], the *carreau* distracts women from their housekeeping chores and the interior of their homes are let go to rack and ruin, leaving much to be desired in terms of cleanliness."[31] One wonders whether he realized the contradiction between his comments and the prevalent ideology which emphasized that lacemaking developed good habits in young girls by promoting tidiness.

The backbone—or perhaps better put, the fingers—of the lace industry were the thousands of women and young girls who made the strips of lace in their homes, and from whose labor the merchants' fortunes were made. Some lacemakers worked year-round, particularly those living in cities such as Le Puy or Craponne; but far and away the most common practice was that women who worked in the fields alongside their husbands or brothers during harvest time and at other moments when they were needed for agricultural chores produced relatively little lace at those times. These women would produce large quantities of lace during the long winter season. (In the highest parts of the Haute-Loire one might be snowed in for five or six months.) Unfortunately, they could not always count on receiving a good price for the lace they had made. Any number of factors beyond their control might affect the value of their product. In an extremely volatile and insecure business, not surprisingly, the lacemakers themselves were in the most precarious position. The lacemakers of Le Puy and its environs were buffeted by the changing winds of Parisian fashion, subject to the impact of war and revolution, and threatened by competition from cheap, machine-made imitations of their artistry. These problems affected the lace merchants and their families as well, of course, but the fabulous wealth they had accumulated from their businesses allowed them to ride out many storms that the lowly lacemakers, usually paid the most minimal wage, could weather much less easily.

For approximately 60,000 women in the Haute-Loire, many of whose circumstances could be described as bare subsistence, wages from lacemaking were an important source of income in the nineteenth century.[32] Significantly, a woman who was asked "Do you work?" knew that she was being asked "Do you make lace?" *Travailler* for the women of Le Puy and the Haute-Loire meant making lace.[33] To establish exactly how much money they derived from this work is difficult if not impossible. Like everything else in the lace business, wages were volatile. One can follow their fluctuations only in the most general manner by examining prefects' reports or documents originating with the Conseils des Prudhommes. A statistical survey taken at the end of the Second Empire suggested a formula based on estimates of percentages that merchant-fabricants paid out in wages in relation to other expenses and profits; but these are very rough gauges of questionable value. In a rough manner these "official" sources suggest a range of fifty centimes to one franc per day as the "average wage" of a lacemaker in the Haute-Loire during most of the century.[34] Whatever the best statistical estimate might be, it is unlikely that the workers with whom we are concerned calculated their earnings in terms of an average wage.

As William Reddy has demonstrated with regard to textile workers in northern France during the same period,[35] given the unpredictability of wage rates, no lacemaker could anticipate with confidence the level of her earnings from one week to the next. She was paid not for her time but for the individual strips of lace whose value differed according to the complexity of the pattern, the quality of her work, and the fashion world's demand as interpreted by the merchant with whom she had contracted. It was not at all uncommon for a lacemaker to work assiduously over the winter months on a pattern that had been in great demand in November only to be told when she delivered her lace in March that, because styles had changed, the merchant could pay only one-half or one-fourth the amount he had paid the previous fall. In Reddy's example, the lacemaker had little recourse when confronted with the merchant's decision. The prefect in Le Puy advised her to bring her complaint before the Conseil des Prudhommes, but local police authorities in the small villages of the Haute-Loire confirmed the lacemakers' claimes that they could not afford the time or the expense for a trip to Le Puy, only to have the Conseil des Prudhommes, whose president was inevitably a lace merchant, decide against them.[36]

During most of the nineteenth century, the majority of the lacemakers in the Haute-Loire, working with well-known, popular patterns, probably made no more than fifty or sixty centimes per day. When times were good, they might have averaged one franc, or a bit more. But there were moments (for example, under the Second Empire, when lace-covered crinolines were all the rage, or during the early 1870s, when every fashionable lady had to have a black lace shawl) when the caprice of fashion drove merchants to offer three, four, or even six francs for a day's product. At these golden moments even the men of the Haute-Loire were reported to have tried their hands at the *carreau*.[37]

Wages in the lacemaking trade were essentially piecework rates. Salaries per se were paid only to a small number of highly skilled lacemakers, the *chantillonneuses*, who worked in the merchants' shops trying out new patterns in order to determine the approximate length of time, quantity of material, and level of skill needed for the work. The *chantillonneuses* and other workers employed full-time in the merchants' stores made approximately thirty-five to forty francs per month.[38] The large majority of lacemakers, however, were paid for each piece of lace produced. For most of the century, women in the Haute-Loire were given thread and patterns by the merchant-fabricant and paid upon delivery of the finished lace (so much for a given length of lace with deduction for flaws). If she lived in Le Puy, the lacemaker would take her lace directly to the merchant's shop. Normally, she would deal only with the merchant who had given her the thread. But if the pattern was one of the traditional ones that all merchants bought, she might shop around for the best price.

One of the most intriguing aspects of the documentation concerning wages is evidence that the lacemakers were not entirely at the mercy of the merchant-fabricants. They did not hesitate to take advantage of favorable conditions to insist on better compensation. Merchants, desperate to beat their competitors to the new pattern that would strike the fancy of the trendsetters in Paris, and pressured by clients to supply the season's hottest item at once, would find that many lacemakers refused to make new patterns unless paid more for their trouble. Even when offered more money, some women preferred to make the old patterns with which they were familiar, although they knew they would be paid very little for this work. To the dismay and perplexity of the fabricants, clearly they were not motivated by money alone.[39] Similarly, industrial inspectors reported that many young women in the Haute-Loire rejected better-paying jobs in the ribbonmaking factories of the region in favor of lacemaking, because the environment in which they worked was more pleasant and they could control the pace of their work.[40]

If the lacemaker lived in the countryside, most transactions with the merchants would pass through the hands of an intermediary, a *leveuse*, who would supply her with materials, pick up the lace, and pay for it. This role was filled frequently by a *béate*, who taught the catechism and lacemaking to young girls and organized evening *veillées* for lacemakers in the small villages of the department. The *leveuses* would take the finished lace to Le Puy or to towns such as Craponne or La Chaise-Dieu that served as pickup points for agents of the Ponot (Le Puy) merchants. Standard practice seems to have been for merchants to allow a 5 or 6 percent benefice to the *leveuses* on the wages they paid to the lacemakers. The *leveuse* would also be paid, of course, for the lace she had made herself. Frequent complaints from lacemakers that they were being cheated by the *leveuses* suggest that these women may have enlarged their compensation by false reporting of rates offered by the merchants and by excessive charges for flaws in the lace. In any case they certainly drew more income from their activity than did the average lacemaker.[41]

The chance discovery of the account books for one merchant-fabricant family, the Avond-Portals,[42] provides a precise description of the activity of the *leveuses* in their employ. The register for the first nine months of 1868, for example, indicates that thirty-five women and fifteen men brought lace into the shop under some sort of arrangement with the merchant. In addition to these transactions noted by name, the books record a large number of anonymous purchases of lace under the title "various credits." For every strip of lace there was a notation of pattern number, length, and wages paid to the lacemaker. Considering the number of transactions recorded, and specific indications of "benefice to the *leveuse*," it appears that about one-fourth of the women worked under a regular arrangement with the merchant whereby they combed the countryside—in most cases notations of Craponne, La Chaise-Dieu, Chalignac, and so forth suggest that each *leveuse* had her own "territory"—and brought packets of lace to Le Puy periodically. Of the nine women who can clearly be identified as *leveuses*, seven were paid a 5 percent benefice and two were given 6 percent. Most of the *leveuses* came to Le Puy once or twice a month, although one of them returned with smaller quantities of lace every week. Together they paid out in wages to individual lacemakers almost 20,000 francs. Mlle Fannie Manson, who delivered the largest quantity of lace (7,040 francs' worth), received the largest benefice, 395 francs. This amount of money, which might have been in addition to payment for lace the *leveuse* made herself, was approximately twice what a skillful lacemaker could expect to receive for a year's work in 1868. Ten women with only one transaction and eight others with five or fewer visits to the merchant's shop may have been selling their own lace or that of their family, because the amount of money paid to them was under 325 francs (and for most, only 100 or 200 francs). No benefice was indicated for any of these transactions.

The eight remaining women present a bit of a mystery. Most came into the shop fairly often—at least once a month for five of them, twice a month for one, and every other month for two others. Half of these women were from out of town (one from Nantes, but the others from towns nearby). All were paid fairly substantial amounts of money (from 550 to 2,235 francs) for the lace they delivered, but none was paid a benefice as such. For three of these women no payment to them was noted, whereas the others were credited with some portion of the amount they had paid out to the lacemakers, from one-third, to one-half, to almost the full amount— one woman who had paid out 750 francs to the lacemakers was paid 696 francs. Clearly, these were not *leveuses* with the usual 5 or 6 percent benefice, yet they seem to have had some sort of regular association with the merchant, because they paid out wages to lacemakers for him, and they were paid as though they were agents of some sort.

Might they have had some sort of arrangement similar to that of the fifteen men who were also credited with bringing in lace to the shop? Only four of these men are identified as having received payment or reimbursement for their activities. In each case this was far more than a benefice would have produced. One man was even paid 100 francs more than the 1,787 francs he had paid out in wages for the lace he delivered. In contrast to the women, the men seem to have received fairly regular payments of substantial amounts of money, as if they were regular, salaried employees or agents of the merchant. Since almost all of the evidence available to me mentions only *leveuses* (or men working as factors in a similar capacity) as the intermediaries between lacemakers and merchants, I am uncertain who these other, apparently more numerous, agents may have been.

In terms of total amounts of money paid out by the company for lace, the nine *leveuses* handled 18,997 francs, compared to 15,075 for the fifteen men. The most active man paid out only 2,022 francs, less than one-third of Fannie Manson's activity. The eight women in the "mystery" category paid out 8,932 francs, while the eighteen women identified as regular clients who sold their own or their family's lace distributed 2,712 francs. I have concluded that all of these agents or clients had a regular arrangement with the merchant because their names were given with each transaction, whereas under the title *avoirs divers* (various credits), the company ledgers record 153 transactions for payment to unnamed individuals for their lace. Altogether these *avoirs divers* total 3,387 francs, but most entries are for small amounts, usually a few francs and even as little as 95 centimes in one case, indicating that individual lacemakers brought their lace to the shop whenever they needed a small amount of money.

Either directly or through these intermediaries, the Avond-Portal company paid 49,103 francs in wages for the lace delivered to them in the first nine months of 1868. If, as has been estimated, an "average" lacemaker might earn 100 to 200 francs per year, the company could be said to have provided work for approximately 250 to 500 women in the Haute-Loire; but in fact, the number making lace for the Avond-Portals was probably larger than this, given the lacemakers who sold their lace over the counter to different merchants on an irregular basis. While suggestive, the evidence we have concerning the income of lacemakers and *leveuses* is not entirely satisfactory. The account books of the Avond-Portal family do offer, along with census data and notarial records, one of the few concrete traces left by these women. At least we can discover their names: for the *leveuses*, usually their full names; for the lacemakers who lived in the countryside, normally a first name (Marie, Paulette, Annie), but occasionally only a nickname ("the deaf one" or "the cripple"). The notations of the *leveuses*, with their deductions for flaws and higher pay for certain strips of lace, may even intimate something about skill levels of individual lacemakers. However, because there were many "Maries" and "Paulettes," one cannot be certain what any one lacemaker was paid by the Avond-Portals in a given year, and even if this were possible, there is no way to determine whether she made lace for sale to other merchants. Whatever the exact amount a lacemaker's income might have been, we do know that in a relatively impoverished part of France, this money was vital to her family's subsistence.

The delicate lace made in the towns of the Haute-Loire and in the most remote hamlets of the region surrounding its commercial hub at Le Puy found its way into an international network of trade reaching clients in England, the United States, and Latin America, as well as the lucrative internal market centered in Parisian fashion houses. Significant fortunes were made in the lace trade in the nineteenth century, and an examination of the generation of these fortunes illuminates several aspects of the lace business.

In the nineteenth century in the Haute-Loire, the threads of fortune led from a dingy peasant farmhouse or a village assembly through the hands of a *leveuse* to the *comptoir* of a merchant on the rue Raphaël in Le Puy to the cash drawer of an haute-couture house in Paris. At each step of the process someone benefited from the lace trade, but the benefits were unequally distributed. The researcher following the flow of money along the lace network from the lacemakers and the *leveuses* to the merchant-fabricant is still bedeviled by the lack of entirely adequate documentation. In part because the lace trade in the nineteenth century was not subject to the same administrative scrutiny as "factory industry," prefectorial records offer only the most general comments about levels of wealth achieved by the merchants. Electoral rolls of the Restoration and the July Monarchy and tax lists for the Second Empire suggest the relative importance of lace fortunes among Le Puy's notable elites.[43] Bankruptcy files (especially those including detailed inventories of the merchant's personal property) underline the risks of a highly volatile trade, but provide valuable insights into the lifestyle that might be enjoyed through the lace trade.[44] Here again, the account books of the Avond-Portal family are invaluable. Using these in combination with notarial acts, recording marriage contracts and financial transactions, and including tax documents describing inheritances, one can obtain a striking impression of the wealth achieved by lace merchants, as well as an interesting look at the uses to which they put their fortunes.

Members of the Avond and Portal families were involved in the lace business at Le Puy throughout the nineteenth century. A Portal was among the four merchant-fabricants representing Le Puy at an exposition sponsored by Napoleon in 1802, and the Guichard-Portal company was described as one of the leaders of the industry in the Haute-Loire during the following decade.[45] For the balance of the century their names do not appear in the front ranks of the great lacemaking families, but they may be taken as typical of the middling merchant at Le Puy, not fabulously wealthy but leading a very comfortable life. Account books from the 1840s through the 1890s describe the activity of the Avond-Portal business, and marriage records and inheritance documents allow us to follow the growth of their fortune. Like the evidence for wages of lacemakers and *leveuses*, the sources concerning the fortunes of the merchants are uneven.

Just as the calculation of an "average wage" for the lacemakers was difficult and of questionable utility, estimates of the annual income of lace merchants are at best unreliable and tend to mask the volatility that is the chief characteristic of the lace market. For example, during 1868, the year for which I have analyzed the *leveuses* registers, we saw that the Avond-Portals paid almost 50,000 francs in wages for the lace they purchased. According to a statistical survey published in 1872, lace merchants averaged a seventeen centime profit on sales for every 100 francs paid in wages.[46] This would suggest that after covering other expenses, the Avond-Portals should have earned roughly 8,500 francs (17×500). In fact it appears that the family was running a substantial deficit that year. In addition to wages for lacemakers and *leveuses*, the Avond-Portals paid 10,679 francs to purchase thread and other supplies for their business, and for the wages of the employees in their shop. Meanwhile, the ledger recording sales to clients in Paris and elsewhere records only 19,683 francs in sales for the year. The ledgers indicate that Paul Portal deposited 21,500 francs in the cash drawer as a "loan for their lace business" in 1868 and another 21,700 francs in 1869. The first of January 1868 there had been an inventory of unsold lace valued at 7,052 francs in the shop.[47] All of these indications of a negative balance in the company's affairs correspond to reports from the prefecture at Le Puy[48] of a sharp downturn in commerce for the years from 1865 to 1868, with the first hint of recovery for lace in the last quarter of 1868. Although the Franco-Prussian War and the Paris Commune would bring the trade to a temporary halt, the early 1870s were one of the true golden ages for lace at Le Puy. These were the years when it was possible for a skillful lacemaker to make as much as five or six francs a day at her *carreau*, and police reported that mothers were keeping their children home from school to work on lace.[49] For these years the bankbooks of the Avond-Portal family record a clear shift in their fortunes. From a negative balance in 1872 of almost 20,000 francs, the company achieved a small positive balance of 4,000 francs in 1874, which they increased fairly steadily throughout the rest of the century.

A favorable balance of more than 70,000 francs in January 1886 seems to have been the high point of their accumulation of liquid capital, but they were able to weather the bad years of the 1880s and '90s because of the prosperity of the 1870s.[50] Any given year or even several consecutive years might seem disastrous. In the spring of 1876, for example, Paul Portal wrote to his brother Louis that it was simply impossible for him to contribute to their mother's pension. The lace in his storehouse had lost three-fourths of its value, many merchants at Le Puy faced bankruptcy, and he would go to Paris to try to start some other business were he able to salvage anything from the sale of his lace business. Paul suggested to his brother that he urge their mother to spend less money, noting that she had spent 5,594 francs the year before, which should have been more than enough![51]

The instability of demand for their products encouraged the lace merchants at Le Puy to try to limit wild fluctuations in the market by keeping close tabs on the fashion world and trying to work out arrangements with their Parisian clients that would help to spread the risk they took when commissioning lacemakers to work on a particular pattern. In letters to André Ware, Vaugeoir et Binot, and other Parisian retailers of lace products, Paul Portal begged that he be kept abreast of the latest shifts in fashion and insisted that his clients agree to pay for all of the lace they had ordered at the contracted price. For his part Portal promised to deliver the special lace patterns exclusively to these clients.[52]

The Avond-Portal experience suggests that timing might be crucial to one's success in the lace business, but that once established, a merchant might do quite well at Le Puy. The evolution of the Portal fortune as we trace it may not be perfectly "typical," but the impressionistic image it conveys is not out of line with what we know about many of the forty or so established merchants who maintained their business through the nineteenth century. Jacques Jean Marie Portal, a goldsmith, the son of an employee at the prefecture, married Jeanne Claudine Sahuc, the daughter of a lace merchant, in 1825. Portal brought 6,000 francs and his bride a dowry of 12,000 francs to the marriage contract. When in 1867 one of their sons, Paul Portal, married Anne Marie Georgette Avond, the daughter of lace merchants at Le Puy who were to bring the newlyweds into their business, he brought approximately 20,000 francs to the marriage. Interestingly, the bride retained her family name and became Madame Avond-Portal. This seems to have been a common practice for young women at Le Puy whose parents were in the lace business. The new couple soon moved into a residence on the fashionable Boulevard St. Louis. When Paul Portal died in 1892, he left an estate valued at more than 100,000 francs to his wife and children. In liquid capital alone, 60,299 francs, he was ten times wealthier than his grandfather had been sixty-seven years earlier. Well might he have thought of lace as the golden thread.[53]

The succession records offer an intriguing guide to what lace merchants did with their wealth in the nineteenth century. Paul Portal had purchased one large house in a suburb of Le Puy, with a garden and so on, worth 48,000 francs. He also owned two rental properties in the countryside at Polignac and Beaulac. This might suggest that late in the nineteenth century, landowning was still considered an important symbol of status for the middle class in France. Perhaps more interesting is evidence that lace merchants at Le Puy were very active investors in French and international financial markets. Paul Portal owned 50,355 francs' worth of stocks and bonds, representing twenty-four different kinds of securities (especially railroad bonds) from France, Central Europe, South America, the Middle East, Africa, and Russia.[54] A rapid survey of the wills of many of the leading lace merchants at Le Puy reveals that all of them made similar investments.[55] Stubborn holdovers from the putting-out system of early capitalism, the lace merchants of Le Puy helped to grease the wheels of industrial modernization in nineteenth-century France. Remarkably, the trail of the lacemakers' thread stretches from rural Velay to Le Puy and Paris to railway construction sites in Argentina and Siberia.

By 1900 there were several indications that the possibility of "striking it rich" in the lace business might be a thing of the past and that the handmade lace industry was faced with a serious crisis; its future as a commercially viable operation was by no means certain. Indeed, although its death was to be a lingering one, a farsighted observer at the turn of the century might have realized that the industry would never recapture the days of artistic perfection achieved during the "Falon era" of the 1830s through the 1850s, nor, despite the occasional short-lived vogue for lace, would the astonishing prosperity of the early 1870s return. Among the factors contributing to the demise of handmade lace were changing tastes in fashion, always a perennial threat to the industry, of course; but following the First World War, women's fashions were much more sleek and trim, never to return to the layer upon layer of lace that had captured the fancy of nineteenth-century trendsetters. And when lady fashion did smile upon lace again, few women looked closely enough to distinguish between the handmade variety produced in the villages of the Haute-Loire and the machine-made imitations that were so much cheaper to produce. Moreover, should a customer demand the "real thing" (that is, handmade bobbin lace), the lacemakers of Le Puy now faced still competition from their far more numerous and less well paid sisters in French Indochina, who had been taught the craft by French missionaires.[56]

Cognizant of the seriousness of the threat to their livelihood, the lace merchants of Le Puy responded to the challenge in a variety of ways, all of which proved ultimately to be inadequate. Many witnesses believed that the Ferry school laws of the 1880s, by evicting the *béates* from their central position in elementary education, had destroyed the traditional apprenticeship system for teaching young girls in the region how to make lace at an early age. Consequently, two deputies from the Haute-Loire, Monsieurs Engerand and Vigouroux, both former lace merchants, sponsored a bill, passed by the Chamber of Deputies in 1903, providing for obligatory lace classes for young girls in the public schools of lacemaking regions.[57] Contrary to the intentions of the sponsors of this legislation, the students spent only a few hours a week learning the craft. Despite evidence that a few of the girls taking these classes produced commendable handiwork,[58] often the women teaching the classes knew only the most basic patterns.

A special school, La Dentelle au Foyer, was founded at Le Puy in 1909 with a program to train young women as expert lacemakers who would serve as teachers in their home villages after several months' internship at the school.[59] Unfortunately, after being converted to an infirmary during World War I, La Dentelle au Foyer failed to attract many students when it reopened in the 1920s, and like the Engerand-Vigouroux law, it was unable to provide the lace merchants with the large pool of labor they had enjoyed in the nineteenth century. Today, a curious tourist requesting assistance at the central police headquarters in Le Puy may be perplexed by the large inscription emblazoned across the top of the building: LA DENTELLE AU FOYER, marking the site of one failed attempt to salvage the past.

In addition to their ultimately unsuccessful experiments with educational reform, the lace merchants at Le Puy turned to the French government in hopes that tariff reform and laws requiring patents and stamps of authenticity would protect their designs from foreign competition and unprincipled imitation from their mechanized rivals in France and elsewhere.[60] As heated disputes raged between France and the United States over war debts in the 1920s, high tariffs on lace that virtually closed the American market to Le Puy's merchants cannot have been the highest priority for French negotiators. Similarly, success in obtaining government regulation of labels for authentic handmade lace neither stopped pirating of designs nor overcame the basic problem that many women who bought lace garments, tablecloths, and so forth simply could not distinguish between handmade lace and the increasingly perfected machine-made product.

In fact, at the turn of the century, several lace merchants at Le Puy became involved in the production of machine-made lace, and they served as champions of the idea that the lacemakers and the machines need not be rivals. Despite improvements in technology, these men argued, the machines, which produced simple patterns very rapidly, and with little difference in quality from handmade lace, could never produce the most artistic designs. Consequently, the "modern" lace merchants urged the region's lacemakers to abandon the simple patterns and concentrate on more intricate work, for which they might receive higher pay without fear that the machines would replace them.[61] Not surprisingly, such merchants were among the supporters of La Dentelle au Foyer's attempts to develop a core of highly skilled lacemakers for the region; and they were heard calling plaintively for the emergence of imaginative new designers to revive the industry through their artistry and leadership as Falon had done in the previous century. While several prominent merchants called for cooperation between the producers of handmade and machine-made lace, the fact that separate patronal syndicates were maintained suggests that their interests were not always identical.

Although the introduction of machine-made lace did extend the life of commercial lacemaking in Haute-Loire, it was not to be the panacea some had hoped for. There were even businesses established in Le Puy to make the machines, and quite a few "factories"[62] took advantage of the region's water power to install machines in abandoned mills along rapidly flowing rivers. By the late 1930s, quantitatively, fourteen times as much lace was produced in Haute-Loire by machines as by women working at their *carreaux*; yet the much smaller quantity of handmade lace sold for 25 percent more money than the total produced by the machines. In 1938 there were twice as many merchants (110 versus 58) dealing with handmade lace as with the machine-made product. At the end of the Second World War the lace machines employed 740 men and women, whereas there were perhaps 20,000 traditional lacemakers, barely one-sixth the number working at the turn of the century. Twenty years later little more than 1,000 would remain.[63]

Lamenting the precipitate decline of lacemaking in the twentieth century, one former lacemaker noted that as economic conditions and lifestyles were progressively ameliorated in the Haute-Loire, fewer and fewer women showed an interest in lacemaking. The young girls admired and tried to imitate the "typist or secretary with her powder, rouge, painted fingernails, and smartly styled hair," not "the poor old lacemakers, with their sunken shoulders, straight hair, and gnarled hands." Women in their forties who knew how to make lace began to hide the fact. "To say that one made lace was to reveal that one came from a very modest family. One was a bit ashamed of it. With a chance for a better life . . . one put away the bobbins and *carreau* in the attic, those objects with which one had had to work so hard for so little."[64]

Notes

Research for this chapter and for my book-length study, *The Threads of Fortune: The Lacemakers of Le Puy*, was funded by a grant from the National Endowment for the Humanities and by smaller grants from the General Research Fund, University of Kansas.

1. ADHL, 2 M 2/1, Préfet Haute-Loire to Conseiller d'État en mission dans la 19ème Région Militaire, 17 Pluvoise, an Neuf de la République Française. Note that all file numbers (côtes) in these endnotes refer to documents conserved in the Archives departementales de la Haute-Loire (ADHL), Le Puy, unless otherwise indicated.

2. ADHL, 163 W 113, "Le dentelle au Puy," excerpted from La Haute-Loire, 26 February 1904. According to a reporter at the Chicago Exposition of 1893, at that time there were 92,000 lacemakers in the Haute-Loire and 127,000 for all of France. According to a census of lacemakers drawn up in 1851, the Velay accounted for approximately one-fourth of all lacemakers in Europe. Cited in ADHL, 163 W 112, Paul Fontanille, LE PUY Centre Dentellier Sa Dentelle Aux Fuseaux, Conservatoire Départemental de la Dentelle, Le Puy, no date, p. 141.

3. According to Jean Merley, Le Haute-Loire de la fin de l'ancien Régime aux débuts de la troisième République, Cahiers de la Haute-Loire, Archives departementales, Le Puy, 1974, pp. 147-48, women headed 53.8% of the lace establishments at Le Puy at the end of the eighteenth century.

4. ADHL, 163 W 112, Paul Fontanille, LE PUY Centre Dentellier, pp. 126-29, provides a colorful description of the lace trade of the rue Raphaël in midcentury based on H. Achard's interviews of elderly persons at Le Puy around the turn of the century.

5. F/12 2428 Archives Nationales, Paris. The prefect wrote to the Minister of Commerce, 18 October 1843, testifying that the merchants' complaints were justified and asking the minister if there was a law he might apply to stop the practice.

6. ADHL, 20 M 47, 21 January 1812, Ministre des Manufactures et du Commerce to Préfect, Haute-Loire.

7. An example of a livret used by the merchant Theodore Falçon at Le Puy in 1856 is found in ADHL, 20 M 47. The livret indicated the date of the order, the quantity to be made, the type of pattern, the agreed price by meter, time allowed for the work, the design number, the type and amount of thread provided, the date of delivery, the amount, by length, of lace made, the weight of the thread worked and unused, the date, and the amount paid to the lacemaker.

8. Relevant correspondence in ADHL, 20 M 22; also 163 W 1, Procès Verbal de la Réunion des patrons et des ouvriers de l'industrie dentellière de la région du Puy et d'Arlanc-Puy-Ambert tenue au Puy le 6 Novembre 1941 sous la présidence de M. Le Préfet de la Haute-Loire.

9. ADHL, 19 MI 3 (2), Hippolyte Achard, Réponses au questionnaire adressée par Mr. le Président de l'Exposition.

10. Jean Merley, La Haute-Loire de la fin de l'ancien Régime aux débuts de la troisième République, pp. 558-61, offers an interesting discussion of the impact of the railroads in Haute-Loire.

11. ADHL, 163 W 112, Fontanille, LE PUY Centre Dentellier, p. 162.

12. ADHL, 163 W 1, Chaleye, 19 November 1941, Préfecture de la Haute-Loire, Conservatoire départemental de la dentelle à la main; Préfecture de la Haute-Loire, "La Dentelle du Puy-Création d'un organisme de développement—Le Conservatoire départemental de la dentelle à la main"; ADHL, 163 W 4, Le Directeur du Conservatoire départemental de la Dentelle à la Main du Velay à M. Le Ministre. Sécretaire d'État à la Production Industrielle, Hotel Carlton, Vichy, no date; and ADHL 163 W 113, "Étude sur la Dentelle du Puy," July 1942.

13. ADHL, 163 W 4, Projet de Lettre à la Production Industrielle, 5 May 1944, Préfet Haute-Loire à Ministre de la Production Industrielle.

14. ADHL, 163 W 107, Paul d'Ivoy, "L'art industriel de la dentelle," excerpted from L'artiste, 1857. Also emphasizing the importance of "cleanliness" in the lacemaking process, and perhaps reflecting an odd, male (?) notion of the nature of menstruation, the man who introduced the use of gold and silver threads for lace made in the Velay in the 1830s claimed that lacemakers who had "disagreeable breath, or at the time of menstruation risked tarnishing the brilliance of the gold or silver, had to refrain then from making lace with those ma-

terials." ADHL, 163 W 112, Fontanille, *LE PUY Centre Dentellier*, p. 118, citing Alphonse Richard as the source of his information. Presumably, women were simply considered "dirty" during their periods.

15. ADHL, 5 Mbis 5, Commissaire de Police, Le Puy, to Préfet, 1 September 1876.

16. ADHL, 163 W 107, M. L. Vigouroux, Député, "Conférence sur La Dentelle à la Main," 23 November 1904.

17. ADHL, 163 W 107, "L'industrie de la dentelle en Normandie," no author or date. This document, although describing lacemaking in Normandy, is part of the documentation, reports and commentaries, concerning the Engerand-Vigouroux law of 5 July 1903, which provided for lacemaking classes in the schools of the Haute-Loire and other regions with similar domestic industries.

18. Ibid.

19. Albert Churand, "La fabrication de la dentelle dans le Velay," excerpted from *Art et Industrie* 12 (March 1936): 2.

20. Bonnie Smith, *Ladies of the Leisure Class* (Princeton: Princeton University Press, 1981), offers an excellent discussion of the movement of middle-class women in northern France from important responsibilities early in the century in the business world to a focus on "domesticity" in the later decades of the nineteenth century.

21. ADHL, 163 E 112, Fontanille, *LE PUY Centre Dentellier*, pp. 126-29.

22. ADHL, 20 M 33, 20 M 38, and 17 M 26. Even those workers' organizations whose membership was largely female often had men as the main officers. Overall, there was little syndical organization at Le Puy, and those with women in leadership positions were very rare.

23. Descriptions of various tasks, activities, and skills involved in lacemaking may be found in ADHL, 19 M1 3(2), Hippolyte Achard, Réponses au questionnaire adressé par M. le Président de l'exposition; ADHL, 163 W 113, P. Mamet, "Au Pays des Dentelles," excerpted from the *Almanach de Brioude*, 1929; and Michele Rocherieux, *La dentelle aux fuseaux en Auvergne et Velay*, I Autrefois, la dentelle . . . , Clermont-Ferrand: C.R.D.P., 1977.

24. Mlle Marguerite Jullien, a prizewinner in 1849, was the one exception I have discovered to this general pattern, and in her "Rapport à Messieurs du Jury de la Haute-Loire" (ADHL, 13 M Exposition 1849), she indicates that she had taken over the business because of the premature death of a young *fabricant dessinateur*, Monsieur Poulhe.

25. ADHL, 2 M2 1, Rapport Trimestriel, Préfet à Ministre de l'Intérieur, 8 January 1859. The prefect noted that children were paid from five to twenty-five centimes for the lace they made. By way of comparison, the same report indicates the following average salaries for other trades in the region: miners, 2F–2F50; woodworkers, 1F50–2F25; carpenters, 2F; cartwrights, 2F25; shoemakers, 1F–2F; masons 1F25–2F25; metalworkers, 2F; blacksmiths, 1F50–2F; locksmiths, 2F; weavers, 2F; tailors 1F50–2F; ribbonmakers and workers in velvet and passementerie, 1F25–1F50.

26. ADHL, 163 W 113, "Délégation Régionale de l'Artisanat de Clermont-Ferrand," Enquête de l'I.S.E.A., 9 November 1945, Département: Haute-Loire, Métier: Dentelle.

27. Churand, "La fabrication de la dentelle dans le Velay," p. 2.

28. Ibid.

29. Merley, *La Haute-Loire de la fin de l'ancien Régime aux débuts de la troisième République*, pp. 120-21. My emphasis.

30. ADHL, 163 W 107, Honoré Bayzelon, Extraits de l'industrie de la dentelle à la main, no date, but from marginal notation probably written in 1906.

31. Hippolyte Malègue, *Éléments de statistique générale du département de la Haute-Loire*, (Paris: 1872), Guillaumin et Cie, p. 166.

32. Since the total population was under 300,000 it is clear that *most* women and young girls in the Haute-Loire were lacemakers at least for part of their lives. Estimates vary from 30,000 to 120,000 for the total number active in lacemaking, but a figure of 50-70,000 is given most commonly.

33. ADHL, 163 W 113, Elisabeth Savy, "La dentelle à la main du Puy en Velay," *Bulletin de l'Association des diplômes aux Exposition national du Travail* 2 (no date): 3.

34. Malègue, *Élements de Statistique Générale du département de la Haute-Loire*, pp. 167-68; Conseils des Prudhommes reports in ADHL, 20 M 9 and 20 M 10; but especially prefects' reports in ADHL, 2 M2 1, regularly include wages for various occupations.

35. William M. Reddy, *The Rise of Market Culture* (Cambridge: Cambridge University Press, 1984), pp. 157-68.

36. ADHL, 20 M 47, Maire, Chorrèlles, to Préfet, Haute-Loire, 8 September 1852, and Commissaire de Police, Craponne, to Préfet, Haute-Loire, 12 October 1853. Although local officials (mayors and police) took the side of the lacemakers in these disputes and provided clear evidence that the lacemakers were being "continually exploited in the most unfair manner," the prefect replied that the lacemakers should come before the Conseil des Prud-hommes, where he believed they would receive an impartial hearing.

37. ADHL, 163 W 113, P. Mamet, "Au Pays des Dentelles," p. 1.

38. This estimate is based on my analysis of the account books of the Avond-Portal family (Musée Crozatier, Le Puy). According to the doctoral thesis of Louis Lavastre, *Dentellières et dentelles du Puy* (Le Puy: Imprimerie Peyriller, Rouchon et Gamon, 1911), p. 64, the *échantillonneuses* might average 50-60 francs per month.

39. Musée Crozatier, Correspondence Avond-Portal, 12 March 1877, Paul Portal to Monsieur Delafond, Paris, and 8 August 1877, Paul Portal to Monsieur Warée, Paris.

40. ADHL, 20 M 17, L'Inspecteur Divisionnaire Charrarriz to Monsieur le Préfet, 30 June 1889, describes the unhealthy conditions for young women in the small ribbon factories of the Haute-Loire.

41. Lavastre, *Dentellières*, p. 15, notes that in 1709 the Bishop of St. Flour had ordered priests to use the confessional to encourage *leveuses* to be more honest in their dealings with the lacemakers. He comments that by the end of the nineteenth century, the merchants had begun to eliminate the *leveuses* as intermediaries. Better means of transportation made it easier for them to pick up the lace directly from the lacemakers. (p. 45)

42. I was very fortunate to stumble across (almost literally) twenty-four account books and ledgers which had been stored in two cardboard boxes in the attic of the Musée Crozatier. A lace designer at the National Conservatory of Lace at Le Puy told me that he thought he had seen these records when searching through the attic for old lace patterns. The director of the museum, who had no idea that the boxes were there, was happy to let me consult them in exchange for my agreement to label each volume with a brief description of its contents. To my knowledge these are the *only* records of this sort in existence. In any case none of the other descendants of nineteenth-century lace merchant families have been willing to make their records public. The financial information in the next few pages was drawn from these accounting registers.

43. ADHL, 4 M 177. These lists must be used with caution. One historian, Jean Merley, *L'Industrie en Haute-Loire* (Lyon: Centre d'histoire économique et sociale de la région lyonnaise, 1972), has been led to underestimate the importance of lace in generating wealth at Le Puy, because second- or third-generation descendants whose wealth originated in the lace business are identified on these lists or in inheritance records as bankers, lawyers, or simply "propriétaires."

44. ADHL, Bankruptcy Files, 41 U 5.

45. ADHL, 163 W 112, Fontanille, *LE PUY Centre Dentellier*, p. 110-11.

46. Malègue, *Éléments de statistique générale du département de la Haute-Loire*, pp. 167-68.

47. Avond-Portal collection, Musée Crozatier, *Leveuses* Registers.

48. ADHL, 20 M 11 (États de l'Industrie); 20 M 9 (Situation Industrielle et Commerciale, Rapports mensuels); and 2 M2 1 (Préfet à Ministre de l'Intérieur).

49. ADHL, 5 Mbis 5, 30 April 1873, Canton de Craponne.

50. Avond-Portal Collection, Bankbooks.

51. Avond-Portal collection, Correspondence, Paul Portal to Louis Portal, June 1876.

52. Avond-Portal collection, Correspondence.

53. ADHL, Notarial Records and Succession Documents, 3 Q 5317, 3 Q 4604, 3 E 520/38, 3 E 474-81, and 3 E 5vo/414, 3 Q 4595.

54. ADHL, 3 Q 4604, Succession Paul Portal.

55. These records are held at the ADHL for the period before 1900. For those who died after 1900, most of the succession documents are at the Hôtel des Impôts in Le Puy.

56. ADHL, 20 M 47, Loi du 10 Juillet 1915, Rapport de Monsieur Lous Oudin, Président de la Chambre Syndicale de Dentelles, 19 November 1922.

57. ADHL, 163 W 107, folder entitled "La Loi Engerand-Vigouroux du 5 Juillet 1903, Rapports et Commentaires qui en ont précéde le Vote."

58. Dozens of notebooks full of examples are preserved in the Archives départementales de la Haute-Loire (ADHL, 163 W 39-43) with notations by the teachers indicating "well-done," "poor," and so forth.

59. J. M., *L'école de perfectionnement de la Dentelle au Foyer* (Le Puy: Imprimerie Peyriller, Rouchon et Gamon, 1914).

60. F 12 7686 and F 12 7622, Archives Nationales, Paris.

61. ADHL, 163 W 113, P. Mamet, "Au Pays des Dentelles," pp. 5-14.

62. Most of these were very small family operations with only a handful of employees.

63. ADHL, 163 W 9, Chambre de Commerce/Corréspondence/1944-1955: "Les principales activités commerciales et industrielles de la Haute-Loire: Inventaire, possibilités d'avenir, industries complémentaires," April 1947; and Rocherieux, *La dentelle aux fuseaux en Auvergne et Velay*, p. 9, graph indicating number of lacemakers active in the region from 1789 to 1970.

64. ADHL, 163 W 113, Savy, "La dentelle à la main," p. 4.

Working Women, Gender, and Industrialization in Nineteenth-Century France: The Case of Lorraine Embroidery Manufacturing

Deploring the misery of female embroiderers at the hands of unscrupulous manufacturers and intermediaries, a public health crusader in 1856 described in melodramatic terms these martyrs to capitalist greed and consumer vanity:

> Enter with me into this mean-looking house on the outskirts of Epinal. . . . Five or six girls huddle around a feeble lamp that gives off a thick, fetid smoke. They are embroiderers.
> Their thin, pale faces and reddened, watery eyes are as much due to their overwhelming fatigue as to their poor diet. They work from four in the morning to eleven in the evening, their eyes fixed on this blackened and creased rag that they cover with arabesques, stars, and blossoms, and surround with jaunty scallops. The completion of the work will yield for each of them 60 or 80 centimes, up to 1 franc, or, very rarely, 1.50 francs for a workday of eighteen to nineteen hours.[1]

While Dr. J. Haxo was absolutely right about the long hours, low pay, and general poverty that embroidery workers endured, his treatise on embroiderers was very much a polemic against the physical and moral degradation of women of the department of the Vosges in France's eastern region of Lorraine. Haxo did not object to the embroidery industry as such; to the contrary, he considered it an economic boon to an impoverished area. What really bothered him was the array of abuses in the manufacture of embroidery that "prevent[ed] working-class girls from becoming complete women, healthy mothers."[2]

The character and condition of working-class women were at the heart of a debate over the merits and failings of the Lorraine embroidery industry to which Haxo

87

contributed in the middle of the nineteenth century. Ostensibly, this debate concerned French economic policy: should the government maintain the prohibition against importing foreign embroidery into France, or should it lift the trade barrier and force the Lorraine industry to compete against its German, English, and especially Swiss rivals? While issues of balance of trade, regional employment, and national industry entered into the controversy, the recurring theme that embroidery manufacturers, retailers, and administrators evoked was whether Lorraine women could or should embroider for a living, and if so, under what circumstances to promote family and social stability. In other words, gender—in this case, the popular belief that women belonged in the home and under male authority—was integral to the discussion of national economic policy.

This study will analyze both the arguments surrounding embroidering as an occupation for women, and the actual experience of female embroiderers in Lorraine. It will argue that working women and gender were crucial influences on the development of the Lorraine embroidery industry, contributing to the persistence of hand methods of manufacturing and a dispersed production structure that were both characteristic of French industry as a whole.

Recent research has shown that, contrary to the model of industrialization that posits inexorable progress toward greater efficiency and output through mechanization and concentration of production, in France hand manufacturing and dispersed structures were often viable alternatives to mass production. Scholars note several factors behind this form of industrial development, including labor supply, the multiple income sources of working-class households, a distinctive work culture, consumer demand fluctuations, and the ingenuity of entrepreneurs.[3] In addition, a growing number of researchers are focusing on the sexual division of labor within working-class families, and the contribution of working women to explain developments related to this pattern of industrialization, notably declining fertility and the absence or peculiar nature of working-class activism.[4] While these works have greatly enhanced understanding of industrialization and of the role of working-class women in this process, none has been able to show how gender—that is, ideas about proper female activity and behavior—as distinct from the sexual division of labor contributed to industrial development. The unique documentation of the debate over economic policy in relation to Lorraine embroidering allows for an analysis of industrialization that integrates the sexual division of labor and gender. This essay will emphasize the economic and family structures that made embroidery a female occupation in Lorraine, and that enabled women to resist manufacturers' efforts to alter the production process at the expense of embroiderers' independence and convenience. It will also show how gender informed the arguments about national economic policy, resulting in the perpetuation of dispersed, hand manufacturing of embroidery in Lorraine.

The Embroidery Industry and the Supply Crisis

Embroidering has a long history in France. For centuries prior to the French

them in the more prestigious agricultural sector, as in Lorraine.[14] Because of the poorer economic conditions, compared to Lorraine, in the area surrounding St. Gall and Appenzell, the sexual division of labor that designated embroidering as women's work did not develop. Finally, wages were lower in Switzerland than in France, due to lower costs of living, which meant that Swiss manufacturers sold their embroidery at lower prices than the French.[15] For all of these reasons Swiss embroidery presented a formidable rival to the Lorraine product because it was finely executed and comparatively cheap.

Not surprisingly, Parisian retailers began to order embroidery from Switzerland, despite the fact that its importation was prohibited by an 1816 law designed to protect the French cotton textile industries. Smuggling Swiss embroidery was relatively easy, however, until Lorraine manufacturers complained to the French government about this violation of the law. From 1846 to 1848, customs officials increased their vigilance, searching retail shops in Paris and confiscating suspected contraband embroidery from Switzerland.[16] But these measures solved neither retailers' demand for fine embroidery nor manufacturers' fears of Swiss competition. Presumably in response to this situation, a few manufacturers in Lorraine tried to increase their output of fine embroidery by introducing a frame method of embroidering to their handworkers. But such a change in production proved fairly costly to manufacturers and unacceptable to most embroiderers.

In order to introduce frame embroidering into the Lorraine countryside, manufacturers had to establish workshops, hire embroidery teachers, purchase frames, and then persuade embroiderers to give up regular earnings during a six-month to one-year apprenticeship while they learned to embroider with a frame. These changes in the labor process represented a form of proletarianization because they increased the number of women solely dependent on wage earning for their livelihoods and increased manufacturers' control over embroiderers.[17] As an embroidery mistress in charge of a workshop with thirty-five embroiderers asserted, "This is advantageous because I supervise them [les surveille]. The work is better done, and in addition they work harder."[18] To be sure, women were learning a new skill by embroidering with a frame, and they even earned minimal wages during the apprenticeship. But how valuable was this skill to workers under the circumstances?

The frame used in France was "rather inconvenient," as the author of a technological dictionary described it.[19] Called a *drum* (*métier à tambour*), this device consisted of a thin wooden hoop covered with wool or flannel cloth. A worker stretched the embroidery muslin across it like the skin of a drum, securing the muslin with a leather belt and a buckle (see Fig. 5). Just mounting the muslin onto the frame took half an hour, according to a report on embroidery at the Crystal Palace Exhibition of 1851.[20] Moreover, frame embroidering was more demanding than handwork, requiring the embroiderer to peer intently at the weave of the fabric and to bend constantly over the frame while she pushed and pulled the needle through the cloth. Manufacturers could promise embroiderers little financial gain for the production of frame rather than hand embroidery, since they were competing with cheaper Swiss products. After several weeks of effort, most rural embroiderers who tried to learn the frame method gave it up. "It took too long to learn," Mademoiselle Poucher, an embroiderer from Lorquin (Meurthe), explained. "We are used to embroidering by hand, and we feared that we might earn no more doing frame embroidery even though the work was more painstaking and more difficult."[21] Other embroiderers asserted that their hand embroidery was just as good as that done on a frame. An embroiderer in Mirecourt (Vosges) said, "I do as well and as quickly embroidering by hand as I would do working on a frame."[22]

For these embroiderers, the frame was merely a means for manufacturers to exploit workers even more, and the women refused to go along with this innovation because it entailed greater hardship for them with inadequate remuneration. Rejection of the frame was one of many strategies that embroiderers used to resist proletarianization. Other efforts included the acceptance of too many jobs, refusal to do jobs that paid too little, total withdrawal from the putting-out system in favor of direct dealings with consumers, and seasonal (occasionally permanent) abandonment of embroidering to do agricultural labor.[23] But in this critical period of economic depression and serious competition, manufacturers seized upon embroiderers' resistance to the frame to further their interests in another way. Accusing embroiderers of being set in their ways and too independent, manufacturers called upon the government to save their foundering industry by protecting it against foreign competition.[24]

Countering the demands of Parisian retailers for free trade that would enable them legally to import fine embroidery from Switzerland for a flourishing domestic and foreign trade in finished embroidery and embroidered goods, Lorraine manufacturers claimed that such a policy would ruin the French embroidery industry and throw thousands of Lorraine women out of work. According to the manufacturers, the reason they could not compete with the Swiss was that French women workers were too obstinate and proud to produce frame embroidery at low wages.

Nonetheless, they argued, this was no cause for destroying an industry that brought prosperity to an entire region and that generated yearly revenues in the millions of francs. Enforcement of the prohibition against foreign embroidery, they concluded, was the only solution to the problem.

Advisors to the minister of agriculture and commerce, Jean-Baptiste Dumas, to whom retailers and manufacturers directed their c posing demands, hesitated to go along with either side until an investigation of the industry was completed and the claims of both sides could be weighed with some knowledge. Thus, in 1851 the ministry appointed a nine-man committee of retailers, manufacturers, and a customs official for this purpose. In their interviews of Lorraine manufacturers, intermediaries, local officials, and embroiderers, the members of the investigating committee tried, albeit feebly, to determine whether sufficient numbers of embroiderers could be persuaded to adopt the frame and thereby satisfy retailers' demand for fine embroidery. Though they never answered this question definitively, the testimony they gathered indicated that manufacturers stretched the truth regarding workers. Many embroiderers, indeed, rejected the frame, but not for the reasons manufacturers gave, while others, particularly in urban areas, accepted the new technique.

What made some women resist this form of exploitation and others acquiesce?

Round frame or "drum" mounted on a stand.
With the kind permission of le Musée de la Broderie,
Fontenoy-le-Chateau (Vosges).

What resources were available to embroiderers to support a collective works manufacturing system that was less exploitative than workshop production? Census data
reveal that significant differences in embroiderers' roles in the family economy and

TABLE 1

Age and Civil Status of Embroiderers

AGE AND CIVIL STATUS	ASPACH 1846		NANCY 1851	
	No.	%	No.	%
Mean age of embroiderer	22	–	30	–
Unmarried	21	100	116	71
Married or widowed	0	0	47	29
Total	21	–	163	–

SOURCE: ADM 6M 89, Listes nominatives de la population, Lorquin, arrondissement Sarrebourg, 1846; ADM 6M 110, Listes nominatives de population, Nancy-ville, sect. 1-4, 1851; ADM 6M 111, Listes nominatives de population, Nancy-ville, sect. 5-8, 1851.

the relative importance of paid industrial work to embroiderers and their families influenced female workers' response to the frame. From this information a clearer understanding of female workers' responses to proletarianization emerges and a basis for evaluating male entrepreneurs' and officials' views about women and their work can be established.

The Condition of Embroiderers

Lorquin (Meurthe), in the eastern reaches of Lorraine, was an area where manufacturers failed completely to introduce frame embroidering. The 1846 census of the commune of Aspach in the canton of Lorquin reveals several salient features about local embroiderers that help explain this failure. All of the 21 embroiderers in this community of 236 inhabitants were young (mean age of 22) and unmarried, and they were all daughters living in their parents' (or in one case grandparents') households (see Table 1). The fathers of embroiderers were almost all involved in agriculture: five were day laborers, two were farmers, two were property owners or pensioners, and one was a peddler. The three female heads of households with embroiderers were day laborers, and one was a property owner or pensioner (see Table 2). Clearly embroidering was *not* the sold means of support for the embroiderers in Aspach, nor was it a lifelong occupation for women. Moreover, as the archives repeatedly indicate, rural embroiderers invariably alternated industrial work with seasonal agricultural labor.[25]

At this time agriculture in Lorraine consisted primarily of smallholdings for the cultivation of grains and common pastures for the keeping of animals.[26] Laboring on the family plot or tending family animals was probably more important for women in Aspach than industrial work, especially after marriage. In addition, some chores appropriate for adolescent daughters, such as minding younger siblings or watching animals in pasture, could be done while embroidering by hand but not

TABLE 2
Occupations of Heads of Households with Embroiderers

OCCUPATIONS	ASPACH 1846		NANCY 1851	
	No.	%	No.	%
Day laborers	7	53.8	21	16.0
Domestic servants	–	–	–	–
Unskilled workers	–	–	14	10.7
Embroiderers	–	–	46	35.1
Other needleworkers	–	–	1	.8
Textile workers	–	–	8	6.1
Laundresses	–	–	–	–
Factory workers	–	–	–	–
Clerks	–	–	1	.8
Delivery/transport	–	–	1	.8
Artisans	–	–	25	19.1
Shopkeepers/merchants	–	–	5	3.8
Liberal professions	–	–	–	–
Farmers	2	15.4	0	0
Owners/pensioners	3	23.1	1	.8
No profession	–	–	8	6.1
Other	1	7.7	–	–
Total	13	–	131	–

Source: ADM 6M 89; ADM 6M 110; ADM 6M 111.

while using a frame. A recent sociological study of a contemporary rural village in Lorraine (in the northern portion of the department of Moselle) reveals that the extensive traditional obligations of married women left them no time for industrial wage earning. Women in Grand-Fraud assumed with marriage enormous responsibilities for food cultivation and household maintenance: they had complete charge of the stable and animals, they did all the gardening, and they helped in the fields when necessary, in addition to performing all household tasks such as food preservation, cooking, cleaning, and child rearing.[27] It is likely, too, that in the middle of the nineteenth century women's productive work on the land was essential to family survival, and that the wages from embroidering were either a welcome cash addition to the family income or the source of a dowry for a single girl. Thus, women's life-cycle stage and their role in the rural family economy help explain why Lorquin embroiderers refused to adopt the frame technique.

In addition, the many opportunities for and importance of sociability while working might have stiffened rural women's resistance to the frame and to the workshop setting it entailed. The testimonies of manufacturers and regional officials indicate that embroiderers often worked together in groups of ten or twelve at a worker's home, in order to share heat and light.[28] Though the questions directed to embroiderers never elicited any comments on this practice, a contemporary embroiderer living in Lorraine today can shed some light on the significance of collective work outside of a workshop. Madame Rapin of Remoncourt (Vosges) remembers that before World War II the *veillées*—evening gatherings of local inhabitants for work and socializing—were lively, cheerful occasions that strengthened community ties while providing a congenial and relaxed atmosphere for needlework.[29] For embroiderers who could survive on hand embroidery, the *veillée* was clearly a better work environment than a workshop.

But embroiderers could not always work under such ideal conditions. A big job with a short deadline required a different kind of collective labor, where a half-dozen or so women joined in on a single project for an intense bout of continuous labor. Madame Rapin and her friends once worked on a piece of embroidery for two days and two nights straight, after which one of the embroiderers climbed on her bicycle in the wee hours of the morning to deliver the completed fabric to an intermediary by 6:00 A.M.[30] The community networks supported rural embroiderers psychologically and practically in ways that would have been difficult to re-create in a workshop.

To be sure, even the sociability of handwork in the home could not banish the stresses and strains of embroidering as a trade. But rural women could call upon the saints to help them through such difficulties. Madame Bonétat of Mirecourt (Vosges), the daughter and granddaughter of embroidery intermediaries, recalls one embroiderer who lit a taper to Saint Jude, the saint of persons in desperate situations, when she had to do a lot of embroidery in an impossibly short amount of time. As she expected, Saint Jude came through, and she finished the job. Other embroiderers invoked Sainte Lucie, the saint of light, to relieve them of the eyestrain that embroidering caused. They did this by filling a carafe with clear water on 13 December, Sainte Lucie's day, and then placing the carafe in front of a candle to refract the light onto the embroidery.[31]

Resistance to the frame and the workshop, then, was possible for rural embroiderers whose first priority was agricultural labor. In addition, the persistent demand for hand embroidery allowed them to continue to work by hand and in the home, conditions that were more agreeable to them for practical and personal reasons. Finally, the rural setting, with its religious rituals and community networks, may have contributed to embroiderers' sense of solidarity against manufacturers' efforts at exploitation.

A brief glimpse at the situation of embroiderers in urban Nancy reveals an entirely different family economy and labor supply compared to those in rural areas, which explains why workers here did both hand and frame embroidering. Nancy was a thriving city with a growing population of over 40,000 in 1851; significantly, the number of female inhabitants greatly exceeded that of males (22,310 females versus 17,979 males), especially among individuals between the ages of twenty and thirty-five, which suggests considerable need and competition for jobs among Nancy women.[32] The census sample from Nancy includes 1,649 individuals from

TABLE 3

Females over 13 Years Old in Occupations

OCCUPATIONS	ASPACH 1846		NANCY 1851	
	No.	%	No.	%
Day laborers	3	3.3	54	7.8
Domestic servants	–	–	9	1.3
Unskilled workers	–	–	7	1.0
Embroiderers	21	22.8	162	23.4
Other needleworkers	1	1.1	52	7.5
Textile workers	1	1.1	5	.7
Laundresses	–	–	10	1.4
Factory workers	–	–	–	–
Clerks	–	–	–	–
Delivery/transport	–	–	–	–
Artisans	–	–	5	.7
Shopkeepers/merchants	–	–	5	.7
Liberal professions	–	–	2	.3
Farmers	–	–	–	–
Owners/pensioners	3	3.3	4	.6
No profession	63	68.5	372	53.7
Other	–	–	6	.9
Total	92	–	693	–

SOURCE: ADM 6M 89; ADM 6M 110; ADM 6M 111.

two densely populated working-class streets in the center of town in 1851. While the 163 embroiderers in the sample, like their coworkers in Aspach, tended to be young and unmarried, their mean age of thirty was considerably higher than that of women in the countryside. Twenty-nine percent of them were married or widowed, while no embroiderers in Aspach were married (see Table 1). For women in Nancy, then, embroidering could be a lifetime occupation, and more families in the city than in rural areas depended on married women's wages (as opposed to their productive functions).

Perhaps most striking in suggesting why many Nancy embroiderers accepted the frame and occasionally peopled embroidery workshops are the data on the occupations of heads of the 131 households with embroiderers. Forty-six households, or 35 percent, were headed by embroiderers, many of them single and living alone, some living with other embroiderers, and several with children (often illegitimate) or other relatives to support (see Table 2). The next-largest single category of heads of households with embroiderers was artisans (19 percent), which was followed by day laborers (16 percent) and unskilled workers (10 percent). Not surprisingly, embroiderers most often lived in poorer, working-class households. Clearly, women and

Embroidering by hand in Nancy (Meurthe), ca. 1905.
From Chambre de Commerce de Meurthe-et-Moselle,
Cinquantenaire, 1855-1905
(Nancy: Berger-Levrault, 1905),
between pp. 40 and 41.

families in Nancy depended more upon the income from embroidering than did the inhabitants of Aspach, and so embroiderers were more likely to adopt the frame technique, which might better ensure steady earnings. Additional reasons for some Nancy embroiderers' acceptance of the frame probably included (1) manufacturers' having more control over workers since they lived and worked in close proximity; (2) a few more women competing for jobs in embroidering; and (3) the greater possibilities of better pay and job mobility for more skilled embroiderers in Nancy than in the countryside.

In general, then, embroiderers' responses to the frame method depended on age, life-cycle stage, and whether productive functions were more valuable than wage earning in the family economy. The situation of the embroiderers expands upon and modifies Louise Tilly's findings in her comparative study of female workers' responses to proletarianization by introducing yet another form of female wage labor during industrialization. Tilly concluded that collective resistance to proletarianization among female workers was likely when (1) women worked away from home rather than under the supervision of a male head of household, (2) they felt solidarity with other female workers, as opposed to being isolated in homes or small shops, and (3) they were more concerned about wage earning than about other family interests.[33]

Lorraine embroidery workers differed from Tilly's samples of urban working-class women in that most of them combined industrial wage earning with agricultural labor. Though embroiderers worked at home, no male family member supervised their labor, because embroidering was an exclusively female occupation. Nor were embroiderers (at least in the countryside) isolated from one another, because local women often worked together. And contrary to the situation of the female cigarmakers Tilly studied, embroiderers were more capable of resisting proletarianization when other family interests prevailed over industrial wage earning. To be sure, the embroiderers' resistance to proletarianization was neither activist nor collective in the sense of an organized strike, such as that the cigarmakers waged, but it was no less effective for being passive and seemingly unorganized. Moreover, persistent demand for both fine and ordinary-quality embroidery throughout the 1850s allowed embroiderers to earn wages through handwork even after they rejected the frame. Thus, the case of Lorraine embroiderers shows that different work organizations, family economies, and gender divisions of labor influenced the motivations for and types of female workers' responses to proletarianization.

It is also possible that embroidery manufacturers welcomed any excuse to desist from innovations—such as frame technology and workshop organization—that were costly and unrewarding. Certainly manufacturers put more concerted energy into lobbying the government to maintain protectionism than they put into restructuring embroidery production, a priority that momentarily won them relief from Swiss competition and the pressure to reorganize the industry. During the 1851 investigation of the embroidery industry, manufacturers argued their case in both market and gender terms, maintaining that protection of the embroidery industry was necessary for economic stability and social order in France. Though their claims about women's role, women's work, and embroidering often were inconsistent and erroneous, gender proved a powerful support for protection of the embroidery industry in Lorraine.

Gender and Embroidering

Those members of the 1851 investigating subcommittee who actually visited Lorraine queried manufacturers and local administrators about social as well as economic issues related to the embroidery industry. At a time when the conventional view of the female role maintained that woman's first priority was family nurturance in the home, subcommittee members (consisting of five bourgeois men) wanted to know how industrial wage labor affected the social behavior of embroiderers and their families. Testimonies and other pertinent archival materials revealed male apprehensions about embroidering's negative effects on family relations and local welfare, but the vast majority of administrators and manufacturers agreed that the work was a necessary source of income for poor families in the region. Indeed, they supported this position with the argument that embroidering was suitable as women's work because it was done in the home. This argument proved particularly useful in manufacturers' theoretical case for protectionism, despite their practical efforts to remove embroiderers from the home by introducing frame embroidery and workshop organization.

Some local officials asserted that embroidering led to immorality and debauchery among girls and young women because it fostered their desire for finery, which, given the low wages embroiderers earned, could be satisfied only through loose living.[34] Equally bad, according to the subprefect of Mirecourt (Vosges), was that girls who embroidered might never learn housekeeping skills and, as he once witnessed, would treat their parents with disrespect.[35] Men holding these views feared that embroidering, as a wage-earning occupation, destabilized families and promoted social unrest, since women had neither time nor training to inculcate good morals among family members.[36] Local administrators' solution to this problem was not to eliminate the embroidery industry but to guarantee that women and girls worked at home and under family supervision so they would learn and perform household tasks.

Embroidering, as a domestic industry, suited these requirements in principle. But in fact, rural Lorraine women regularly abandoned embroidering and left the home to do agricultural labor. An intermediary in Roechicourt (Meurthe) complained to the subcommittee that she could never find enough embroiderers at harvest time because women were "forced by farmers to work in the fields."[37] Clearly, agricultural labor took precedence over embroidering because it contributed to the survival of the family farm and to regional economic and demographic stability. But how did local administrators reconcile this practice with the ideal of women in the home? Indeed, they strongly condemned other instances of embroiderers working outside of the home. For instance, the mayor of Fontenoy-le-Chateau (Vosges), the only small town the subcommittee visited in which frame and workshop embroidering were common, asserted that "the meetings of workers on leaving small workshops, and in which they chat about their intrigues, might have contributed to their moral decline." Similarly, the subprefect in Commercy (Meuse), who thought that embroidering did not harm women's morals since they worked at home and alone, said, "It might be different if they were gathered in a workshop."[38]

An important distinction between agricultural labor and embroidering away from home for Lorraine women was that field work was a family affair and occurred under male supervision. By contrast, when embroidering brought women together outside of family influence, local officials feared for female morality and docility. Patriarchal control, then, along with economic necessity, justified women's work outside of the home in the case of agricultural labor. However, male attitudes toward the sexual division of labor permitted no such flexibility for men. When the subprefect of Mirecourt learned that a few adolescent boys in his district had renounced farm labor to earn money by embroidering, he protested that the latter occupation "accords neither with [the boys'] age nor with their sex, and even less with the development of their health and their physical strength."[39] What the subprefect suggested here was that agricultural labor—rough, tiring, taking place outdoors, and the mainstay of family and regional economies—was "men's" work, while the sedentary, painstaking, indoor, and secondary occupation of embroidering should be left to women. The rigidity of occupational sex-typing was less important than the belief that men should be the chief breadwinners and should be in control of family labor. It was precisely this position that embroidery manufacturers successfully exploited to support their case for protecting the industry in 1851.

Lorraine manufacturers argued for maintaining prohibition by asserting that embroidery benefited France because it allowed women to work at home under familial supervision and shielded from immoral influences outside the family. Echoing the position of manufacturers during the investigation of 1851, the prefect of Meurthe wrote to the minister of agriculture and commerce in 1854: "Beyond the resources it procures for the poor class, especially during the season when other types of work are lacking, embroidery offers the incomparable advantage of providing work for women and girls in the very heart of the family, without requiring their meeting in workshops where health and morals are only too often imperiled."[40]

However, at the same time the prefect, along with the manufacturers he supported, was extolling embroidering for allowing women to work at home where their morals were safe, market forces threatening Lorraine embroidering were moving women out of the home and into the workshop. As the census data suggest, manufacturers' chances of procuring fine embroidery were greatest where women were most dependent on embroidering for wage earning and where women and girls might work outside of the home. Yet manufacturers supported their case for protectionism with arguments positing an opposite situation for female embroiderers— wage earning subordinated to family productive interests and work in the home. Manufacturers tried to address this inconsistency by establishing schools where girls could learn valuable skills of embroidering (presumably the frame technique) and where teachers, clerics, and bourgeois ladies would supervise pupils at all times and give them Christian readings and lessons while they worked.[41] But the fundamental conception of domestic womanhood won the day for embroidery manufacturers. They concealed their economic interest in removing embroiderers from the home behind their rhetoric on embroidering as a form of home manufacture and therefore a suitable feminine occupation. In 1851 the argument that embroidering contributed to female morality and family stability was more effective in serving entrepreneurial interests than were the efforts to train embroiderers to use a frame and compete with Swiss producers.

Of course, gender arguments were not manufacturers' only justification for maintaining protectionism. Manufacturers reiterated to the commission and to the minister of agriculture and commerce how important their industry was to the French economy, how formidable Swiss competition was because of factors out of French control, how patriotic and good-hearted manufacturers were in providing employment for so many thousands of poor women, and how utterly disastrous a free-trade policy would be for France as a whole.[42] These assertions were very persuasive, particularly given the strong precedent of protectionism in French economic policy. But the argument about embroidery allowing females to work in the home, thus preserving domestic and social tranquility, was also integral to the protectionist cause.

When the commission ended its investigation of the white embroidery industry, it decided in favor of protectionism. It concluded that the industry was too valuable in terms of revenue and jobs to expose it to the rigors of foreign, especially Swiss, competition. Gender, too, appeared in the commission's recommendation to the minister of agriculture and commerce, as members indicated the importance of embroidering in providing the type of work that allowed women to help with family and farm, which in turn fostered social order. "Embroidery . . . is . . . (what one looks for so often today) one of a small number of jobs that, reserved especially for women, also combines with agricultural labor. . . . There is then a humanitarian and political interest of the first order [in embroidery]; for where there is work, tranquility reigns."[43]

The history of the Lorraine embroidery industry in the mid-nineteenth century shows how manufacturers' efforts to control workers, and workers' strategies to evade proletarianization, resulted in a standoff during a critical period that preserved the putting-out structure of embroidery manufacture. Rural women continued to divide their time among household responsibilities, agricultural labor, and embroidering by hand at home, while manufacturers, shielded from Swiss competition, still found ready markets at home and even abroad for Lorraine embroidery. Embroiderers remained overworked and underpaid, but they again engaged in passive resistance when, during the 1850s, regional prefects tried to implement a workbook (*livret*) requirement to prevent workers from accepting more than one job at a time. This attempt to make embroiderers carry workbooks in which all their jobs were inscribed failed utterly.[44]

The situation, of course, eventually changed. As a result of several factors, the 1860s marked a steady decline in the number of embroiderers in the department of the Meurthe.[45] In the first place, embroidery as an important part of feminine dress went out of style. Second, the Civil War in the United States deprived French embroidery producers of a major market. Third, the French government finally adopted a free-trade economic policy that forced Lorraine embroidery to compete with foreign goods, including machine-made embroidery from Switzerland. Finally, industrial developments in Nancy and other parts of the Meurthe meant that increasing numbers of women found more remunerative types of industrial-age employment than embroidering.[46]

However, domestic and workshop embroidery manufacturing never disappeared completely from Lorraine. In the later decades of the nineteenth century, manual embroidering continued to sustain families in the less industrialized department of the Vosges.[47] In fact, in this comparatively poor economic setting offering few agricultural and wage-earning opportunities, frame embroidering flourished, and even men took up embroidering in some villages.[48] These developments reinforce the findings of this study—that forms of manufacturing during industrialization were various and mutable within the framework of manual technologies and nonfactory capitalist organizations. The conditions of workers and their interaction with employers influenced the forms and structures of manufacturing, and not necessarily in the direction of mechanization, concentration, and mass production.

In addition to showing how the sexual division of labor within the family and rural women's resistance to work intensification contributed to the persistence of hand and dispersed manufacturing in embroidering, this study also reveals the importance of gender in the making of French economic policy and in the development of French industry. Gender was embedded in the controversy surrounding embroidery manufacture and trade in Lorraine, which was part of a long-standing political conflict over national economic policy. Previously regarded as a gender-neutral subject, the debate over free trade versus protectionism that continued throughout the nineteenth century in France actually embodied male notions about female character and behavior and the respective roles of men and women in society. Feminist scholars have argued recently that this is not at all surprising—that gender is incorporated more or less explicitly in all social, political, economic, and cultural institutions.[49] The debate over economic policy with regard to the embroidery industry is noteworthy in the openness of the discussion of gender and helpful in illuminating this fundamental basis of social organization and politics. In addition, the case of Lorraine embroidery hints at the tension between gender and the actual experience of working women and the means by which bourgeois men could maintain and enhance their power through the construction of gender.

The Lorraine embroidery industry during the mid-nineteenth-century crisis offers a view of the resources mobilized by workers and employers to protect their respective interests. Rural embroiderers relied upon agricultural labor, the still-viable market for hand embroidery, and possibly community solidarity with other embroiderers to resist the manufacturers' introduction of the frame. For their part, manufacturers' most potent resources were their connection with the state and the arguments about women's proper place and French economic stability that they used to support protectionism. The very failure to impose the frame upon some rural embroiderers became a useful weapon in the manufacturers' campaign against free trade. This case indicates how important the examination of working-class women and gender can be to the understanding of industrialization in the nineteenth century.

Notes

This chapter originally appeared as an article in the *Journal of Women's History* 2, no. 2 (Fall 1990): 42-65.

1. J. Haxo, *Populations industrielles de la France. La broderie et les brodeuses vosgiennes* (Epinal, 1856), pp. 49-50. By comparison, Haxo indicated that cotton weavers or spinners earned 75 centimes to 1.20 francs for twelve hours of work. Ibid., p. 25.

2. Ibid., p. 40.

3. Alain Cottereau, "The Distinctiveness of Working-Class Cultures in France, 1848-1900," in *Working-Class Formation*, ed. Ira Katznelson and Aristide R. Zolberg (Princeton: Princeton University Press, 1986), pp. 111-54; Alain Faure, "Petit atelier et modernisme économique," *Histoire, économie et société* 4 (1986): 531-57; Ronald Aminzade, "Reinterpreting Capitalist Industrialization," in *Work in France*, ed. Steven Laurence Kaplan and Cynthia J. Koepp (Ithaca, N.Y.: Cornell University Press, 1986), pp. 393-417; Charles Sabel and Jonathan Zeitlin, "Historical Alternatives to Mass Production," *Past and Present* 108 (1985): 133-76.

4. Elinor Accampo, *Industrialization, Family Life, and Class Relations* (Berkeley: University of California Press, 1989); Gay L. Gullickson, *Spinners and Weavers of Auffay* (New York: Cambridge University Press, 1986); Louise A. Tilly, "Paths of Proletarianization," *Signs* 7 (1981-82): 400-17. Scholars of protoindustrialization (rural manufacturing for export markets) often address the issue of the gender division of labor in the home of protoindustrial workers. However, these authors tend to view protoindustry as an early phase of industrial capitalism that either leads to a factory system or simply disappears. Such works are not helpful in explaining how women and gender contributed to the success of dispersed manufacturing as a part of modern industrialization. See, for example, Franklin F. Mendels, "Proto-industrialization," *Journal of Economic History* 32 (1972): 241-61; Peter Kreidte, Hans Medick, and Jurgen Schlumbohn, *Industrialization before Industrialization*, trans. Beate Schempp (Cambridge: Cambridge University Press, 1981); and several articles in *Annales ESC* 39 (September–October 1984). For a critique of the protoindustrialization model that raises intriguing questions about patriarchy and the sexual division of labor, see Anna Cento Bull, "Proto-industrialization, Small-Scale Capital Accumulation and Diffused Entrepreneurship," *Social History* 14 (May 1989): 177-200.

5. Ernest Lefébure, *Broderies et dentelles* (Paris, n.d.), pp. 84-162; Henri Noiret, *Musée retrospectif de la classe* 84 (n.p., n.d.), pp. 40-79.

6. Archives Départementales de Meurthe-et-Moselle (hereafter ADM) 9 M 28, Industries diverses, An IX-1939. The report on embroidery and lace industries for the 1851 Exhibition in London indicates that white embroidery started in France just before 1789, but after suffering during the revolutionary years it revived under Napoleon and proceeded, with minor setbacks, to flourish under the Restoration (1814-1830) and the July Monarchy (1830-1848). France, Commission française sur l'industrie des nations à l'Exposition universelle de

1851, *Travaux de la Commission française sur l'industrie des nations* (Paris, 1854), vol. 5, pp. 89-91.

7. ADM 9 M 28.

8. ADM 9 M 28; France, *Travaux*, vol. 5, pp. 2-121; Archives Nationales (hereafter AN) F[12] 2357-58, Enquête sur les dentelles et broderies, 1851-1857.

9. France, *Travaux*, vol. 5, p. 101.

10. AN F[12] 2357-58.

11. Ibid.

12. Ibid.

13. Ibid.; AN F[12] 6884, Broderies de coton, dentelles, 1833-1899 (douanes). Though French documents frequently referred to the embroidery frame used in Switzerland, descriptions of that frame were few and rather vague. It appears that the Swiss manufacture consisted almost entirely of the higher grades of embroidery, while Lorraine produced a wide range of quality, from "rich" to "ordinary" embroidery. Ibid.

14. Ulrich Pfister's research on two rural Swiss communities in the late eighteenth century lends credence to this hypothesis. In a community of small, independent property holders, a gender division of labor evolved whereby males cultivated land and females engaged in rural textile manufacturing. However, in a community with little independent landholding, men, women, and children all worked in rural industry, particularly cotton spinning, and no gender division of labor developed. Ulrich Pfister, "Work Roles and Family Structure in Proto-industrial Zurich," *Journal of Interdisciplinary History* 20 (Summer 1989): 83-105.

15. AN F[12] 6884.

16. Ibid.; Villermé fils, *Les Douanes et la contrabande* (Paris, 1851).

17. Christopher Johnson defines proletarianization as the "increase . . . in the number of wage laborers in a given population and their increasing domination by capitalists," in "Patterns of Proletarianization: Parisian Tailors and Lodeve Woolens Workers," in *Consciousness and Class Experience in Nineteenth-Century Europe*, ed. John M. Merriman (New York: Holmes and Meier, 1979), p. 67.

18. AN F[12] 2357-58.

19. C. Laboulaye, *Encyclopédie technologique. Dictionnaire des arts et manufactures de l'agriculture, des mines, etc.*, 2nd ed. (Paris, n.d. [1845?] vol. 1, n.p. [499?]).

20. AN F[12] 6884. It is possible that Lorraine manufacturers also introduced large, rectangular frames, which stretched embroidery fabric across simple wooden slats, or vise frames. However, the vise frame was very expensive, and the slat frame often stretched the embroidery fabric too much or too little. The rectangular frame, like the round frame, often rested on a stand. Laboulaye, *Encyclopédie*. Two separate French committees appointed by the minister of agriculture and commerce to investigate the embroidery industry found Lorraine manufacturers to be either unwilling or unable to implement in France the exact technique of Swiss embroidering. AN F[12] 2357-58; AN F[12] 6884.

21. AN F[12] 2357-58.

22. Ibid.

23. An embroiderer from Metz (Moselle), obviously fairly skilled, said she had once been offered four francs to embroider a pillowcase very extensively. "I refused to accept it," she declared. "I would not have earned fifty centimes a day on it." Similarly, Madame Bonlarron of Mirecoat (Vosges) also rejected certain unfavorable rates: "I give you the example of a petticoat that was proposed to me for fifteen francs, and which I refused because it did not pay enough." A few workers dispensed entirely with intermediaries and manufacturers and dealt directly with their bourgeois female customers. Paraphrasing the testimony of Mademoiselle Roland, St. Mihiel (Meuse), the written account reads: "She works neither for intermediaries nor for merchants of Paris or Nancy. In view of how little workers earned, she decided ten years ago to work for direct and individual requests of women needing embroidery. . . ." Women who embroidered independently did not necessarily earn more than other workers, but they had more control over their time and made at least as much as those who

worked for intermediaries. Two unmarried sisters from Bains (Vosges) could not say whether they earned more by embroidering for private individuals, "because we do not work consistently all day. We embroider only after we have done the necessary housework." Unfortunately, the investigation that elicited the above statements by embroiderers did not address itself to the women who quit embroidering for other occupations, though manufacturers and Lorraine officials attest to this common occurrence. AN F^{12} 2357/58.

24. Embroidery manufacturer Auget Chedeau asserted that, compared with Swiss embroiderers, French workers "are not very intelligent; they are generally very routine." A manufacturer in Nancy lamented, "The workers lay down the law to us a little. . . . They do [the work] which seems most profitable, and leave the rest undone." F^{12} 2357/58. A regional newspaper representing the interests of embroidery entrepreneurs reported, "Compared to Swiss workers, French embroiderers want to work at home and when they want. They are more difficult to supervise. . . ." *L'impartial de la Meurthe et des Vosges*, 16 February 1851.

25. AN F^{12} 2357-58; ADM 8 M 28, Expositions nationales des produits de l'industrie française à Paris, 1834-1849; ADM 9 M 4, Statistique industrielle, 1827-1834; ADM 9 M 5, Statistique industrielle, 1835-1840; ADM 9 M 7, Situation industrielle, 1849-1859; ADM 9 M 28.

26. Société Lorraine des Études Locales dans l'Enseignement Public, *Histoire de Lorraine* (Nancy, 1939), pp. 656-58.

27. Hugues Lamarche, Susan Carol Rogers, and Claude Karnoouh, *Paysans, femmes et citoyens. Luttes pour le pouvoir dans un village lorrain* (Le Paradou, 1980), pp. 73-77. See also Martine Segalen, *Mari et femme dans la société paysanne* (Paris, 1980).

28. AN F^{12} 2357/58; Haxo, *La broderie*, pp. 49-50.

29. Interview with Henriette Rapin, Remoncourt (Vosges), 27 May 1986.

30. Ibid.

31. Interview with Evelyne Bonétat, Remoncourt (Vosges), 27 May 1986.

32. Odette Voilliard, *Nancy au XIXe siècle 1815-1871. Une bourgeoisie urbaine* (Paris, 1978), pp. 3-4.

33. Tilly, "Paths."

34. One of many examples of this attitude came from a welfare officer in Metz (Moselle) who told the subcommittee: "I would never advise a mother to give her daughter a calling that . . . being a luxury occupation, leads the worker to accustom herself to ideas of luxury and dress." AN F^{12} 2357-58.

35. The subprefect reported in 1863 that too many girls devoted themselves exclusively to embroidering and never learned housekeeping skills. Families encouraged this, since they wanted the wages daughters earned from their needlework, and so the mothers of these girls performed all domestic tasks unassisted, allowing the embroiderers to work unimpeded. Not only did these embroiderers never learn to keep house, according to the subprefect, but they also became imperious and disrespectful of their mothers. The subprefect asserted that he overheard an embroiderer demand that her mother polish the girl's boots. "Doesn't one find in this convention between mothers and daughters, in this degradation of the mother, one of the causes of family dissolution . . . ?" Ibid.

36. Lorraine officials were not alone in these attitudes. See also Baron de Gérando, *Des progrès de l'industrie, considérés dans leurs rapports avec la moralité de la classe ouvrière* (Paris, 1842), pp. 73-76, in AN F^{12} 2361^a Arts et manufactures, 1845-1883; Charles Dupin, *Le petit producteur français*, vol. 6, *L'ouvrière française* (Paris, 1828), p. 44; Jules Simon, *L'ouvrière* (Paris, 1861), pp. 15, 103-104.

37. AN F^{12} 2357-58.

38. Ibid.

39. Archives Départementales des Vosges (hereafter ADV) M 292, Tissage et bobinage 1885-1890.

40. AN F^{12} 6884. In a pamphlet published in 1854, a supporter of the Nancy embroidery manufacturers wrote: "[Embroidering] has the great advantage of solving a problem that has

preoccupied many statesmen: that of homework, which permits the mother of the family to combine with breadwinning work [her] presence inside the household and her moral influence on the family by watching over [it] all the time." Bernard, *De la broderie. Broderie de Nancy. Broderie de Paris. Broderie suisse* (Nancy, 1854), p. 14.

41. AN F^{12} 2357-58. See also A. Deniau, *De la nécessité d'un conservatoire de broderie à Nancy* (Nancy, 1862), p. 15.

42. AN F^{12} 2357-58. AN F^{12} 6884.

43. AN F^{12} 2357-58.

44. ADV M 292; ADV M 242, Livrets d'ouvriers, 1856-1870; ADM 9 M 28; ADM 8 M 22, Législation et conditions du travail, 1854-1900.

45. ADM 9 M 7, Situation industrielle, 1849-1859; ADM 9 M 8, Situation industrielle, 1860-1861; ADM 9 M 9, Statistique industrielle, 1862-1863; ADM 9 M 10, Statistique industrielle, 1864-1868.

46. Ibid.

47. Odette Voilliard, "Le Travail des brodeuses lorraines au XIXe siècle," *Actes du colloque sur l'artisanat* (Besançon, 10-12 juin 1960) (Paris, 1961), pp. 121-35.

48. ADV Recensement de population, Fontenoy-le-Chateau, canton Bains, 1886. See also the Musée de la Broderie, Fontenoy-le-Château (Vosges).

49. Joan W. Scott, "Gender: A Useful Category of Historical Analysis," *American Historical Review* 91 (December 1986): 1053-75.

The Calico Painters of Estavayer:
Employers' Strategies toward the Market
for Women's Labor

In the eighteenth century the calico industry, which produced chintzes and printed calicoes, was one of the leading sectors of the western European economy. In the course of the century England, France, Belgium, Holland, western Switzerland, Germany, Spanish Catalonia, and Bohemia all witnessed the birth of hundreds of cotton-printing manufactories.[1]

This type of product had originally appeared in the previous century. It was imported from India, and its price made it a luxury item: in 1670 one had to be a "person of quality" like Molière's Bourgeois Gentilhomme to be able to boast about possessing "a dressing gown made of chintz," for these first decorated calicoes were hand-painted. However, from the end of the seventeenth century, Dutch, French, and English workshops began to print cotton fabrics using engraved wooden blocks. This produced important gains in productivity and brought down production costs. In France and England the producers of woolen and silk cloth demanded and obtained a prohibition on the manufacture and use of printed calicoes. Yet only the ban on manufacturing was respected, whereas there was an active smuggling trade, and both countries were flooded with goods arriving from many different sources, particularly ones located in Holland and Switzerland.

For it was true that, quite apart from the added attractiveness of printed calicoes to the more snobbish consumers because of the very fact that they were banned, their use value was really greater than that of the rival fabrics used for clothing and furnishings: their lifespan, the brightness and variety of their colors, and their durability when washed were all clearly superior for a price that was some 20 percent less.

When the ban was lifted in the middle of the eighteenth century, the western European market was extremely buoyant. This was to permit an exponential growth both in the volume of production and in the profits made. For a time there was a real printed-calico craze, which encouraged even the most incompetent to set up as improvised manufacturers. The celebrated Casanova, in person, opened a workshop in the very heart of Paris in 1759. Around twenty women workers were employed

"Les Travaux de la Manufacture," calico designed by J. B. Huet, 1784;
detail showing the *pinceauteuses* (female workers applying painted
decoration to calico).

there, whom, in his *Mémoires*, he did not fail to mention as being particularly se-
ductive! More seriously, large firms, which were among the most important concentrated manufactories of the period, prospered on a continuous basis: for example,
the businesses of Peel at Manchester, of Oberkampf at Jouy near Paris, of Dollfus at
Mulhouse, of Fazy at Geneva, and of Pourtales and Du Pasquier at Cortaillod near
Neuchâtel in Switzerland. During the second half of the eighteenth century, each of
them employed a workforce of about a thousand persons to print between 500,000
and 1,000,000 meters of cotton cloth per year. Calico printing thus contributed in
a significant fashion, albeit less spectacularly than mining, metallurgy, or spinning
and weaving, to the start of the Industrial Revolution.

The social history of calico printing remains relatively underresearched, whereas
in fact the number of men and women workers that were employed in it at the end
of the century was considerable: for the whole of western Europe it was somewhere
on the order of 100,000 to 150,000. This figure continued to increase until the
1830s, reaching around the 200,000 mark before falling off thereafter.[2]

In addition, apart from its quantitative importance, calico printing constituted
an original example of the combination of old and new forms of the division and
organization of labor: calico printing was both a craft and a mass industry. It was

heir to Indian artisanal techniques and also provided an opportunity for the application of innovations in mechanics (printing with rollers), in chemistry (the use of new dyes, mordants, and bleaching agents), and in motive force (the steam engine).

This same complexity is also to be found in the makeup of the labor force. The essence of what constituted the technical originality of the manufacturing process at the end of the century depended upon workers—designers, engravers, printers, and colorers—who had a common set of characteristics: male, highly skilled, well-paid, work concentrated within the walls of the manufactory, long occupational careers, stable employment, and high geographical mobility, with these last two characteristics not necessarily being naturally contradictory. Studies of the calico-printing labor force have concentrated on these workers.[3] But in all the manufactories this skilled labor represented only a fifth of the total workforce. The rest was made up of workers with very different characteristics: young children of both sexes (aged between 6 and 11) and, above all, female labor dividing up into two distinct components: the more skilled—the *rentreuses* or assistant printers, who did work similar to that of the male printers—and the others, possessing no skill whatsoever, called *pinceleuses* or calico painters.

It is this latter occupation that we want to look at here in the context of one of the great manufactories of the eighteenth century: the Fabrique-Neuve at Cortaillod.[4] It was founded in 1752 by C. A. Du Pasquier (manufacturer) and J. L. de Pourtalès (merchant) and employed about 800 men and women at the end of the century, before going into decline until its eventual disappearance in 1854. Up to 1820 this firm was very representative of its branch, and thus it allows us to analyze the sexual division of labor within calico printing with respect to two sets of factors: on the one hand the techniques employed and their various requirements in terms of age, physical force, and occupational training; and on the other the interplay of the offer and demand for labor on the regional, and even national and international, labor market. Such interrelations can be drawn out in all their complexity only within a monograph. This alone allows us to go beyond general schemes of explanation applicable to whole regions or branches and to take into account the combination of forces creating a concrete interplay, in the long and in the short term, between factors of production that are both internal and external to the firm.[5]

Calico Painting: Technical Backwardness and Labor Requirements

The calico painters represented about a third of the labor force employed by the printing manufactories and a quarter of their wage bill. In certain respects, however, by the second half of the eighteenth century they were an anachronism. Originally brush-work constituted the principal technical method of cotton-fabric painting, as practiced in India.[6] One of the fundamental innovations that the European manufactories had introduced consisted in replacing this brush painting by a much more rapid printing process using engraved wooden blocks. However, not all colors could be obtained by block printing: only black, puce (brownish purple), violet, red, and pink mordants could initially be applied by this process. For a long time blue, made from indigo, could be obtained only with brushwork. Indeed the indigo-blue preparation contained arsenic sulfide as well as a considerable quantity of lime. When exposed to the air, the latter made a fat coppery crust form on the surface of the preparation, which would have clogged the fine engravings on the wooden blocks or on the copper plates which succeeded them. Application by brush was consequently the only possibility: the crushed willow shoots which served as brushes allowed the oxidizing crust to be eliminated and only indigo of an appropriate consistency to be applied.

Blue brushwork was extensively used in the manufactories, but other colors were also obtained by this process, for instance green, which was produced by mixing a rusty yellow made from iron dissolved in vinegar with indigo blue. Green brushwork figures appear most frequently, along with those in blue, in the fabric patterns of the Neuchâtel manufactories in the second half of the eighteenth century. To a lesser extent brushwork could also be used for applied yellow made from Persian seed.

Brushwork also made it possible to obtain resistant areas on the fabric by applying certain colors in such a way that another color, applied to the whole cloth, took only on the remaining white patches. In this way one could obtain, for example, a yellow resist under blue. In fact, only a small proportion of resistants were applied by brushwork: most of them were block-printed. Finally, brushwork also enabled fabrics that were already block-printed to be touched up or their designs to be embellished.

By contrast with block printing, brushwork required no particular skill. It was simply extremely time-consuming and as such was typical of older modes of production. The *Encyclopédie Méthodique* noted significantly that "in Persia and in India labor costs practically nothing, hence the time given over to these types of work [painted calicoes] is not something to be taken into account. Here [in Europe], on the contrary, time is what is most precious . . . one has to find how to save time if one is to be able to make any profits."[7] *Saving time* was the aim of block printing, which could technically rival most of the tasks carried out by brushwork, save where indigo blue was concerned. From this point of view, resorting to brushwork thus constituted an archaism that was denounced as such by the Basle calico printer Ryhiner as early as 1766: "Brushwork takes longer and is less precise; block printing is quicker and produces a more uniform product."[8] For a long time, however, brushwork was preferred by the majority of manufacturers, which explains the place within the manufactories' labor force occupied by the calico painters until at least the beginning of the nineteenth century.

The recruitment and employment of the calico painters were part of the training and orienting of the workforce. This general process took effect in workers' lives from the age of six years and up.[9] By the age of six, boys and girls could get themselves taken on as *tireurs* or printers' assistants. Their work consisted principally in spreading out the paint in the frames where the male printers and the female assistant printers dipped their blocks; in pulling (*tirer*, hence the French term *tireur*) each successive section of the fabric to be printed in front of the printers; and in getting the many different blocks needed by the latter from the storeroom. These children were paid by the printers or assistant printers themselves. The latter were sometimes their own parents, and the children worked under their supervision in the same workshop. They were thus able to acquire the first rudiments of the trade, and began to get used to factory discipline.

Toward the age of eleven, a first parting of the ways separated the destiny of the boys from that of the girls: the boys became young laborers, the girls calico painters. At about fifteen the children arrived at a second parting. The boys remained laborers or began an apprenticeship as assistant printers, which prepared them to become fully fledged printers at about twenty-one, while the girls remained calico painters or began an apprenticeship as assistant printers, but unlike the boys, they never were allowed to go on to become full-fledged printers. The women workers who remained calico painters could in the course of time rise to the "first tables," to which the most difficult and the best-paid tasks were entrusted as they demanded the most experience. As for the most skilled trades—designers and engravers—they were not concerned by this process. All the workers so employed were male, and their course was without variation: an apprenticeship lasting about three or four years began at about age fifteen, followed directly by practice of the trade.

In sum, the sexual separation of the different tasks was absolute after the age of eleven: males performed the most-skilled jobs or those needing the greatest physical force. These two criteria were operative simultaneously in explaining the difference between the printers (who applied the first printing block) and the female assistant printers (who applied the second and subsequent blocks). These two tasks were practically identical, although the printers' wages were one and a half times higher than those of the assistant printers. However, the first-application printing blocks were much larger and heavier (3 to 4 kgs) than those used by the assistant printers (1 to 1 1/2 kgs), leading to a considerably greater labor productivity on the part of the printers.

As for calico painting, we have seen that it was in fact carried out by three categories of women workers:

- Adolescents doing a job that fit into a lifetime career that progressed from being a printer's assistant (6-10 years old) to being a calico painter (11-15) and finally an assistant printer (16–ca. 60).
- Young women, between 11 and 20 or 25, doing temporary work before getting married or being taken on as farm servants.
- Women who worked as calico painters throughout their lives, staying for twenty, thirty, or even forty years in the same manufactory.

The thing that all these calico painters had in common was their low level of skill: the basic requirement was meticulousness and precision, experience being necessary only for the most difficult items. Training took place on the job, and virtually any woman or girl could get herself taken on overnight as a calico painter in a calico-printing manufactory. This led the manufacturers to adopt a specific strategy toward recruiting calico painters and organizing their labor time.

By the 1770s, Neuchâtel calico printing was at the end of a very rapid phase of growth which had witnessed the creation of more than a dozen firms of all sizes in the three previous decades.[10] The number of workers employed was over the 2,000 mark, with 80 percent of them concentrated within four communes in the Vignoble area, namely Boudry, Cortaillod, Bevaix, and Colombier. The local, and also regional, labor market was completely saturated: the principality of Neuchâtel then had only 40,000 inhabitants, of which 10 to 15 percent lived in the Vignoble area. As a result these manufactories resorted very early to immigrant labor. Between 1754 and 1793, the percentage of workers at the Cortaillod Fabrique-Neuve who came from the Vignoble area fell from 52 to 21 percent, that of workers from the rest of the principality remained constant (33 as compared to 32 percent), while the proportion of workers from Switzerland rose from 10 to 32 percent of the workforce, and those from abroad (France and Germany) from 0 to 7 percent.

In fact, the situation was different for each category of workers, the most skilled being the most mobile. In 1793, 49 percent of the designers and 43 percent of the printers were born outside the principality as compared to only 28 percent of the calico painters. As regards the skilled workers, the manufacturers frequently developed a hiring strategy that reached beyond the principality to Geneva, Switzerland, or right over to Paris or Nantes. The calico painters, on the contrary, were normally recruited within a limited radius, unless they belonged to a family of which the head—either father or husband—was himself a skilled worker. Thus the tension in the labor market was the greatest for this category of workers. In 1776 the Fabrique-Neuve alone employed no fewer than 160 calico painters, whereas that same year the village's entire population was only 800 (an increase of 60 percent from midcentury).

To loosen up the labor market, the Neuchâtel manufacturers first resorted to decentralizing part of the calico painting: they gave out work to women living in distant villages. This system rapidly came up against its inherent limitations, however, which were technical in nature: only small items such as handkerchiefs or shawls could be worked upon individually by women working at home. Guinea cloths, *baftas*, or *salemporis*, all of which measured twelve square meters or more, could be worked upon only in manufactories.

That was why in the 1770s the manufacturers adopted a new solution to the shortage of calico painters, namely the locating of calico-painting workshops on the east of Lake Neuchâtel, in what are today the cantons of Vaud and Fribourg. Although these areas were only a few kilometers away from the Neuchâtel Vignoble, their economic and social structures were actually noticeably different. The economy was still predominantly agrarian. Cereal growing, which was the main form of agricultural activity, was carried out by a landowning, or less frequently a land-renting, peasantry, which worked small farms with geographically dispersed landholdings. A few large estates employed wage labor. Livestock farming, like winegrowing, was relatively rare.

In this setting of small-scale cereal production, it would seem that the demographic pressure prevalent in the eighteenth century gave rise to or accentuated a situation of underemployment. The decennial rate of natural increase of the Vaudois population had varied between 5.8 and 8 percent since 1740, producing emigration both toward the canton's towns and abroad. Various attempts were made to use this surplus labor for industrial purposes, but we know little about them. Thus attempts were made in the canton of Fribourg to introduce the earthenware industry and cloth, ribbon, and stocking weaving, but, for reasons little understood, these attempts met with little success, save for straw weaving, which developed only at the end of the century. In this respect the situation was scarcely different in the area corresponding to today's canton of Vaud. Thus in the 1770s the Neuchâtel manufacturers undertook to set up calico-painting workshops in an area which had never seen any significant industrial activity before, in order to be able to put hundreds of women to work under centralized supervision.

The Hunt for Calico Painters

The Creation of the Calico-Painting Workshops

The Cortaillod manufactory established its first outlying calico-painting workshop in Estavayer-le-Lac in February 1777.[11] For a long time this establishment was managed by Dominique Perrier du Cotterd, who belonged to one of the town's old burgher families. His role consisted in recruiting and paying the labor force from funds provided by the Fabrique-Neuve, keeping the accounts and dealing with correspondence, and exercising authority over the calico painters and their forewomen delegated to him by the manufacturer. On the other hand he was not in charge of the technical side of things. Supervision and control of production were carried out by the forewomen, former calico painters from Cortaillod whose experience and competence had led to their being promoted to a supervisory role (see Fig. 8).

At Estavayer the role of forewoman was filled between 1777 and 1810 by the Bonny sisters, Marie and Suzanne-Esther, who had begun working at Cortaillod as calico painters in 1771. Their wages were relatively high, rising from 222 livres per year in 1777 to 235L in 1780 and then to 269L between 1795 and 1810. Thus for more than thirty years the Bonny sisters provided the main element of technical management at the Estavayer workshop.[12]

In return for the capital he invested and his own work, Perrier du Cotterd for his part received a remuneration equal to 18 percent of the wages paid to his workers (forewomen excluded). He was succeeded by his younger son, Perrier-Dorrington, in 1802, who was in turn replaced by the ex–army chief administrator Georges-Antoine Endrion between 1804 and 1810, the year in which the workshop was closed.

Between 1777 and 1810, Estavayer produced painted calicoes worth a total of 215,000 livres. In its first year of functioning, the wages and profits paid out amounted to 5,500L, representing the decoration of 4,000 pieces of cloth, or 16 percent of the Fabrique-Neuve's production. They subsequently varied between 5,000 and 10,000 livres in the period until 1805 (see Fig. 9). C. A. Du Pasquier opened a second calico-painting workshop at Chevroux in the canton of Vaud in 1786. By 1789 its volume of production was close to that of Estavayer. In 1791, 3,600 pieces of cloth were painted there, representing an added value of 4,946L.

In the following year a third workshop was founded at Grandcour (Vaud). It was, in fact, the result of the decentralization of the workshop at Chevroux, where, prior to 1792, many workers from Grandcour had been hired. Between 1792 and 1794, the

TABLE 1

The Activity of the Calico-Painting Workshops, 1777-1810

	NUMBER OF PIECES OF CLOTH PAINTED	WAGES OF CALICO PAINTERS	WAGES OF FOREWOMEN	MANAGERS' SHARE OF PROFITS	TOTAL
Estavayer 1777-1810	141,000	169,956	14,597	30,593	215,146
Chevroux-Grandcour 1786-1800	47,000	72,772	4,559	10,916	88,247
Portalban 1789-1792	1,000	1,800	0	280	2,080
Total	189,000	244,528	19,156	41,789	305,473

SOURCE: Cortaillod Fabrique-Neuve: Ledgers, Registers of goods sent to Estavayer

work was done in a number of different rooms which were relatively unsuited to calico painting, but in 1795 all the fifty or so calico painters at Grandcour were brought together in a specially built spacious hall with six windows, one per worktable.

The workshops at Grandcour and Chevroux were managed by Lieutenant Müller until they closed in 1800. Their links with the Fabrique-Neuve were practically identical to their ties with Estavayer. Müller's remuneration amounted to only 15 percent of the wage bill, but the forewomen's wages were very close to those of the Bonny sisters. Between 1787 and 1800, Marie Nicolet earned about 230L a year to manage Chevroux. At Grandcour Jeanne-Marie and then Suzette Benoît were successively in charge between 1792 and 1800, with wages varying between 210 and 290L. In 1789 and 1792, the Fabrique-Neuve in addition made use of the calico-painting workshop at Portalban. It had been founded in 1778 by a rival Neuchâtel firm and employed 35 workers (see Table 1).

Thus, between 1777 and 1810 the workshops that the Fabrique-Neuve set up in the cantons of Vaud and Fribourg alone painted 189,000 pieces of cloth of a total length of about 4,000,000 meters. The wages paid out added up to more than 300,000 Neuchâtel pounds, a figure which is suggestive of the importance of these establishments in their respective local economies and societies. If, on the other hand, we follow step by step the stages in the workers' recruitment, by an inverse process we will discover the resources that this rural society was able to offer as a precondition for the development of industrial employment.

Recruitment of the Workers

The calico painters were mainly recruited from among the young peasant girls of the area. The local labor market in fact had a structural labor surplus. Food crises

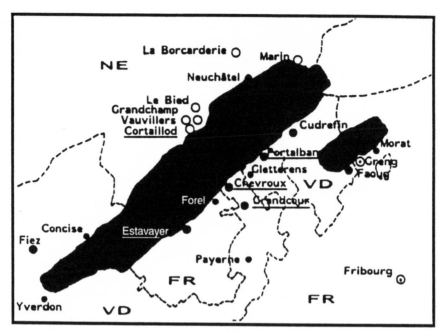

Neuchâtel calico printing and its outlying establishments at the end of the eighteen century:

○ = Neuchâtel manufactories   ● = calico-painting workshops working
⊙ = manufactories managed   for Neuchâtel manufactories
    by people from Neuchâtel   • = other population centers

accelerated the movement away from agriculture by increasing the requests for employment in the calico-painting workshops: "As the harvest has been a small one," wrote Müller in July 1792, "everybody is trying to protect himself from the distress which will certainly be acute next year amidst the poor peasantry. . . . As there are a lot of young girls about, it will be easy to get pupils." The situation was the same at Estavayer: "Here we have a lot of destitute poor who have no idea of where next to turn: they have no money or other resources. Some would like to take up calico painting," wrote Perrier du Cotterd in October 1793, adding that twenty or so girls were in this situation.

Under these conditions the managers of the calico-painting workshops could easily recruit the workers they needed. These are the terms in which Perrier du Cotterd presented the progress he had made in recruiting in the first months of 1777 to Claude-Abram Du Pasquier. January 31: "Our affairs seem to be going well. I will have a good collection of girls." February 12: "I already have forty girls all ready for work; I'll manage to get sixty for this first year." February 19: "I have sixty-four girls ready to work. I think we should stop there for now." February 26: "We should come to an agreement about how many workers we want to take on this year, for if I really

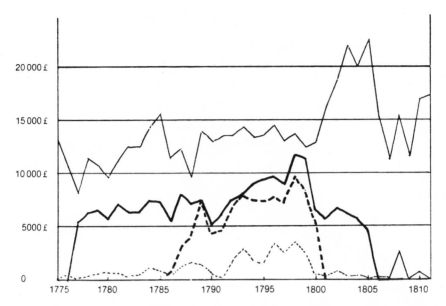

The evolution of the total wage bills for calico painting. Light solid line = annual wages
for table workers at Cortaillod; light dotted line = items put out on a piecerate basis (Cortaillod area); heavy solid line = wages at Estavayer (1); heavy dotted line = wages at
Chevroux-Grandcour (2).

(1) These figures include the wages of the calico painters, the profit share of the workshop's manager (18% of the previous figure), and the wages of the two forewomen (445£
from 1777 to 1782, 480£ down to 1805, 403£ in 1808, and 151£ in 1810).

(2) These figures include the wages of the calico painters, the profit shares of the workshop's managers (15% of the previous figure), and the wages of the forewomen (from 201
to 497£ according to the year in question); Portalban figures for only 3 years: 1479, 463£
in 1790, and 138£ in 1792.

go out to get them in the local villages, I am going to bring back all the girls who go
to the neighboring manufactories." April 3: "Our girls are going along satisfactorily.
Some get fed up, others come back. Our ten worktables (each of eight workers) are
not yet full." April 14: "I have nine full tables at the moment." April 21: "The ten
tables are full and I have six girls too many. I will take my workforce up to a hundred." Thus despite some early turn over and the limits imposed on the area of recruitment by the proximity of the rival workshops, Perrier du Cotterd was able to
take on one hundred young peasant girls for industrial work in less than three
months. Even if one knew nothing else about the exact social origins of the workers
recruited, this in itself would say much about the labor resources that a region of
small landholdings, such as the one along the shore of Lake Neuchâtel, could offer
to industry in its first stages.

The number of calico painters at Estavayer subsequently stabilized at around one
hundred until 1805, save for the years 1798 and 1799, when there were slightly

more. These figures, it should be noted, take into account only those working at the tables: several dozen other women were employed in their homes, but the number of pieces of cloth that they painted was marginal (see Fig. 9).

It was just as easy to recruit workers at Chevroux and Grandcour. In 1786, the year of its opening, Chevroux employed 32 calico painters. Grandcour had 12 in 1792 and 48 in 1795. Together these two establishments had about 100 workers, "women and children," in the closing years of the century, and still about 60 in 1800, the year in which their operations fell by half. Taken together, all the calico-painting workshops working for Cortaillod employed between 200 and 250 workers in the 1790s, when their operations were at their height. This was a figure which, when added to that of the manpower employed by the other similar workshops in the area, ended by creating a degree of tightness in the labor market and thus posing problems for the managers of the calico-painting workshops.

The large-scale recruitment of calico painters indeed led to fears that the general wage level might rise. As early as January 1778, Perrier du Cotterd denounced "the hiring sessions which soaked up all available labor and put up the daily wage for workers and farm servants." The same hostility can be detected in this further remark that Perrier du Cotterd addressed to C. A. Du Pasquier in May 1783: "You would have difficulty in imagining how spiteful and nasty everybody becomes when they see that things are not going well at the manufactory!" "Everybody" here clearly refers to that class of big farmers and rural landowners who, although they were in a minority in the local economy, could not but view in an unfavorable light an employer who competed against them in the labor market and pushed up wages. A fear of the same order was expressed in the obligation imposed upon young girls entering the calico-painting workshop at Chevroux "first to have to prove to the baron of Grandcour that this didn't mean they were neglecting their work in the home or in the fields." In fact, it is likely that most calico painters worked only between the ages of twelve and twenty or twenty-five. They then left industrial work either to get married or to get themselves taken on as farm servants.[13] Agricultural wage rates, however, were no higher than those in the calico-painting workshops. For instance, in the area around Gilly and Rolle in the Vaud, a day's wages for a washerwoman or a grape picker were often no more than four sous in the period 1756-57.[14] But the prospect of being taken on for the year was no doubt more attractive than the rather too uncertain pay to be earned in the workshops.

Another source of tension in the labor market was the fact that the different calico-painting workshops came to compete against each other in the search for labor. In the region of Lake Neuchâtel, the manufacturers, who were all relatives, associates, or friends, passed rules forbidding the enticement of each other's female workers away from their factories. Thus even when they obtained permission to leave, the hand painters could be refused employment in the other factories, alerted by the "good offices" of the duplicitous boss whom they wanted to leave. The employers, however, took into consideration human circumstance, as the following letter proves. The message, with its exceptionally jocular tone, was addressed to the management of Cortaillod by the boss of a neighboring factory:

Sirs,

We have just learned that the reason A. Heyer [a female worker at Cortaillod since 1786] has asked us for work in the imminent campaign is her imminent marriage to Jean-Pierre Giroud, our printer. We hope that for a reason as legitimate as this, you will not prevent the wife from following her husband and thus conforming to the Holy Scriptures.

When among our women workers some exceptional Beauty is found in the same circumstance relative to one of your people, we will be equally careful not to hinder the fulfillment of this precept.

Bovet, Robert & Co.
Boudry, 3 January 1798

Simply to judge by their population figures, the localities where the workshops were established did not contain sufficient reserves of labor. Thus some of the calico painters working at Chevroux came over every day from Grandcour (2.5 km), Forel (2 km), Gletterend (2.5 km), and beyond. At Estavayer many of the workers came from distant villages and had to lodge with the locals during the industrial season. At Chevroux, Müller asked the owners of the Fabrique-Neuve to warn him "a few days before the beginning of the season, so that he could have time to assemble his little division."

So the calico-painting workshops' areas of labor recruitment ended up overlapping. Portalban opened in March 1778 after having recruited painters who had been employed at Estavayer the previous year. In the same year the Deluzes, from the Bied, who were trying to set up an establishment in the area, "went the rounds of the villages to try and hire the girls [from Estavayer] by offering them a higher wage rate." In March 1780 it was the Verdans, who employed labor at Chevroux, who were "trying to tempt away all the Fribourgeois girls that they can"; Perrier du Cotterd had to take the affair before the bailiff, who forbade the Verdans to recruit them. Inversely, in April of the same year, it was the forewomen of Estavayer who, "seeing that they didn't have enough workers, went to get others in the vicinity of Portalban."

In conclusion, the labor market was a scene of contrasts throughout this period. The region had reserves of labor from which the calico-painting workshops were to draw abundantly, but for various reasons shortages and competition emerged. It was as a response to this situation that the manufacturers established an organization of labor which also presented a number of ambiguous characteristics: they aimed both to mobilize and to retain their workers by adopting the model of the manufactory at Cortaillod and forms of organization better adapted to the local labor market.

The Organization of Work

Operating decentralized units of production posed two types of problems for the manufacturer. The first was related to the control of the quality of the products; its acute nature derived from the fact that the painting operation took place right in the middle of the manufacturing process, whereas its results could not become evi-

dent until the latter's conclusion. The second, closely linked to the first, was a function of the complexity of managing the calico painters' labor time, which was itself
necessarily irregular given the role assigned to the calico-painting workshops.

The Control of Quality

The exercise of this control rested in the first place, as at the Fabrique-Neuve, on
the organization of the workers into a hierarchy of "tables" according to the type of
work and the skills required. The tables around which the different groups worked
were from ten to twelve feet (three to three and a half meters) long and from three
to four feet wide. Each table consisted of eight workers, but there were also half-
tables of four. Each piece of cloth was thus painted collectively by a group of workers, the size of which varied. The best workers, who were capable of carrying out the
most difficult pieces of work (the "fine items"), sat at the first tables; they were
sometimes paid a day rate. The last tables were filled by the apprentices, who were
always paid a day rate. The tables were also differentiated by their specialization in
certain types of work. Thus applying resistants and painting with blue were carried
out by different workers: in 1778 Estavayer had seven tables for the application of
resistants and four for painting with blue. Finally, some workers worked at home. In
their case it was a question of part-time work, which implied the existence of other
sources of income.[15] The number of girls and women working as outworkers was no
doubt quite high, although difficult to quantify, and in addition subject to very
strong annual, even seasonal, fluctuations.

By comparison with the situation obtaining at Cortaillod, the possibilities of op-
timizing quality were, however, thwarted by two factors. One was caused by the
physical absence of the technicians—the colorists and engravers—capable of resolving the problems posed by the storing and use of the paints. The other stemmed
from the workers' not being immersed in an ordered industrial environment such as
that provided by the manufactory at Cortaillod. Control of the work performed thus
necessitated the combined intervention of the manufacturers at Cortaillod and the
forewomen at the site of production.

The general framework of this control was defined by a set of regulations like the
one established by C. A. Du Pasquier for Estavayer in 1779:

> Wages will not be paid for work on all pieces of cloth that are stained, whether with
> blue or resistant or green or with whatever color. Work on all pieces of cloth badly
> finished in blue, green, rusty yellow, etc. will be paid at reduced rates, and to be able
> to judge this we will inspect them here, and we will be careful to note our findings
> regarding those which prove to be faulty so that a deduction can be made on the
> next payment. As for the application of resistants, the Bonnys will be careful to note
> all those which have been badly worked or stained in order to have them washed
> immediately, if they are not finished, and if they are finished they should be sent to
> us separately so that we can see if having them washed is appropriate, and as it is not
> possible to see everything before they have been dipped in blue, if any pieces were
> found to be faulty owing to poor workmanship or stains, we will send them back once

they are finished so that the work can be given to those having done the original job, and they will repair them as well as they can.

It was up to the forewomen to exercise part of the control defined by these regulations. As a result they played a more important role than their equivalents at Cortaillod. This role was first a technical one: it was a matter of resolving the problems posed by the storing and the use of the paints, notably the indigo. If the latter remained exposed to the air too long, it oxidized and became unsuitable for use with the brushes. If it was too thick, it did not penetrate the cloth; if it was too liquid, it caused smudging. Humidity and temperature levels also played an important role. This called for careful supervision of the heating of the buildings, especially at Estavayer and Chevroux because of the lakeside humidity during winter. The forewomen were supposed to resolve this type of problem even if, as appears to have been the case, they didn't always have the necessary skills. Thus, in 1793 Müller reminded Jeanne-Marie Benoît, the forewoman at Grandcour, that "the blue must be stirred every evening and the cups [used by the calico painters] changed every morning." To this Benoît retorted that it was not her fault: if the blue was bad, it was because it had "long since" been in that state at Cortaillod. Or again in 1799 Perrier du Cotterd's youngest son noted that "despite all the care taken by the Bonny sisters to render the blue more liquid, it has not been possible to make it penetrate and get into the cloth."

The second function of the forewomen, and the more important of the two, was to "manage and train the calico painters," a matter of instructing the apprentices and of distributing, controlling, correcting, and paying for the work performed by the workers.

The training of the workers was made difficult by the high turnover of the workforce in the calico-painting workshops. In addition, the young calico painters recruited between the ages of ten and twelve had no experience working in a manufactory, whereas at the same age those in the Neuchâtel manufactories had already worked as printers' assistants, that is, as helpers to the printers and assistant printers. The clumsiness of the apprentices is indeed frequently alluded to by the members of the workshops, although they brought up the subject only most cautiously. Drawing too much attention to it would have been tantamount to encouraging the managers of the Fabrique-Neuve to limit their deliveries of pieces of cloth to be worked up, as they often threatened to do. The forewomen could also recommend that those apprentices whose workmanship seemed unlikely to improve be sacked.

The forewomen also had to divide up the work in accordance with the skills of each worker, to whom they assigned a place in the hierarchy of tables, and to control the quality of the labor supplied; and, if the need arose, they had to correct the defects or "to hand out the pieces of cloth again when things had been forgotten."

The forewomen of Estavayer left only purely technical information about their work. The atmosphere of a hand-painting workshop is better described by the testimony of another supervisor, Louise-Frederick Verda. She was the daughter of an owner of the Neuchâtel factory of Boudry, whose father wanted to see her keep busy and to earn her wage in the environment of the hand painters. At nineteen years of age, she kept a journal in which she recorded her experience, which lasted several months. Here we have three extracts, which evoke more the atmosphere of a workplace in a female poorhouse than a factory; especially striking is the length of the workdays.

> Wednesday 25 March 1817: Papa proposed that I inspect some forty of the painters. He claims that they work more under my supervision than they would ever do under the aegis of good will alone. . . . This new occupation will help me to exercise my patience, for I will not hide from myself that it takes a lot of patience to spend the lovely season of summer shut up from five o'clock in the morning until eight o'clock in the evening with a swarm of female workers who do not have the feminine delicacy of their designation and who have given up everything that our sex is interested in or, even worse, who never knew anything about it and who live in the most disgusting unconcern.

> ? March: I got up this morning at daybreak. I took myself off to my post, where I stayed faithfully until seven o'clock in the evening, without any interruption other than that given to the working girls taking their meals.

> Friday 11 April: Nothing is more monotonous than how I employ my time. There I am seated with my knitting in my hands. . . . I am going to examine the work of those under my supervision very seriously. I scold them, if necessary, with a severity which I didn't think myself capable of. And would you believe, that's how I spend the most beautiful hours of the day.

Finally, it was the forewomen who distributed the tickets to the calico painters. These tickets were credit vouchers, printed on the backs of playing cards, which corresponded to the value of the working up of a piece of cloth, for example between twelve and twenty-four sous in 1787. In principle the workers exchanged these vouchers for cash from the manager every two to four weeks, but the poorest converted them more quickly. Thus on May 19, 1795, Müller noted that "as everything is expensive this year, the workers are obliged to change their tickets as soon as they have finished a piece of cloth." The delay in paying the tickets also allowed the quality of the labor supplied to be checked in the meantime. To impose a reduction upon a worker for poor work was equivalent to "holding back tickets," an operation which was the source of many protests.

The responsibilities of the forewomen were thus quite important. However, the extent to which they were able to supervise the quality of the work was limited because of the distance which separated them from the rest of the calico-printing process. In fact, the essential elements of control had necessarily to take place within the Fabrique-Neuve, since it was only at the end of processes that were carried out there later that certain defects might appear. The role of the managers of the calico-painting workshops was itself minimal. Basically they merely gave out cash in return for the tickets and, in respect to the labor process, simply transmitted the observations of the managers of the Fabrique-Neuve to the forewomen, who knew how to read and write fluently.

In sum, it seems that despite the forms of control which were instituted, defects were markedly more frequent than in the calico-painting workshops at Cortaillod itself. This reflected the fact that, quite apart from the technical reasons already mentioned, the demand for quality was partially contradicted by the way in which the manufacturer decided to use the time of his calico painters.

Use of the Workers' Time

The length of time worked, on a daily but also annual basis, is the main target of an employer's policy regarding the management of the labor market. It is therefore important to be able to separate out as precisely as possible what in this area is the product of technical constraints, of economic conjuncture, and of employers' and workers' strategies.

THE WORKING DAY

The length of the workday was identical to that of the workers at Cortaillod: it lasted from sunrise to sunset. This made for a very long day, at least in summer, but despite this there is no trace to be found of any protest or of attempts to avoid this work in documentation deriving from either the employers or the workers at the calico-painting workshops. On the contrary, the workers asked to be able to work beyond sunset on "short days." The authorization to do so was given only with much reluctance by the manufacturer because he feared that a lack of light would encourage defective workmanship and that candle wax would stain the calicoes. The following exchange of letters is particularly revealing about what the aspirations of the calico painters could be.

On October 14, 1798, Müller wrote to Henri Du Pasquier:

> All the girls at Chevroux and Grandcour came to beg me to write and ask you to be so kind as to grant them candles and permission to work after daylight, that is to say those girls who know how to work best in the two workshops, and not those working at home. The forewomen have promised them that they would stay up with them and would take care of the candles and make sure that the work was of good quality. They add, and with reason, that during the grape-harvesting season they saw that work continued after daylight in all the manufactories in your districts, that this year they had little hemp to spin, and that they would be very pleased to earn enough to buy coffee. . . . So I have done my duty toward the girls![16]

H. Du Pasquier gave belated and reluctant satisfaction to this request:

> As it pleases your workers at Chevroux and Grandcour to work after daylight, we consent to this and will pay for the necessary candles. But we ask you to advise the two forewomen not to give out new candles until the remaining candle-ends have been used up and to make sure that none are pilfered. One candle is enough for two workers, that is to say they must so organize themselves that they are in even numbers at each table. Be so good as to tell them, above all the workers and the fore-

women, that if they are to be allowed to continue to work after daylight, the work must be done as well as that done during the day, and that they must be careful to avoid stains from both paint and tallow. If the work is well done, we will ensure that it is not in short supply and we will not leave them unemployed for long this winter!

This exchange is instructive in several respects. First, it shows that if the wages earned by the calico painters were low, they could nonetheless be a complement to other forms of income (hemp and cotton spinning, grape harvesting, and haymaking), and that when taken together their standard of living allowed them to include a product such as coffee in their patterns of consumption. Coffee was already a part of the area's "social minimum" despite the fact that it was very expensive.[17] Second, and above all, it contradicts the impressions that often derive from the normative rulebooks that governed the first forms of industrial work.[18] Here one notes no traumatizing rupture with the normal conditions of work in rural society, where many forms of work were carried out by candlelight. In fact, the calico painters aspired not to the rhythm of agricultural work but to the rhythm of work in a manufactory; and it was their employer who was reluctant to accord them the "pleasure" of working after sunset, as it was little in his economic interest.

THE CAMPAIGNS: FLEXIBILITY AND ITS UNINTENDED EFFECTS

It was equally with reference to the situation obtaining at Cortaillod that both the calico painters' aspirations concerning the length of the working year, known as "the campaign," and the employers' policy toward it should be understood. In an average year the campaigns at Estavayer were as long as those at Cortaillod, the period of winter unemployment caused by climatic factors being generally two to three months in both cases.

The campaigns at Estavayer, however, were much more often interrupted for one reason or another than those at Cortaillod. Layoffs could, first, derive from unfavorable meteorological conditions: if bleaching of the calicoes was held up at Cortaillod, all calico painting came to a halt. Storms or fog could also make it impossible for the boats to cross the lake and thus prevent Estavayer from being supplied with calicoes and dyeing materials. All in all, breakdowns in supplies were frequent. In 1778, Perrier du Cotterd complained of not having materials to work with on March 17, May 17, June 26, July 1 ("Still nothing . . . "), August 29, October 7, November 17, and December 23. These interruptions sometimes lasted for quite some time: "We have been without work for a whole week for those applying resistants, and for two days for everybody else. You have abandoned us completely," complained Perrier du Cotterd on October 30, 1786.

The interruptions were particularly frequent at the beginning and, above all, at the end of each campaign. It was at these times of year that the manufacturers preferred to make their workers bear the risks of the economic conjuncture. Thus in 1800 the manufacturer warned that he "would do everything to employ the workers [at Estavayer] without interruption for a part of the year if this was possible, but to achieve this they would have to start working late [in the year]." Thus while the campaign normally began in February or March and went on until December or January of the fol-

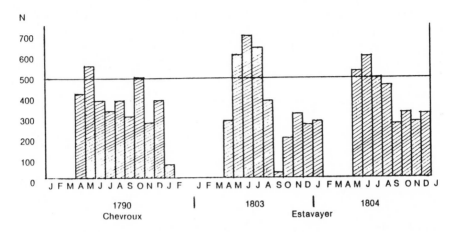

The monthly breakdown of operations in the calico-painting workshops. N = the number of pieces of cloth sent to Cortaillod by the calico-painting workshops. The delay between receipt of the calicoes by the workshops and their return was between two and four weeks.

lowing year, in times of slump it could start only in April (in 1790) or even in May (in 1808) and finish in November. In between times, operations were often irregular from one month to the next. It can be observed, for example, that at Chevroux in 1790, as at Estavayer in 1803-1804, the consignments of painted calicoes for Cortaillod culminated in spring and summer, two-thirds of the year's work being carried out between April and August. September was always marked by a clear decline in production, as most of the calico painters went grape harvesting.

Alternation between calico painting and agricultural work aided a more flexible hiring policy. This was why the manufacturer on occasion encouraged the latter type of work; thus even before the start of the 1801 campaign, he recommended that Perrier du Cotterd "make all the workers stop working during the grape harvest for at least a fortnight, during which many of them will be able to find employment elsewhere."

On the other hand, discontinuity in the offer of work could produce two harmful consequences. First, it could prompt the calico painters to seek employment in other workshops. There was a remedy to this danger: a private agreement between manufacturers, which will be analyzed below. Second, work in the fields could damage the manual dexterity that was particularly required for calico painting. This is what lies behind the following appeal made by Müller on June 13, 1793: "We are short of blue. I am sending a boat across with this note to get some, for the girls who have no blue to work with are going to get themselves taken on by the peasants to do haymaking and will leave the manufactory like bees leave the hive when they swarm. They will stay perhaps longer than we would like, and in addition they will spoil their hands for brushwork!"[19]

The manufacturer was conscious of these unintended consequences. That was why he tried to guarantee the calico painters a minimum quantity of work relatively independently of the commercial conjuncture, still without abandoning the regulatory role he had assigned to the calico-painting workshops. Thus in April and May 1790, despite "the poor state of business," he sent over enough calicoes for painting "of the sort that he normally had decorated by block printing." In 1800, when it was even more seriously affected by the economic crisis—the stocks in the warehouses of Vaucher, Du Pasquier, and Company by then represented two years' worth of production—the Fabrique-Neuve continued to ensure Estavayer a level of production that was above a strict interpretation of Cortaillod's needs, although of course considerably reduced. The managers of the Fabrique-Neuve assured Perrier du Cotterd that "if they followed only their own interests it would soon be to their advantage to dismiss seven-eighths of their workers and to cease to work with him altogether. The only reasons which make them continue are the hope that their business will improve and the pleasure they take in working with him."

The management of the calico-painting workshop's labor force thus appears to have been complex, with the ideal of flexibility aimed at by the manufacturer often being moderated, if not reversed, when the unintended consequences of its application were taken into account. In addition, management of the labor force also had to allow for the individual and collective reactions of the workers. These were rarely spectacular, but they have left sufficient traces for us to glimpse the place occupied by the workers within the dynamic of social relations.

The Balance of Forces in the Labor Market between Employers and Women Workers

For those who worked in them, the calico-painting workshops constituted a more attractive model of employment than what the surrounding economy could offer. There were, however, two exceptions to this situation: the Fabrique-Neuve itself, which was sufficiently close to constitute a point of reference regarding wages and employment, and the neighboring workshops, which offered the possibilities of competitive hiring. In both cases the workers tried to play the laws of the market to their own advantage, while the manufacturers on the contrary strove to thwart them.

Wages

The workers' protests centered above all on the problem of wages. The wage rates in the calico-painting workshops were not in themselves very different from those at Cortaillod. In the first year Estavayer was open, the workers there received 3,966L for the painting of 5,599 pieces of cloth. According to an extremely precise calculation carried out by C. A. Du Pasquier himself, wages for the same work at Cortaillod would have been 3,936L. However, from 1779 onward, C. A. Du Pasquier lowered the piece rate at Estavayer by one to two sous for each piece of cloth. As a result, that year the painting of 7,172 pieces of cloth at Estavayer cost him

4,836L as against the 5,224L that the same work would have cost at Cortaillod. In both cases, however, the difference was slight.

The wages paid in the calico-painting workshops were lower for a number of reasons. The first of these was that the workers were on balance less skilled and therefore performed easier and lower-paid work. This phenomenon was particularly clear when the workshops first opened. In March 1777, Perrier du Cotterd noted that although the seventy-odd girls that he had just taken on were "full of good will" and "were quite good for beginners," they earned very little. In order not to discourage them, he proposed to pay them a day rate for a trial period of six weeks, giving "five sous a day to the best, four sous to the next best, and two sous to the very young." By comparison, the daily wage rates for the same month of March varied from thirteen sous (first table) to seven sous (eighth table) at the Fabrique-Neuve. Relatively quickly, however, the experience gained by the apprentices allowed them to paint better-paid calicoes. Yet taken as a whole, the calicoes remained less well paid. Thus in 1779, it was mainly Guinea cloths which were decorated at Estavayer, with two different reds on blue or over a resistant, paying fourteen sous. These were worked on from only the fifth to the eighth tables at Cortaillod, whereas the first four tables painted Guinea cloths which were either all blue or contained three different reds, and these were paid twenty and eighteen sous respectively. The day rates received by a minority of the workers at Estavayer were also constantly lower than those at Cortaillod. In May 1779 they were less than nine sous at Estavayer, while at Cortaillod the first two tables earned fifteen sous a day and the sixth, twelve; roughly speaking, the highest day rates paid to the calico-painting workshops were equal only to the lowest wages at Cortaillod. In addition, faulty workmanship needs to be taken into account. Wages at Estavayer were subject to far from negligible reductions on that account: in 1778 Claude-Abram Pasquier valued the "redoing" of omissions or defects at Cortaillod at 200L, or 5 percent of the wages paid to the painters at Estavayer.

As the campaigns were also shorter than at Cortaillod, the average annual wage was low. In 1778 it was 50L at Estavayer (forewomen's wages not included); in 1781 it rose to 63L as compared to that year's figure of 100L at Cortaillod. This average wage subsequently increased markedly: in 1790 it was 59L at Estavayer and 72L at Chevroux-Grandcour. It reached 92L in all the calico-painting workshops taken together in 1796 and was 93L in 1800. This increase for the most part reflected the overall increase in the workers' skill and working time, but it was not bigger than the increase in the wages of the table workers at Cortaillod for similar reasons. In 1796 the latter earned 152L, whereas average annual earnings of the outworkers were only 60L; in 1800 the table workers earned 160L and the outwork had practically disappeared. What is more, average annual earnings figures disguise considerable disparities. In 1796 at least a quarter of the table workers at Cortaillod earned more than 200L, while another quarter, including mainly the apprentices, earned less than 100L. These disparities were at least as great in the calico-painting workshops, but overall the gap between wage levels in the workshops and in the Fabrique-Neuve continued to exist. This was to be the cause of numerous demands emanating from those who worked in the former.

As early as 1777, Perrier du Cotterd informed C. A. Du Pasquier that "several girls had already asked him why he didn't want to pay them as much as was paid on the other side of the lake." More frequently the workers complained about the calicoes that they were given to paint, accusing them of being "bad." By this they meant that the difficulty of their execution was not proportionate to the piece rate. This depressed their earnings, as workers were paid mostly for the job and not for the day, unlike the workers at the first tables at Cortaillod. From 1779 onward the workers demanded both easier pieces of work such as handkerchiefs and for more to be paid by the day. Finally, the workers also asked for more regularity in the sending over of the calicoes. The managers of the calico-painting workshops constantly echoed this request, but it is true that this time, as they were paid on a percentage basis, their own interests were also directly concerned: "You should think about their small earnings, and even more about my own," wrote Perrier du Cotterd blandly in 1778, while demanding employment for his workers who had been laid off for too long.

Working-class protest took several forms. The most frequent was the simple expression of a grievance that the manager of the workshops was asked to trasmit to the manufacturer. Thus in 1794 the calico painters at Chevroux and Grandcour asked Müller "through a very humble request to ask the manufacturer to fix the rates [the wages] higher than they are." But shows of rather more lively discontent can sometimes be discerned in the correspondence between managers. In 1779 Perrier du Cotterd noted that

> the girls are complaining bitterly. The first tables will only earn 3.5 batz [= 7 sous] at most this fortnight. I have got some who want to leave and who are stirring up trouble to get others to follow them. Such a scene of "trouble," in which the leading actor was besides a former worker from Seigneux [Vaud] who worked at your place, I believe, with her husband, caused a terrible uproar in the manufactory. I was sitting down, otherwise I would have given her a kick in the ass. She argued with the Bonny sisters, accusing them of cheating on badly finished work and saying that you didn't cheat as much. She told our girls that you paid more for the job than at Estavayer. We came close to a revolt. She ended up by climbing down, saying: "I will go to Cortaillod, where they don't look over the work so closely." Imagine what a sensation this created, and what I had to say to refute her falsehoods!

In several cases, finally, these protests took the form of ceasing or refusing to work. The first of these two modes of action, which was by far the most common, went together with falling back upon other sources of income, notably money deriving from agriculture, for a far from permanent workforce. Thus in October 1779, "disgusted by the bad designs" that they had been sent, a "large part" of the Estavayer workers left the workshop to go grape harvesting. Perrier du Cotterd was obliged to ask the manufacturers to send him better designs by return boat that would be likely "to reward the girls whom he still had and to make those who had flown off regret their action." Other forms of action more clearly took on the characteristics of a strike, the means of collective pressure by organized workers. Thus in 1787 twelve workers from Grandcour stopped working for more than a week to protest the deductions (for faulty work) that the manufacturer was asking Müller to take out of their wages. The latter characterized these workers as being "able," that is to say with considerable length of service and experience behind them; he pleaded for the cancellation of the deductions, declaring that he would be able to replace the workers only with girls "of lesser quality." We do not know if his plea was granted by the manufacturer.

The most significant instance of collective action of which we have a record took place in March 1796. Over the previous year, food shortages had pushed the price of corn up to over 70 percent of its price level in 1784-1793. On March 3, 1796, fifty workers from Chevroux wrote a letter to H. Du Pasquier that they signed collectively:

Sir,
    We are writin' you this to tell you that we canot work on the peeces that you are sendin' us for the prise that were payd. If you do not want to hincrease the prises we all wish to stop workin' for we canot earn our livin' bred is to deer, the prises are much badder than last year, and you pay much less, so Sir try and fix things so that we can at least live, if not we are all goin' to leave, so Sir we are expectin' you to hincrease the prises.

Signed
The girls of the manufactory

On March 9, H. Du Pasquier sent his reply to Müller:

Please tell the workers at Chevroux (who wrote to us to say that they didn't wish to work if we didn't increase prices) that we continue and will continue to pay as last year, and not a sou more, and to require that the work be perfectly carried out, and if it is not it will be subject to the deductions that we judge fit. If they are not in agreement, we will send only goods for Grancour in future and we will do a good turn to more than 60 calico painters at Cortaillod, Bevaix, and Boudry who have asked, and who ask every week, for work and to whom we will give the pieces of cloth destined for Chevroux if the workers of said Chevroux no longer wish to work at the rate we pay, for it is certain that we will not increase it.[20]

The end of H. Du Pasquier's letter confims that one of the principal issues at stake in creating the calico-painting workshops had been to create secondary pools of labor at some distance from Cortaillod so as to be able to play off those working at Cortaillod against those in the "reserve armies" so created. However, this strategy could have been upset by the presence of other manufacturers in the labor market, to wit the sponsors of the neighboring calico-painting workshops, toward which workers left idle for too long could turn in search of work. In order to eliminate this danger, which threatened them all, the Neuchâtel manufacturers deliberately distorted the interplay between the offer of and the demand for work by coming to a common agreement on the hiring of their calico painters.

TABLE 2

The Flexibility of Employment: Annual Variations
in Total Wage Bills, 1790-1799

YEAR	TABLE WORKERS AT CORTAILLOD (%)	INDIVIDUAL ITEMS (CORTAILLOD)	ESTAVAYER (%)	CHEVROUX- GRANDCOUR (%)	TOTAL WAGES OF ALL CALICO PAINTERS (%)
1789/90	+5	−42	+20	+33	+8
1790/91	+1	+770	+27	+38	+21
1791/92	+1	+50	+5	+21	+10
1792/93	−5	−39	+13	−5	−4
1793/94	+1	−19	+4	−3	0
1794/95	+7	+118	+3	+7	+11
1795/96	−10	−27	−17	−16	−14
1796/97	0	+40	+52	+46	+25
1797/98	−4	−29	−4	−15	−9
1798/99	+4	−86	−43	−40	−27
Average of absolute variations for the period					
1790-1799	±3.8	±122.5	±18.8	±22.4	±12.9
1778-1804	10.6	N/A	16.3	27.1 [1787-1799]	13.2
1760-1777	12.2	N/A	N/A	N/A	

The Alliance between the Neuchâtel Manufacturers

The Neuchâtel manufacturers managed the labor market on a genuinely collective basis. They agreed first to cushion any hiccups in the economic conjuncture by guaranteeing a minimum amount of work to their fellow employers' workers in case of need. The letter that H. Du Pasquier sent to the Bonny sisters on February 7, 1797, illustrates this aspect of their agreement perfectly: he told them that the Bovets of Boudry had proposed "to give employment to the workers of Chevroux and Grandcour for a few weeks until he had work to give them and that he had consented to this proposition, being very glad that they would be able to earn something." Such agreements were frequent and sometimes involved large quantities of calicoes. For example, in September 1787, Bovet and Son from Boudry sent 322 pieces of cloth to be painted at Chevroux and 200 to Estavayer. Inversely, on April 27, 1792, Louis Verdan from Grandchamp asked Henri Du Pasquier to do him the "great service" of having painting done in his workshop at Portalban, "as it was presently without pieces needing to have resistants applied," and assured him that "he would be most pleased if on a similar or other occasion he could in return be of use to him."[21]

This spirit of agreement could on occasion go so far as to take on an air of connivance for fraudulent purposes. In 1790 Abram Verdan from La Borcarderie, who possessed another manufactory at Fribourg that was subsidized by the town's authorities on the condition that it employ a certain minimum number of people, proposed to H. Du Pasquier that he buy "simply for form's sake" the workshop at Portalban that Du Pasquier then owned, "which would help him to make up the numbers of those he was supposed to employ," taking into account the agreements he had signed with the Fribourg authorities. "It goes without saying," he added, "that all my workers would work on your behalf."

The organization of an employers' alliance also had as its objective to prevent the workers from being able to play upon the competition existing between the Neuchâtel manufacturers over wages and hiring. This possibility effectively existed, and the workers knew how to use it when necessary, but the manufacturers made a serious effort to limit it to a bare minimum. Thus in February 1788, Jean-Pierre Du Pasquier, cousin of the Cortaillod Henri Du Pasquier and himself a calico printer at Bied, asked Müller to have a number of pieces painted for him at Chevroux. His calico painters had threatened to go on strike, and he had decided to deprive them of work to keep them at bay, for if he failed to do so they would "try and get him by the throat." This form of conduct, in which H. Du Pasquier readily took part, succeeded, for after having worked for Le Bied up until the end of April, Müller was able to tell H. Du Pasquier on May 6, "Your cousins were very happy with the work we did for them: this little foretaste of things to come has made the calico painters once again recognize their duties."

Another episode that says much about the employers' front took place in the period of the workshops' decline. In 1801 work stopped at Chevroux and Grandcour, which in the previous year had still employed about sixty workers. Forty of these were taken on at the Fabrique-Neuve. Twenty workers remained. Deluze, Petitpierre, and Company from Le Bied asked H. Du Pasquier's permission to employ them at a time when the buildings that the latter continued to rent to Samuel Bonny were not being used. Du Pasquier's reply once again reflects the connivance which had always gone on between the manufacturers behind their formal respect for the rules of free competition in the labor market: "If it were only a question of employing these women, I would gladly consent, but were our workers from those areas to hear that you were employing people there, they would immediately ask to return there and by this arrangement we would be deprived of forty calico painters whom we need at the moment, given the few workers of this sort that we have in the vicinity. I must therefore ask you . . . not to employ them, but please without letting him [S. Bonny] *know that it is I who am the cause of the hindrance.*"

In reality, however, little was at stake in this exchange because of the time at which it occurred. Since 1800 the demand for calico painting had gone into a clear decline, for a number of different reasons: the crisis situation that had hit the Neuchâtel calico-printing industry after a decade of prosperity; the sharp increase in the price of indigo because of the wars and the Continental Blockade that followed, which led quite simply to a complete interruption in the supplying of the Fabrique-Neuve between 1803 and 1809; changes in fashion, which now favored abundantly decorated work less than in the past; and finally, the evolution of techniques which led to much greater use of block printing for the application of blue. By 1811 H. Du Pasquier could write: "Most of the work that we do today contains no brushwork." This was a somewhat exaggerated statement when it was made, but it indicated the future of the industry in correct terms. Between 1790 and 1799, the annual wage bill given over to calico painting had been 32,000L (24 percent of the total wage bill at the Fabrique-Neuve). For the period 1800-1809 it fell to 21,000L (18 percent of the total), for 1810-1814 to 16,000L (13 percent), and in 1815-1819 to 12,000L (8 percent). By 1821, calico painting had come to a complete and definitive end, both at the Cortaillod Fabrique-Neuve and in the other Neuchâtel manufactories.

Faced with this rapid decline which rendered obsolete their former strategy, the manufacturers relocated the calico painting that they had previously decentralized back to Neuchâtel: Chevroux and Grandcour closed in 1801. Estavayer closed for the first time at the end of 1805. Some of the workers who had been employed there went to work at Cortaillod; the others were dismissed and thereafter were hired only on an irregular basis. On November 6, 1810, a boat left Estavayer loaded with eighty-two pieces of cloth that the last thirty-five workers had painted for Cortaillod. Endrion tried "to console the workers as best he could, but felt that even the best reasoning could not replace bread."

In the long term, the results of the location policy for the calico-painting work-shops were visible in the evolution of the size of the workforce at Cortaillod itself and of its wages. The number of calico painters working at tables fell sharply from the 1776 figure of 150 and subsequently varied between 100 and 120, despite an increase in production; as for the wage rates, they were perfectly stable between 1779 and 1800. The decrease in the offer of work in the Cortaillod area must certainly have contributed to this.

In the short and the medium term, the creation of the calico-painting workshops constituted an efficient means of managing the labor market. Looked at from this point of view, its results appear clearly in the annual variations in the total wage bill paid out to the workers of Cortaillod, Estavayer, and Chevroux-Grandcour (cf. Table 2). The flexibility of the wage bill indeed appears to be very different in each establishment. If the firm is considered as a whole, the arithmetical average of the annual variations, increases and decreases included, was about 13 percent between 1760 and 1804 without much long-term change (12.5 percent between 1760 and 1777, 13.2 percent between 1778 and 1804). However, whereas the table workers at Cortaillod had borne nearly all the consequences of these fluctuations up to 1777, they subsequently constitute a protected core at the heart of the system which had been erected. From 1778 to 1804 they were subject to employment variations of only 10.6 percent, and, above all, in the 1790s, when all the outlying calico-painting workshops were functioning, the figure fell to 3.8 percent. This figure was much lower than production variations at the Fabrique-Neuve, which were running at 9 percent per annum in this period.

A second group of wages was made up by what the account books call "individual items paid to calico painters." This covered the payment of the work carried out by either the outworkers in the Cortaillod area or the workers at the Fabrique-Neuve working after daylight in the manufactory or at home. These wages were normally paid out for extra work designed to respond to abrupt changes of either an annual or a seasonal nature in the economic conjuncture. Thus they were subject to considerable variation: over the period 1790 to 1800, they varied between 219L (1791) and 3,458L (1798) (see Table 2).

The case of the calico-painting workshops at Estavayer and Chevroux-Grandcour seems to fall between the two already discussed. Between 1790 and 1799, the average annual variation in the wage bill was 18.8 percent at the former and 22.4 percent at the latter. The function of these establishments thus appears clearly in the figures: given an average annual variation of +/–12.9 percent for all wages paid for calico painting, they were designed to keep the wage bill paid out to the table workers at the Fabrique-Neuve (+/–3.5 percent) as stable as possible while also avoiding the haphazard temporary recruitment of auxiliary workers implied by the sharp variations undergone by the entry "individual" (+/–122.5 percent).

Thus a whole hierarchy of jobs was created within the firm, with the stability of some depending on the instability of others. This represented a solution to a general problem common to all firms, namely flexibility of employment. In the case of the Fabrique-Neuve, which was representative of the firms in its branch of the economy, it is striking that the most peripheral parts of the labor force had also kept several of the characteristics of the world of traditional production. One could doubtless make similar remarks about other industrial branches of the period such as the iron and steel industry.[22] The first industrial revolution thus consisted of transitions in varying degrees of flexibility between old and new forms of work and of the organization of labor, at least when each sector is considered in its own right. Such flexibility could be found even within individual firms themselves.

Throughout the eighteenth century, European calico printing for its part combined separate forms of work. The history of the creation and the subsequent disappearance of the Neuchâtel calico-painting workshops is a witness to the way in which an entire banch of industry passed from youth to maturity. The creation of these establishments in fact coincided with a phase of extensive growth of production, characterized by an increase in capitalization in an unchanging technical environment. The labor recruitment that this type of growth necessitated rapidly came up against a problem of optimal size: it is significant that no calico-printing firm in the eighteenth century markedly overstepped the threshold of 800 to 1,000 workers. The creation of the calico-painting workshops by the Neuchâtel manufactories was an attempt to cross this threshold by managing separately, on the one hand, a hardcore of manufactory workers that alone was fully concerned with the rhythm, the constraints, and the wages that went with highly productive industrial work, and, on the other, a peripheral labor force that could be supplied (and in the event of crises reabsorbed) by the world of traditional rural occupations. It is striking that the workers in the calico-painting workshops had all the characteristics that M. J. Piore attributes to the principal occupants of "social roles outside the workplace" within dual economies:[23] they were *young females of peasant and foreign origin*.

Much was at stake with this peripheral labor force. The attention that was fastidiously paid to it by the manufacturer is sufficient proof of this. Yet it was always the printing sector *strictu sensu* which was the site of the principal *innovations* and therefore of the real *profits*, and the overall evolution of the division and organization of labor in the last analysis depended upon the same sector. It was the adoption of roller printing at the beginning of the nineteenth century—a major innovation that gave the industry the look it has today—which prompted the disappearance of women and children from the factories. In fact, this innovation was to create a veritable change in the center of gravity of the industry's occupational skills. A certain number of men's jobs were promoted: those of designer, mechanic, and roller engraver. Some did not change status, notably those requiring physical strength, while, on the other hand, all the jobs linked to the old process of block printing were deskilled. The printers and above all the female assistant printers now finished off work only on particularly complex cloths printed by roller, such as finishing fabrics or fancy handkerchiefs. As for the printers' assistants, they disappeared completely in the name of productivity after being replaced by a simple machine called a "mechanical puller." The percentages of men, women, and children in calico printing went respectively from 18 percent, 47 percent, and 35 percent in the 1790s to 65 percent, 35 percent, and 0 percent in the 1840s, while at the same time the average annual length of cloth printed by a worker rose from about 2,000 to 5,000 meters.

In the case of calico printing, women's participation in industrial work appears to have been a transitory phase in the Industrial Revolution. It lasted only as long as its degree of technical evolution allowed the manufacturers to come to terms with the traditional mode of production, which was both rural and artisanal and in which women had participated on an equal footing. The history of women's intervention in the Western economy is thus far from linear, as it is the result of the permanent confrontation shaped by technical, economic, and demographic parameters that opposes it to male labor. This, by way of conclusion, pleads in favor of a history of women's work which does not take merely half of the world into account, even if it is the better of the two.

Notes

An earlier version of this chapter appeared in *Revue suisse d'histoire* 36 (Basle, 1986): 121-56. The present text was translated from the French by Andrew Lincoln.

Translator's note: The word "chintz," deriving from the Sanskrit *chitra*, meaning "variegated," was the original seventeenth-century English term for the painted cotton fabrics imported from India. Its meaning subsequently shifted in line with the technological evolution of the industry, and it came to refer to cotton cloths fast-printed with designs of flowers, etc. in a number of colors. The term "calico" derives directly from the city of that name on the coast of Malabar and originally (1578) referred to all cotton cloths imported from the east before taking on its meaning in this article of plain white unprinted cotton cloth. American readers should note that in eighteenth-century English usage, that term did not imply any distinction between fine cotton cloths, such as muslin, and coarser ones.

1. The most recent general assessment of this branch of industry is the study by S. Chassagne and S. D. Chapman, *European Textile Printers in the Eighteenth Century: A Study of Peel and Oberkampf* (London: Heinemann Educational Books, 1989), p. 256.

2. P. Caspard, "La fabrique au village," *Le mouvement social* (October 1976): 17; Chassagne and Chapman, pp. 3ff.

3. Cf. among recent studies bearing on workers of *indiennage* A. Dewerpe and Y. Gaulupeau, "Perrier, Champs, Voet et les autres. Les ouvriers de la manufacture de toiles peintes d'Oberkampf à Jouy-en-Josas (1760-1815)," in *Mémoire de maîtrise* (Paris, 1975), pp. 235ff.; S. Chassagne, A. Dewerpe, and Y. Gaulupeau, "Les ouvriers de la manufacture de toiles imprimées d'Oberkampf," *Le mouvement social* (October 1976): 39-88. Fiscal and design elements of the early industry are found in J. M. Schmitt, *Aux origines de la Révolution industrielle en Alsace: Investissements et relations sociales dans la vallée de Saint-Amarin au XVIIIe siècle* (Strasbourg: Istra, 1980), pp. 340-70, and "Les artistes à la fabrique: Graveurs et dessinateurs au service des éstablissements Hausmann du Logelbach à la fin du XVIIIe," *Annuaire de la Société d'histoire et d'archéologie de Colmar* (1980-81): 103-26. For studies on an important calico manufacture, see S. Chassagne, *Oberkampf: Un entrepreneur capitaliste au Siècle des Lumières* (Paris: Aubier, 1980), pp. 226-63, 350, and "Les ouvriers en indiennes de l'agglomeration rouennaise (1760-1860)," in *Travail, métiers et professions en Normandie* (Nogent-sur-Marne: Société parisienne d'histoire et d' archéologie normandes, 1984), pp. 125-39. An unusually intimate view of workers is found in two articles by P. Caspard, "Mon cher patron. Lettres d'un ouvrier suisse [designer] à ses employers (1770-1811)," *Milieux* (October 1980): 50-63, and "Gérer sa vie? Etude statistique sur le profil de carrière des ouvriers de l'indiennage (1750-1820)," *Revue du Nord* (January 1981): 207-32. For a study of labor unrest, see C. Simon, "Wollt ihr euch der Sklaverei kein Ende machen?" in *Der Streik der Basler Indiennearbeiter im Jahr 1794*, Allschwil (diff.: Simon, Unt. Schellenberg 185, CH-4125 Riehen), 1984, 145 pages.

4. On the history of this enterprise, see P. Caspard, *La Fabrique-Neuve de Cortaillod: Enterprise et profit pendant la Révolution industrielle, 1752-1854* (Paris/Fribourg: Publications de la Sorbonne and Editions universitaires de Fribourg, 1979). The organization and even the division of work were homogeneous in manufacturers of *indiennes* of the eighteenth century. The material given here applies, in general, not only for Swiss workers but also for the 30-40,000 *pinceleuses* estimated in Europe as a whole at the end of the century.

5. "Tout vient de la micro-économie," recalls the convincing appeal of F. Jequier. "L'histoire des patrons, est-elle réactionnaire?" *Etudes de lettres*, Lausanne, April 1979, pp. 1-34. The present study draws part of its inspiration from the group of monographs dealing with similar historic problems. For more theoretical and general points of view on the sexual division of work in earlier periods, consult R. Wecker and B. Schnegg, eds., *Frauen: Zur Gedschichte weiblicher Arbeits- und Lebensdingungen in der Schweiz*, special issue of *Revue suisse d'histoire* (1984, no. 3); M. Perrot, ed., *Travaux de femmes dans la France du XIXe siècle* and *Métiers de femmes*, special issues of *Mouvement social* (October 1978 and July 1987); and J. C. Rabier, ed., *Travail et travailleurs dans l'industrie textile* (Paris: CNRS, 1987).

6. On the technique of brushwork, see J. Persoz, *Traité théorique et pratique de l'impression des tissus*, vol. 4 (Paris, 1846); P. R. Schwartz, "La coloration partielle des étoffes," in M. Daumas, ed., *Histoire générale des techniques*, vol. 3 (Paris, 1968), pp. 704-27; and "Contribu-

tion à l'histoire de l'application du bleu indigo dans l'indiennage européen," *Bulletin de la Société industrielle de Mulhouse* 2 (1953): 63-79.

7. Roland de la Platière, "Toiles Peintes," in *Encyclopédie méthodique* (Paris-Liege, 1785), p. 374.

8. J. Ryhiner, "Traité sur la fabrication et le commerce des toiles peintes," in D. Dollfus-Ausset, ed., *Matériaux pour la coloration des étoffes* (Paris, 1865), p. 67.

9. On the formative years of different categories of workers in *indiennage*, see P. Caspard, "Gérer sa vie?" pp. 208-12.

10. On *indiennage* in Neufchâtel, see ibid., and A. Dreyer, *Les toiles peintes en pays neuchâtelois* (Paris/Neuchâtel, 1923).

11. Without indication to the contrary, the following pages are based on examination of the archives of the Fabrique-Neuve de Cortaillod, in the Archives de l'Etat de Neuchâtel. The series most heavily used are the correspondence received and sent, the Grouds' account books, the registers for the workers, and the invoices for merchandise sent to Estavayer, Chevroux, Grandcour, and Portalban.

12. It is noteworthy that they both remained unmarried. It was always preferable, if not crucial, for women workers to remain single if they wished to be promoted to managerial positions. This is one of the recurrent themes of Perrot, ed., *Métiers de femmes*.

13. Numerous testimonies to this pattern may be found, for example: 23 February 1788, Letter of Müller ("Il convient de prendre toutes les années quelques apprenties, pour remplacer les filles qui vont en service et celles qui se marient"), or 11 January 1797, Letter of Deluze et Cie, du Bied; copy of the letter to Perrier du Cotterd, 21 February 1800.

14. G. De Lessert, "Quelques prix de la main-d'oeuvre et des denrées au XVIIIe siècle," *Revue historique vaudoise* (1913): 254-56.

15. At the moment of liquidating Estavayer, in 1810, Endrion evokes their case in emphasizing that there were differences among the workers sitting at the tables; as for these, they "ne sont pas dans la misère."

16. The same request was formulated by Perrier du Cotterd on 8 October 1781: "Les jours deviennent courts. Nos filles gagnent peu. Elles désirent de veiller."

17. In 1798 coffee cost 10L per pound at Neuchâtel. On practices of consumption at Cortaillod, see P. Caspard, "Une communauté rurale à l'épreuve de l'industrialisation: Cortaillod de 1750 à 1850," *Bulletin du Centre d'histoire économique et sociale de la région lyonnaise* 4 (1974): 1-35. One finds here a Swiss Romand echo of the theme "la jeune fille et le café," frequent in Germanic countries in the eighteenth century. Cf. the "Coffee Cantata" of J. S. Bach (B.W.V. 211, c. 1735): "Ah, how sweet the coffee tastes / Lovelier than a thousand kisses. / Coffee, coffee I must have; / If you would offer me refreshment, / Ah, then, pour me out some coffee!"

18. Cf. A. Melucci: "Action patronale, pouvoir, organization. Règlement d'usine et contrôle de la main-d'oeuvre au XIXe siècle," *Le Mouvement social* (October 1976): 139-59, and A. Biroleau, *Les Règlements d'ateliers, 1798-1936*, Introduction by A. Cottereau (Paris: Bibliothèque nationale, 1984), 82 pp.

19. Similar remarks on 11 June 1778 and 26 April 1794: "Les ouvrières, faute d'ouvrage, ont été obligées d'arrêter un jour et demi, allant à d'autres ouvrages qui leur gâtent la main."

20. Since the harvest was abundant, the price of a measure of wheat from Payerne fell, from the end of summer, from 4L 10s. to 1L 18s. (Information furnished by Müller himself.)

21. Numerous other examples show the pervasiveness of this practice.

22. Cf., for example, G. Verron, "Les structures sociales d'un établissement sidérurgique avant la Révolution industrielle: La forge de Port-Brillet (Mayene)," *Le mouvement social* (January 1967): 63-94, and D. Woronoff, *L'industrie sidérurgique en France pendant la Revolution et l'Empire* (Paris: Editions de l'EHESS, 1984), p. 592. See especially pp. 157-201, for the distinction between workers who were "internes and externes."

23. S. Berger and M. J. Piore, *Dualism and Discontinuity in Industrial Societies* (Cambridge: Cambridge University Press, 1980), p. 18.

Patrizia Sione 8

From Home to Factory:
Women in the Nineteenth-Century
Italian Silk Industry

For most Italian scholars who dealt with industrialization and the working class in Italy, women's work was one of the parameters of industrial change. For some, it was the revealing clue that "advanced" change had failed to happen; for others it was precisely the opposite—the very sign that industrialization had occurred. In both cases, industrialization was understood as the concentration in factories of workers who performed partial tasks at power-driven machinery.[1] In late nineteenth-century Italy, textiles, particularly silk production, were the most important industrial sector. Silk remained the largest export item from the Italian peninsula from the early nineteenth century to World War I.[2] Historians who saw in the relative importance of the textile industry the sign of Italy's "delay" in achieving industrialization comparable to that in England, pointed to the presence of women in the workforce as evidence of the sector's "backwardness": these workers were of rural origin and poorly paid, often mixed domestic with factory work, and were by definition unskilled.[3] Other historians rejected such categorization and its underlying assumption that rural workers were inherently backward. They claimed that women's presence in factories signaled the accomplished revolution by industrial capitalism. Citing Marx and Lenin, they insisted that while unskilled and poorly paid women in textiles were from rural families, they were nevertheless the typical proletariat of the factory system. They had no control over their work, they labored close together in factories, and they were subjected to discipline. Thus women working in textiles at the end of the nineteenth century were elevated to the ranks of the modern proletariat.[4]

Both positions were looking to the factory worker as evidence of industrialization, and both concentrated their attention on women in factories. Great numbers of them did work in textiles, particularly in the silk industry in the province of Como, in Lombardy, which was the leading silk-production center in Italy. In 1873, an official source indicated that in the Como area more than 32,000 out of the 37,000 silkworkers were women, a quarter of them children below the age of twelve,

137

but an estimate raised the total figure to 50,000 including domestic work.[5] Twenty-two years later, in 1895, when a large part of production was mechanized, millworkers numbered more than 46,000 of whom at least 33,000 were women in factories.[6] Most worked in the countryside, in myriad mills scattered among dozens of industrial villages. In 1873 there were silk mills in 206 out of 508 municipalities included in the province of Como, and most were villages.[7] This situation seems to validate the view that unskilled rural women were typically employed when industrial production was mechanized.

Reality is more complex. As many contemporaries had pointed out, long before the advent of the factory, many rural women and men performed domestic industrial work, not only in silk but in other branches of textiles and in the metal trades.[8] Recently Italian historians seem to have taken notice, especially after a wave of rejuvenated interest in rural industry helped them to redefine "industry" in broader terms that included decentralized and small-scale production.[9] The conviction took firm hold among Italian historians that Italy's "road to capitalism" was of a very special nature, setting Italy apart from the other Western countries.[10] Some found evidence that much of Italian industrialization and the working class originated in the countryside.[11] Thus a recent study on the "protoindustrial phase" of the silk industry pointed out that women constituted most of the workforce in the "first stage" of industrialization.[12] Still, taking a further step allows us to grasp more of the complexities of women's experience of industrial work.[13]

An examination of women's work in the silk industry in all of its branches, from the late eighteenth to the late nineteenth century, reveals the falsity of several key notions about rural women's work in factories. According to a consolidated "model," female industrial work would be the end result of a linear course of development from skilled to unskilled work, where skilled work is male, unskilled is female, and where rural work is by definition unskilled. Women's experience in silk subverts these notions, in the first place because of the continuity of female work throughout the industry's history, from the predominantly decentralized phase in the eighteenth century through manufacture and the factory. In addition, women working in particular branches of the silk industry at home—particularly reeling—possessed a high degree of skill, which was employed subsequently in the manufacture and even in the factory. These skills were one of the important factors in the localization of the factory in the Como district.[14] In other branches, such as weaving, women's work underwent a more complex process of change. Urban women's skills did disintegrate with the advent of the factory, but before that happened, they were passed on from urban to rural domestic working women. In other words, many rural female workers who operated power looms in 1895 replaced other urban and rural women who had performed skilled work at home.[15]

Reeling and weaving were only two of the many steps in the complex silk-production process, which included distinct branches of the industry, all of which were present in the Como district. For clarity, it is necessary to outline them here. The silk thread used for weaving cloth was an animal product, generated by silkworms that formed cocoons. A filament had to be extracted from these shells before it could be processed and become a manageable thread, ready to be spun, dyed, and woven. Thus the silk industry included an agricultural phase of production, dependent on the activity of rural workers who tended the mulberry trees, on whose leaves the silkworms fed, and the insects themselves, until they became pupae and started spinning their cocoons.[16]

The cultivation of mulberry trees and the rearing of the silkworms, called sericulture, were done by families of *mezzadri* (sharecroppers) who lived on the hilly uplands close to the Como lake, north of Milan. Men tended the trees, but the rest of the family joined them in early spring to rear the silkworms, from the hatching of the eggs to the larval stage until the pupae formed the cocoons. It was a delicate process that required constant attention and care. To hatch, eggs needed controlled conditions of temperature, humidity, and light; the larvae needed a constant supply of leaves, for they ate voraciously through successive stages of sleep and growth, and had to be fed every few hours. The families of *mezzadri* customarily made room in their own homes for the trays on which the hatching eggs were placed, sometimes even putting them in their own beds. Then they gathered the leaves and made sure the supply was abundant, and when the larvae turned into pupae, they provided the brushwood branches which the insects ascended. The worms produced a gummy, flossy silk thread, about 4,000 yards long, which they spun continuously for three days, until a hard, compact shell was formed. The families of *mezzadri* collected the cocoons, making sure there were no stains, holes, or other defects caused by the larvae's premature death.[17]

Reeling was the following step, in which a filament had to be extracted from the cocoons after the pupae were killed (usually by suffocation). It had to be done quickly, or the delicate cocoons would spoil. As the thread was heavily agglutinated, four or five cocoons were placed in a vat containing warm water, so as to dilute the gum and loosen the main strand. A worker (always a woman) gently brushed the shells, found the ends of a few filaments, gathered them with a slight twisting motion so as to form a continuous, uniform, round strand, and passed it through a guide in order to clean off the gum and dirt. The thread was finally wound on a reel, ready for shipment. In this form (the so-called "raw silk") most Lombard silk was exported until the mid-nineteenth century, and it was deemed among the best available on the international market. The ability and expertise of the *trattrice* (the reeler) were pivotal to achieving high quality, for it was up to her to obtain a continuous, durable, and even thread.[18] The operation had to be performed quickly enough that the warmth of the water would not spoil the silk; the right number of filaments had to be joined together to form a thread with the proper thickness; and the thread had to be stretched and twisted delicately, so as to make it strong but smooth. The reeler was customarily helped by a child, who turned the simple machinery for winding the filaments on reels as they were being extracted. Reeling could be performed at home, and in fact most reelers were members of the same sharecropping households in which cocoons were produced. Throughout the eighteenth century and well into the nineteenth, women reeled silk in huts or on the porches of their homes, using wood fire to heat the water in the vats. The operation lasted only during the warm and dry summer months (on average 60-70 days), because silk was easily damaged by humidity, but even then work was halted in case of rain.

The operation called "throwing" (*torcitura*), which was peculiar to silk, included three different procedures: twisting, in which a single strand was slightly twisted and then cleaned of lumps by passing it through a slit; doubling, in which two threads were wound together; and throwing, which consisted of spinning the doubled threads, giving them a swift, tight twist. The thread to be used in the weft for cloth weaving was only slightly spun and was not twisted before doubling, so that it became soft and flossy, giving fullness to the fabric. This was called tram. The thread for the warp, called organzine, had to be strong, and was formed of two strands which were twisted separately in one direction, then twisted together in the opposite. Throwing was obviously independent from agriculture and required much less skill than reeling. It was done in small mills, scattered in the silk-producing areas. Lombard throwers were the first European silk producers to introduce a simple hydraulic throwing machinery, in the mid-eighteenth century, and water remained the main source of energy until the 1870s. Throwers preferred to take advantage of the abundant sources of energy offered by the numerous streams descending the pre-Alpine valleys in the Como area. However, *incannatura* (winding) was for a long time done by hand, as it was the preparatory operation that transferred raw silk from reels to spindles, to be taken to the spinning mill. Adult women usually did this work in their homes.

Silk weaving requires less explanation, as from a technical point of view it did not differ substantially from wool or cotton weaving, save for the fact that it was more difficult to perform. The quality of the thread influenced the final results, but according to the ability of the weaver, the fabric might turn out more or less full, shiny, and light. Weaving became of some importance only at the end of the eighteenth century in the city of Como. Dyeing, performed right before weaving by skilled workers, became more widespread in Como at the same time as weaving, but it was an ancient craft that dated back to medieval times.[19]

Women were present in all of these branches at least from the early eighteenth century. In reeling, women were able to mix agricultural work with industrial skills in the domestic phase through manufacture. As I will show, women had considerable skills which were transmitted from one generation to another. The adoption of machinery did not destroy these skills, as the work process was not substantially altered by the concentration in small mills or by the application of steam power. The fundamental change occurred in the sexual division of labor within rural households, and in the relative weight of income from industrial and agricultural work.

Initially women worked in reeling as a complement to agricultural activity, with which it was integrated. In the same households the raw material was produced and processed for further elaboration. The type of land tenure was well adapted to sericulture and reeling, for sharecroppers by contract had to provide the work necessary to tend the mulberry trees and produce the cocoons, in addition to grains or grapes.

This contract was common in the hilly area between the large capitalistic estates in the plains farther south and the small plots on the mountains. *Mezzadri* (also called *massari*, later *pigionanti*) were entitled to keep half of the products, including the mulberry leaves and the cocoons, but they had to perform many accessory tasks for the upkeep of the tools, roads, and buildings.

Women in sharecroppers' households ended up performing industrial work at reeling for a number of reasons. Such activity not only did not interfere with agricultural work, but was somehow its natural extension. Women continued to help with agricultural tasks before and after the silkworm-feeding season, and the reeling season did not last but two months. Reeling work was paid in cash, which was a welcome addition to the family support. Also, reeling was such a delicate operation, calling for a high level of dexterity, that women's acquired familiarity with handwork became crucial in their being assigned the task. Landowners obviously reaped great advantages from encouraging women's industrial work. The family unit could provide the constant care that productive silkworm rearing required, plus the buildings, the tools, and the labor force for the transformation of raw materials. Owners thus avoided heavy capital outlay and upkeep costs, while at the same time they enjoyed the increased land value through a type of industrial activity that did not interfere substantially with agriculture. Thus Lombard reelers between the early eighteenth and the early nineteenth centuries performed a variety of tasks at home, including agricultural and industrial work.

The type of land tenure under which rural women performed industrial work as a complement to agriculture changed in time with the success of mulberry cultivation and sericulture. Landowners requested that more and more mulberry trees be planted on their property, and at the same time imposed harder contracts. They increased their demands on the *mezzadri* by asking that a rent be paid in a fixed amount of grain. Formally, the sharecropper was still entitled to half the leaves and cocoons. But landowners took for themselves the right to sell the leaves and cocoons on the market and split the cash with the sharecroppers, which gave them the opportunity to cheat and pay much less than they owed. In addition, landowners started to request that *mezzadri* provide a fixed number of days of work on additional tasks, in exchange for little cash. Sharecroppers as a consequence had less time for the cultivation of grains, grapes, and mulberry trees, for tending silkworms, and also for taking care of their own gardens. So at the end of the rural year, when the balance was drawn, the landowner was inevitably able to show that the sharecropper was in debt. As a result, owners could compel sharecroppers to work harder and tie them to the land in times of great expansion of raw silk sales. Between 1734 and 1846, the number of mulberry trees in the Como province increased from 78,000 to 3 million.[20] The economist Stefano Jacini observed that the whole region had quickly become a "big mulberry orchard," and recalled the old adage which says that "the shade of the mulberry tree is the shade of gold."[21]

One of the consequences of this development was that greater numbers of women were involved in silkmaking. In addition, more and more owners invested some of their increased capital in rudimentary hydraulic machinery for winding silk during reeling. Thousands of small mills (*filande*), located mostly in old huts on landowners' property, dotted the Como countryside. Women would reel, while men took care of starting and feeding the wood fires under the vats. Still, millwork was seasonal and a supplement to agriculture, even though at this point few members of sharecropping families did exclusively agricultural work. Carlo Ravizza, a contemporary Catholic priest, vividly described the mixing of agriculture and industry, which he favored because it supposedly helped to avoid the evils of a factory system like that of Manchester.[22] At harvest time, he wrote, in the Lombard hilly countryside everybody left their occupations and helped out: "women left the *filande*, men left the looms and the ploughs."[23] And silkmaking was not the only temporary wage work among these populations, as it was common for men to migrate at the end of the summer and hire themselves out in construction or on some big farm as wage laborers. Women would go work in the great rice fields farther south in the Po valley.[24] Landowners were partly responsible for the persistence of this mixing of various types of work, as they still could not or did not want to expend capital on the construction of large buildings, where silk would be protected from humidity. At midcentury, most of the work was still done exclusively in the summer. It involved about 18,000 workers in the Como province.[25]

The concentration of female workers in "mills"—which were actually little more than huts—and the use of hydraulic machinery did not change the work process and the tasks assigned to reelers. Like many other women who continued to perform this job at home, mill reelers did work that required a considerable amount of skill. They soon earned a reputation for their expertise in handling silk. Their ability according to foreign silk buyers as well, was unsurpassed. Women gained and customarily passed on their skill from generation to generation. While men took care of agricultural tasks, women reeled silk and taught young girls the "art," and older women looked on and prepared meals. The expertise of the family unit reached such a level that whole families (the *bigattieri*) were called to silk-producing areas in other Italian states to tend mulberry trees, rear silkworms, and reel silk. But individual workers also migrated to perform their wage work in better conditions. Expert female silk reelers moved for the duration of the reeling season to nearby provinces, such as Bergamo, in whose *filande* they could demand better wages.[26]

Such ability was not lost even when steam was introduced as a source of power for the engines and of heat for the vats. First introduced in Como in 1815 by a Frenchman, steam-powered machines were a great improvement, for they allowed the production of a constant source of heat, which made silk of much better quality.[27] But it was not applied extensively—in 1856, only 144 reeling mills out of a total of 3,088 used the new source of energy.[28] Only after the great crisis of the 1850s, when a devastating illness of silkworms almost halted production, did a new group of silk entrepreneurs introduce better tools, employ capital, construct larger mills, and use steam extensively. As a result, much of the work available to women became long-term and full-time. Although some landowners protested this infringement by industrial interests upon their activity, women entered reeling mills in greater and greater numbers. They were induced to accept new employment also by the constant worsening of agrarian contracts. Industrial income was now so crucial in sharecroppers' households that an observer declared that plots of land had become "just a dwelling, not a source of income" for rural populations in manufacturing Lombardy.[29] As a consequence, from the 1860s on, most reelers and winders engaged exclusively in industrial work, and their income became necessary for the family survival. Although they lived in a rural home, they worked in a factory, to which they dedicated all their energies even after marriage. In 1873, a local doctor reported that most women left work in the mills not before the age of thirty, after marriage and several pregnancies.[30] And in a letter he had sent to the mayor of Como in 1867, the *prefetto* lamented nursing women's habit of taking infants with them into the factories.[31] Still, factory work did not alter the reelers' reliance on their skills. In 1884, the silk manufacturers' journal reported that reelers, although very skilled, were not paid enough by their employers, who would have everything to gain from raising workers' wages. The journal even published a series of articles celebrating reelers' work.[32]

If women's work in silk reeling was skilled but domestic and mixed with agricultural activity until the 1860s, throwing required much less skill, and remained domestic in some operations while it was quickly mechanized in others. In any case, great numbers of women were employed in this branch of the silk industry from the early eighteenth to the late nineteenth century and beyond. Also in this case, however, the work women performed in steam-powered factories was a continuation of tasks that had been performed at home for a long time. And again, as contemporaries observed, the factory system took advantage of work habits and accumulated familiarity with industrial activity acquired before, and transmitted from generation to generation. The throwing operations outlined above required a preliminary step, called *incannatura*, which consisted of winding the reeled silk onto spindles. Then the silk was taken to the spinners, either in the homes of rural workers or in small mills in the countryside. Throwing became mechanized early, while *incannatura* remained domestic for a long time, as it was a simple operation that could be done when agricultural activity stopped. In 1748, the Mori brothers obtained tax exemptions from the Como authorities and installed new hydraulic spinning machinery.[33] A century later, in 1855, while most throwing was done by machine, four-fifths of production was accomplished with machinery moved by water, very little moved by steam.[34]

From the times when spinning was a hand operation, *incannatura* was the domestic activity of women, both the wives of artisans and male hand spinners living in mountain villages up north, and the wives and daughters of *mezzadri* farther down in the hilly region.[35] The number of women employed in this operation could only be estimated, but everyone agreed that it was substantial. In 1774, Marco Paolo Odescalchi reported that in the *circondario* Ponte (a subdivision of the Como province) alone there were 2,619 people working at spinning, of whom 2,310 were women working at home at *incannatura*. In the village of Canzo, the spinning mill had 20 male and 60 female workers, and in addition employed 300 women at domestic *incannatura*.[36] An estimate also indicated that 18,000 domestic winders were to be added to the 1,200 to 1,700 throwing mill workers laboring in the *dipartimento del Lario* (in the Como area) between 1800 and 1810.[37]

Incannatura, like reeling, remained a domestic, albeit crucial, task in silk production. In 1856 someone observed that, although Lombardy was a manufacturing region, it would have been necessary to enter rural homes to find evidence of industrial work.[38] According to opportunity, women were able to alternate reeling with *incannatura* or even throwing, because until the mid-nineteenth century women worked in manufacturing mills only eight or nine months a year. According to some sources, there were women who alternated reeling work in the summer with *incannatura* in winter, thus extending industrial work to a year-round occupation. *Incannatura* could very well have been done while taking care of agricultural tasks.[39] Still, other sources later implied that domestic work at *incannaggio* left very little time for agricultural work.[40] It is obvious, however, that when all these branches adopted steam power, many women accepted conditions of work that compelled them to dedicate all their energies to one occupation only. At the end of the nineteenth century, a devastating agricultural crisis, combined with a harder land contract, impoverished rural families, who had to rely more and more on women's industrial income.[41]

Much as had happened in reeling and throwing, women's skills in weaving were passed on from home to factory, but in this case the transferral was physical and geographical. Work opportunities were taken from urban domestic weavers (women and men) and offered to rural factory girls, but first domestic hand silk weaving was encouraged among rural workers. Urban women entered into competition for jobs with rural domestic weavers first, then with rural factory operatives. The transferral of skills was far more swift and traumatic.

Women participated in Como's silk industrial activity after 1737, when the region fell under Austrian domination and the empire eliminated guild regulations and much of the tax burden on manufacturing. As the Austrian government promoted and protected the production of cloth to be "exported" within its territories, many raw and spun silk merchants in Como favored local throwing and weaving. At the same time, the introduction of machinery in rural throwing mills, favored by the great availability of water as a source of energy, contributed to the increase in spun silk production. In the course of the eighteenth century, more and more reeling and throwing mills appeared in the city of Como, while merchants were encouraging the production of cloth they knew could be favorably sold at the Vienna and Frankfurt fairs. Women were particularly present in the reeling and throwing mills and in *orditoi*, the small workshops where they prepared the warp to be given out to weavers. Until the mid-nineteenth century, however, as in the countryside, most winders and warpers worked at home, either on their own or for the family workshop. In 1835, when the silk industry had become the major economic activity in the city and in the countryside, there were thirty-five reeling mills in Como, employing 1,346 people, of whom 70 were men, 676 were adult women, and 600 were girls. Fifteen throwing mills employed 100 men and 160 women, in addition to about 1,000 winders in the countryside. At this point throwing and reeling mills were already abandoning the city for better conditions in the countryside, while weaving was taking root within the walls of the city. Warpers were not included in this count, although they represented a considerable proportion of working women in Como.[42] Weaving, however, was to become the major urban branch of the silk industry. In the following ten years it increased 50 percent, thanks to the empire's tariff protection and better commercialization. In 1847, thirty-six "firms" (of merchant-entrepreneurs) gave work to 2,372 looms in the city, of which 1,930 were located in private homes.[43] Many women worked at looms in 1847, but their participation was as unstable as the weaving industry itself. In addition, it was overshadowed by the predominant role traditionally played by men and by the particular structure of production.

Domestic weaving in Como had a peculiar organization, deriving in part from Austria's abolition of guild regulations. Production had broken up in a multitude of workshops, directed by master weavers who owned a few looms and paid their workers (the *lavoranti*) by the piece. Many weavers worked independently in their homes, helped by family members, and owned their own looms. When demand was high, often spouses and children in these households tended looms as well. Merchants (called *fabbricatori*) organized the distribution of raw material among the workshops and the commercialization of the finished product. They bought the silk thread in the countryside, had it made into warp in urban workshops, gave it out to the weavers, collected the woven cloth, and sent it to distant markets, where their agents had taken orders. The length, weight, and difficulty of execution of the silk cloth determined the compensation, according to specified rates. *Fabbricatori* and master weavers gave their workers an advance in cash against the final compensation, but usually retained a sum for expenses on tools and warp. This system resembled traditional putting-out, but merchants were also entrepreneurs who owned small *orditoi*. It was a sort of pyramidal structure, at the base of which *lavoranti* were the most numerous element.[44]

This structure was loose and unstable, as production and producers expanded and contracted over the decades. Intense competition, the market instability typical of a luxury item, and frequent political and military upheavals subjected the industry to crises marked by sudden downturns in production and prices and widespread unemployment. Merchants therefore favored the domestic hand-weaving system, as it produced flexibility in the use of labor and eliminated both the cost of training workers and large expenditures of capital on machinery.[45] Many silk producers specialized in plain fabrics, and reduced production costs by not introducing significant technical improvements and by encouraging the survival of decentralized hand weaving. *Fabbricatori* had limited expenses, as they provided weavers only with the warp and the small advance against final compensation. In turn, weavers provided the tools and trained the labor force by teaching weaving to their children.

Women's work in weaving was to be significantly affected by the system's instability. There was great competition among weavers, who would sometimes work for minimal wages in order to obtain an order from *fabbricatori*. Master weavers tended to reduce their laborers' compensation as much as possible. In addition, *fabbricatori* did not hesitate to terminate a weaver's contract when they found someone willing to work for less. As a result, weavers were in constant danger of economic ruin, subject to unemployment and low wages. During a crisis, *lavoranti* lost work and migrated or lived on charity; some independent weavers reverted to the condition of *lavoranti*; and small masters surrendered extra looms and kept only one in their home. As sudden and devastating as an economic crisis might be, a reversal of fortune might spur an explosion of activity. Credit being more available, *lavoranti* could abandon masters and set up business in their homes, alone or with the help of family members. Independent weavers added one or two looms and had their wives and children work at them. Just how fluid the situation could be was evident in some data derived from registries of weavers. Taking 1847 as a time of boom and 1857 as a time of crisis, the proportion of productive units with just one loom increased from 9.9 percent to 38.2 percent, while the numbers and proportion of small productive units and of their workers decreased significantly.[46]

Inevitably, women's presence in silk weaving fluctuated widely but remained always elusive. Women contributed directly to domestic production, but contemporary accounts of the industry slighted them, while celebrating independent male weavers. It was the male household head who went to see the *fabbricatore*, picked up the warp, bargained on the price, collected the advance, and finally went to deliver the finished cloth, often having to argue about complicated calculations of weight, size, and quality of silk.[47] The male household head was normally in charge of the operations of the small family business. However, all the members of the family had to cooperate. Women might work outside the home in warping mills, help at home in accessory tasks at the loom, or weave at home with their husbands. Precisely what women chose to do depended on market conditions and specific circumstances.

The 1847 Chamber of Commerce census of active looms, the only one to annotate the names of weavers, is typical of a situation of economic boom, when we assume more women wove. Nevertheless, it shows that married and unmarried women contributed wages to the household well before the advent of the factory system. Out of 2,286 weavers, 552 (36.4 percent) had female names. These were not just young unmarried daughters of male weavers. A substantial 43.5 percent of all the female weavers were married, working with—but not necessarily for—their husbands at home. Experience taught weavers that working for a *fabbricatore* was precarious, and the family members likely tried not to depend on one merchant. Only half of married women declared that the husbands were their master weavers, while 23 percent worked for master weavers other than their husbands, and 17 percent (41) were self-employed. The diversification of *fabbricatori* was more pronounced in the case of single women, only 36 percent of whom worked for someone with the same last name.[48]

The larger proportion of married women working for a male household head resulted from the temporary nature of their help to their husbands, who otherwise would have only one loom or no loom at all. Their unmarried daughters, by contrast, tended to find employment in someone else's larger workshop. That male weavers could rely on their wives in times of increased opportunity for work is evidence that urban women had been trained in the "art," either in cooperation with husbands or as unmarried breadwinners for their family of origin. The registry cannot tell us, of course, how work and cash were distributed in the family, but it is clear that women were able to choose weaving when necessary. It is likely, therefore, that women possessed a variety of skills, and in times of boom they worked at the more remunerative type of activity.

Until the end of the century, no other registries are available that describe women's roles as accurately as the 1847 registry did. However, all sources indicate that if anything women's contribution increased, for all took for granted that urban women contributed to the family economy and great numbers of them wove. After the unification of Italy, available statistics reveal that the proportion of working women remained high. In 1871, women constituted 43 percent of the employed population of the city, and working women made up 68.5 percent of the total female population.[49] The contribution of women, including married women, to the family and to the silk industry was significant. In 1878, a report of the Chamber of Commerce investigating a wave of strikes tried to estimate the average income for a typical family of four, and assumed that three people worked, wife included.[50] An 1890 report by the Lega di Resistenza (a workers' militant association) also took for granted that women contributed wages by weaving, which it calculated as a contribution to the family income.[51]

Urban women's work, like men's, was jeopardized when the silk industry started to move to the countryside in the 1870s. Merchant-entrepreneurs increasingly allocated weaving to rural homes, supposedly to avoid the relatively high wages and labor unrest of urban workers, and in order to cut costs following the 1873 depression. Thanks also to the emergence of a new, militant weavers' association, the Società di Previdenza, the demand was spreading among workers that fabbricatori pay uniform rates for all. Also, weavers were trying to halt the downward trend of wages. The fabbricatori's response was to try to take work away from city weavers. Their aim was to re-create in the countryside the same system of domestic industry that had flourished in the city of Como, but at significantly lower costs because rural workers supposedly lived inexpensively. In the villages, a labor force versed in textile production willingly worked at cheaper, less fine fabrics.[52] The strike movement in 1877, organized by the Società di Previdenza, involved thousands of urban and rural weavers and induced merchants to yield to their demands for equal rates in the city and in the countryside. However, it also strengthened fabbricatori's resolve to move more looms to rural homes. By 1878, the number of looms in the city had declined to 5,500 from 6,500 in 1872, and the number of workers from 12,000 to 10,000.[53] Only two-fifths of all the hand looms were in urban homes; the rest were distributed in rural homes in sixty surrounding villages.[54] At the same time, many entrepreneurs started to erect mills and employ women at power looms.[55] Still unable to invest capital in factories and machinery, some entrepreneurs opted for a mixed system—they gave out work in rural homes and ran power looms in a large factory in the countryside.[56] In the words of an entrepreneur, the movement of 1877 had "brushed away doubts and uncertainties," convincing silk producers to introduce some power looms in small rural mills. Still, the number of both hand and power looms for the production of plain silks increased. "With power looms," the entrepreneur made clear in 1881, "we intend only to increase and complete our production, not to substitute a new weaving system for the other already in existence."[57] By 1893, Como entrepreneurs gave work to 6,264 weavers at hand looms, 976 at power looms. Most of the hand looms were located in the countryside.[58]

In moving to the countryside, *fabbricatori* and entrepreneurs alike were trying to take advantage of the rural population's experience in textile production, of which they were perfectly aware. Rural weavers were the sons and daughters of sharecroppers, who had often looked for temporary work in Como to supplement income from agriculture. In times of prosperity they were able to find employment as simple *lavoranti* in small workshops.[59] Thus, *fabbricatori* were extending on a larger scale an old practice, for they had customarily sent skilled urban weavers to train workers in the countryside. It was also because of this practice that *fabbricatori* knew they could invest some capital in looms to be rented out to the sons and daughters of sharecroppers. As an entrepreneur observed, there were many advantages in perpetuating the domestic system for the production of the better grades of fabric, while resorting to power looms for plain silk.[60]

The developments in silk weaving at the end of the nineteenth century illustrate the complex history of women's skills during industrialization. Women's skills survived the factory for a long time, as they did in rural reeling and throwing, for as we have seen, the introduction of the power loom in the countryside was not sweeping and swift—in 1893 the great majority of rural looms were operated by hand in workers' homes, even though a supposedly cheap labor force was available. The developments in weaving are made more complex mainly by the existence of an urban system of production, in which men and women cooperated. Although urban women earned lower wages than male weavers, it was not feasible for merchants to shift all the work from urban men to urban women. Many urban women, like men, had to succumb to a more devastating fate than their rural counterparts.

Notes

1. Useful discussions of Italian historiography of industrialization are Andreina De Clementi, ed., *La società inafferrabile: Protoindustria, città e classi sociali nell'Italia liberale* (Rome: Edizioni Lavoro, 1986); Giorgio Mori, ed., *L'industrializzazione in Italia, 1861-1900*, 2nd ed. (Bologna: Il Mulino, 1981); but see also Volker Hunecke's discussion in his *Classe operaia e rivoluzione industriale a Milano, 1859-1892* (Bologna: Il Mulino, 1982).

2. Luciano Cafagna, "La rivoluzione industriale in Italia, 1830-1900," in Mori, *L'industrializzazione*, pp. 92-93.

3. The best example of these positions is Giuliano Procacci, one of the Marxist historians of the Italian Community Party school, who accepted the neo-Gramscian preoccupation

with Italy's delay in accomplishing the Industrial Revolution. They tended to celebrate the male skilled working class of the metal, chemical, and steel industries—the "true proletariat"—that provided the rank and file on which the party and its union thrived. Procacci, *La lotta di classe in Italia agli inizi del secolo XX* (Rome: Editori Riuniti, 1978), stressed the backwardness of women's work in textiles, p. 15.

4. Stefano Merli, *Proletariato di fabbrica e capitalismo industriale* (Florence: La Nuova Italia, 1976).

5. Stefano Bonomi, "Intorno alle condizioni igieniche degli operai e in particolare delle operaie in seta della Provincia di Como," *Annali Universali di Medicina* 674 (August 1873): 229.

6. Ministero di Agricoltura, Industria, e Commercio, *Statistiche industriali. Lombardia* (Milan, 1896), pp. 184, 190, 198, 201, and 203. The figure on women is an elaboration from actual and estimated counts.

7. Bonomi, "Intorno alle condizioni," p. 227.

8. Giovanni Cantoni, "Sulle sorti dei contadini in Lombardia," reprinted in Carlo G. Lacaita, ed., *Campagne e contadini in Lombardia durante il Risorgimento* (Milan, 1976); Cesare Cantù, *Storia della città e della Diocesi di Como*, 2 vols. (Florence, 1856); Carlo Cattaneo, "Rettificazione all'ultimo articolo sull'incanto delle sete a Londra," *Annali universali di statistica* 40 (1834); Eugenio Corbetta, "I contadini e l'industria," *Cooperazione e industria*, January 15, 1869, reprinted in Luciano Cafagna, ed., *Il Nord nella storia d'Italia: Antologia politica dell'Italia industriale* (Bari: Editori Laterza, 1962); Giovanni Frattini, *Storia e statistica dell'industria manifatturiera in Lombardia* (Milan: Bernardoni, 1856); Alessandro Garelli, *I salari e la classe operaia in Italia* (Turin, 1874); Giuseppe Gatti, *L'agricoltura e gli agricoltori del circondario di Como* (Como, 1882); Stefano Jacini, *La proprietà' fondiaria e le popolazioni agricole in Lombardia*, 3rd ed. (Milan-Verona: Civelli Giuseppe e Co., 1857); Pietro Pinchetti, *L'industria della seta sul finire del secolo XIX. Statistiche e note* (Como, 1894); Carlo Ravizza, *Un curato di campagna: Schizzi morali* (Milan, 1852).

9. I am referring to the well-known body of literature on "protoindustrialization." As Luciano Segreto pointed out in "La protoindustrializzazione nelle campagne dell'Italia settentrionale," *Studi Storici* (1988):253-73, Italian historians were slow to move beyond the neo-Gramscian paradigm. A French historian was the first to investigate rural domestic activity in relation to "industrialization" in northern Italy: Alain Dewerpe, *L'industrie au champs. Essai sur la proto-industrialisation en Italie du Nord, 1800-1880* (Rome: École française de Rome, 1985).

10. Also thanks to Maurice Aymard's illuminating essay "La transizione dal feudalesimo al capitalismo," in *Storia D'Italia. Annali. 1. Dal feudalesimo al capitalismo* (Turin: Giulio Einaudi editore, 1978).

11. See, for example, Franco Ramella, *Terra e telai: Sistemi di parentela e manifattura nel Biellese dell'Ottocento* (Turin: Giulio Einaudi editore, 1984), and Roberto Romano, *La modernizzazione periferica: L'Alto Milanese e la formazione di una società industriale, 1750-1914* (Milan: Franco Angeli, 1990).

12. In his community study of the Como silk district in the eighteenth and early nineteenth centuries, Raul Merzario sought to test the protoindustrial model, and concluded that rural domestic workers did not sever the ties with the land. *Il capitalismo nelle montagne: Strategie famigliari nella prima fase di industrializzazione nel Comasco* (Bologna: Il Mulino, 1989).

13. At this point I should clarify my use of terms. By "industry" I mean the processing of raw materials, either by hand or by machine, for the production of goods to be sold on a market. In the artisanal form of industry, the worker performs all the operations necessary for the production of the goods, and usually retains for him/herself the form of payment. By "domestic industry" I mean the processing of raw materials in the home for wages, although historically it appeared in the natural economy, as production for household consumption. By "manufacture" I mean the organization of production that is founded on the division of manual labor, under the direction of the same capitalist.

14. Luciano Cafagna even claims that in Lombardy many industrial skills and work habits were first developed by workers in silk production, and then passed on to other industrial branches. "La rivoluzione industriale," p. 92.

15. The secondary literature on the silk industry in the Como area is quite extensive. The most important works are by Stefano Angeli, *Proprietari, commercianti e filandieri a Milano nel primo Ottocento* (Milan: Franco Angeli, 1982); Bruno Caizzi, *Storia del setificio comasco. L'economia* (Como: Centro Lariano per gli Studi Economici, 1957); Kent Roberts Greenfield, *Economia e liberalismo nel risorgimento: Il movimento nazionale in Lombardia dal 1814 al 1848* (Rome-Bari: Editori Laterza, 1985; translation from *Economics and Liberalism in the Risorgiment: A Study of Nationalism in Lombardy* [Baltimore: The Johns Hopkins Press, 1934]); Giovanni Grilli, *Como e Varese nella storia della Lombardia* (Azzate: La Varesina Grafica, 1968); Raul Merzario, *Il capitalismo nelle montagne: Strategie familgiari nella prima fase di industrializzazione nel Comasco* (Bologna: Il Mulino, 1989); Dante Severin, *L'industria serica comacina durante il dominio austriaco, 1737-1859* (Como, 1960), and *Storia dell'industria serica comasca (XVIII-XX sec.)* (Como, 1960); Sergio Zaninelli, ed., *Annali dell'economia comasca. Da un sistema agricolo a un sistema industriale. Il Comasco dal Settecento Al Novecento*, 2 vols. (Como, 1987).

16. My discussion of the technical details of silk production is based on "Silk," in the *Encyclopedia Britannica*, 9th ed., 1887, vol. 22, pp. 55-66; "Silk Factories in Italy" and "How Italian Silk Operatives Live," from a report of the Royal Commission of England on Technical Instruction, *American Silk Journal* 3, no. 8 (August 1884): 138-39, and 3, no. 12 (December 1884): 202-203; Ignazio Lomeni, *Varietà agrarie, economiche e tecnologiche* (Milan: Società degli Editori degli "Annali universali delle scienze e dell'industria," 1834).

17. Rosa Cavalleri gave a vivid description of sharecropping families working at sericulture in her autobiography, written with the help of Mary Hall Ets, *Rosa: The Life of An Italian Immigrant* (Minneapolis: University of Minneapolis Press, 1970). She migrated to the United States from a Lombard silkmaking village at the end of the nineteenth century.

18. Melchiorre Gioia, *Discussione economica sul Dipartimento del Lario* (Lugano, Switzerland: G. Ruggia and Co., 1835), p. 126.

19. Luigi Brenni, *L'arte dei tintori* (Como, 1942); Franco Brunello, *L'arte della tintura nella storia dell' umanità* (Vicenza, 1868). Luigi Ponci, *Tintura della seta: Studio fisico-chimico della seta* (Milan, 1876).

20. Merzario, *Il capitalismo*, p. 100.

21. Stefano Jacini, *La prorieta' fondiaria e le popolazioni agricole in Lombardia* (Milan-Verona: Civelli Giuseppe and Co., 1857), p. 55.

22. Throughout the nineteenth century, the English town remained a powerful symbol—usually with negative connotations—in Italian imagery of industrialization.

23. Ravizza, *Un curato di campagna*, p. 248. He was probably referring to men's cotton weaving, which according to Alessandro Garelli in 1847 occupied 29,000 people in the Lombard countryside during winter. Leydi, *Como e il sui territorio*, p. 28.

24. Some mill owners allowed women to leave the mills during the rice "season." Ravizza, *Un curato di campagna*, pp. 66-84.

25. Severin, *L'industria serica comacina*, p. 133.

26. Ravizza, *Un curato di campagna*, pp. 253-54.

27. Cantù, *Storia dell città di Como*, p. 515.

28. Frattini, *Storia e statistica*, p. 57. More research should be done on this point, but it is likely that at the time most reeling mills were still in the hands of landowners, whose willingness to invest in productive industrial activities was limited.

29. Ministero di Agricoltura, Industria, e Commercio, Giunta per l'Inchiesta Agraria e sulle Condizioni della Classe Agricola, *Relazione sulla X° Circoscrizione*, report prepared by Stefano Jacini, vol. 6, I (Rome, 1882), p. 223.

30. Bonomi, "Intorno alle condizioni igieniche," p. 233.

31. Letter dated June 21, 1867. *Affari Politici Diversi, no. 2249, Statistiche*, Municipal Archive, Como State Archive.

32. *La Seta*, 1884.

33. Severin, *L'industria serica comacina*, p. 23.

34. Frattini, *Storia e statistica*, p. 66; Greenfield, *Economia e liberalismo*, p. 163.

35. Merzario, *Il capitalismo nelle montagne*.

36. Merzario, *Il capitalismo nelle montagne*, p. 109 and 139.

37. Merzario, *Il capitalismo nelle montagne*, p. 110.

38. Frattini, *Storia e statistica*, p. 56.

39. Cantoni, "Sulle sorti," in Lacaita, ed., *Campagna e contadini*, p. 44.

40. Antonio Garelli so maintained in 1874. Roberto Leydi and Glauco Sanga, *Mondo popolare in Lombardia. 4. Como e il suo territorio* (Milan: Silvana Editoriale d'Arte, 1978), p. 28.

41. On the great agricultural crisis of the 1880s, see Gino Luzzatto, *L'economia italiana dal 1861 al 1894* (Turin: Giulio Einaudi editore, 1968), pp. 169-71.

42. Caizzi, *Storia del setificio comasco*, p. 54.

43. Caizzi, *Storia del setificio comasco*, p. 55.

44. They made up between 77.2 percent of the total weavers in 1787 and 67.1 percent in 1847. This is my elaboration of data from registries, as published by Alberto Guenzi in "La tessitura domestica a Como tra Sette e Ottocento," *Archivio Storio Lombardo*, 1978, p. 247.

45. As an entrepreneur explained in 1861, both boys and girls were introduced to silk-work while young, in households or in workshops. "Workers themselves taught young men and women—that is, apprentices—to introduce them to weaving and turn them into accomplished workers." From the answer that Nessi and Barberini gave to a request for information for a local industrial survey, Municipal Archive, VIII, file 30, 2249, Como State Archive.

46. See note 44.

47. Antonio Romano, a master weaver himself, left a vivid description of this painful ritual in a guide for weavers, *Riforma sulla fabbricazione del setificio* (Como, 1874), pp. 143-44.

48. *Elenco dei telaj, dei tessitori in seta battenti nel mese di marzo 1847 nel circondario di questa Camera di Commercio in Como*, Camera di Commercio, 77, Como State Archive.

49. There were 8,304 working women out of a total female population of 12,128. "Censimento della Popolazione, 1871," Letter of the President of the Census Committee to the Municipal Assembly, Como, May 10, 1872, Como State Archive.

50. "Risposta fornita alla Commissione d'Inchiesta per gli Scioperi del Ministero dell'Interno" (answer to the Interior Ministry Investigative Committee on Strikes, April 1878), in Guenzi, "La tessitura," 234.

51. Lega di Resistenza, *Sull'avvenire degli Operai Tessitori della Fabbricazione di Como*, compiled by Aristide Bari (Como: Tipografia Cooperativa, 1890), pp. 14-16.

52. Rural workers were also employed in numerous wool, linen, and cotton manufactures. Pietro Pinchetti, *L'industria della seta sul finire del secolo XIX* (Como, 1894), p. 112. In 1876 in the province of Como, 46,634 workers were employed in the various branches of the silk industry, of whom 13,818 were in weaving. Ministero di Agricoltura, Industria, e Commercio (MAIC), *Statistiche industriali. Lombardia* (Milan, 1896), p. 186.

53. Pinchetti, *L'industria della seta*, p. 105.

54. Letter of the President of the Chamber of Commerce to the Ministry of the Interior, February 28, 1878, file 369, Chamber of Commerce, "Controversie di lavoro," Como State Archive.

55. The number of power looms increased slowly from 250 in 1870, to 686 in 1890, to 976 in 1893. Hand looms still numbered 6,264 in 1893. See *Statistica Industriale. Lombardia*, p. 201. In 1904 there were still 7,972 hand looms, while there were 5,213 power looms. Caizzi, *Storia del setificio comasco*, p. 78.

56. The brothers Tasco adopted this system and used the workshops for training their la-

bor force. See Ministero di Agricoltura, Industria, e Commercio, Comitato dell'Inchiesta Industriale, *Atti. Deposizioni scritte. Trattura, Stagionatura, torcitura e tintura della seta*, Categories 1, 2, 3, and 6 (Rome, 1874), p. 21.

57. Gedeone Bressi, "Tessuti di seta," in *Esposizione industriale del 1881 in Milano. Relazioni dei giurati. Le industrie tessili* (Milan, 1883), reprinted in Mario Romani, *Storia economica d'Italia nel secolo XIX* (Milan: Adlo Giuffrè editore, 1970), p. 1,183.

58. MAIC, *Statistiche industriali*, p. 203.

59. Giuseppe Gatti, *L'agricoltura e gli agricoltori del circondario di Como* (Como, 1882), p. 78, and Ugo Tombesi, *L'evoluzione di un'industria italiana: La tessitura serica a Como* (Pesaro, 1899), p. 24.

60. Inchiesta Industriale, *Atti. Tessitura della seta*, category 6, § 3. Deposition by Marinoni Giovanni, p. 21.

Jean H. Quataert 9

Survival Strategies in a Saxon Textile District during the Early Phases of Industrialization, 1780-1860

Strategically placed along key historic trade routes that moved goods around Europe, the Oberlausitz Margravate of Saxony by the eighteenth century had become an indispensable link in the commercial and transportation networks of the continent. Its favored geographic location at the crossroads of traffic going east-west as well as north-south tied the remote territory directly into the growing manufacturing and export sectors of Europe. During the so-called Atlantic Stage of European economic development, the territory was a major supplier of woven linen cloth for the advancing world market. Capitalizing on tandem social changes in the countryside of the south Oberlausitz, merchants in Britain, Spain, and other countries that also owned colonies had moved textile production beyond the city gates, and growing numbers of agricultural smallholders were simultaneously becoming small manufacturers. Oberlausitz linenwares produced by these rural cottagers became an essential part of the flowing colonial trade of cloth, cutlery, and hardware from Central Europe in exchange for indigo, rice, sugar, and tobacco. Destined principally for Hamburg, London, and Cadiz, the linen cloth subsequently was reexported by the colonial powers to clothe the slaves in the West Indies and North and South America and to sack sugar, cotton, tobacco, and dyes.[1]

An accumulating series of technological and organizational changes upset this older economic order, which, while dynamic in its own right, nonetheless had grown up around a connected web of customs and traditions steeped in the forces of nature and geography. Beginning around the last third of the eighteenth century, parts of the manufacturing sectors in Britain turned to new machine technology, inanimate sources of energy, and centralized spaces for the organization of production. In those industries initially shaped by economic innovations, prices fell, productivity rose dramatically, and overall demand increased, generating ever-widen-

153

ing markets for the goods. The new economy of industrial capitalism promised to restructure productive tasks and rerank economic sectors, as well as overturn existing relations between developed and less-developed regions. It posed a major challenge to important hand-weaving regions such as the Oberlausitz territory in Saxony, inaugurating in effect a protracted "period of transition" to the industrial economy, the end of which—full industrialization or ruralization, to mention merely the two outer poles—was not fully predictable solely from the region's eighteenth-century economic profile.[2]

Much of the scholarly literature treating the broad theme of economic development in Europe pays insufficient attention to these important decades of transition, highlighting the final outcome of a region's development rather than the transition processes themselves. Yet, examination of the precise mechanisms of adaptation by groups speaking for hand-weaving interests in the Saxon Oberlausitz sheds important new light on broader themes in European economic history during the critical time period preceding widespread introduction of mechanized factory production in the various German states. Indeed, the example of the Oberlausitz Margravate rectifies what Pollard sees as a major shortcoming of economic theory. Economists, he notes, have failed to assess adequately "the relationship which was by far the most important and dynamic in nineteenth-century Europe: the trade implications of the industrial revolution, as a process which took place most unevenly at different stages and differing speeds as between regions, sectors, and countries."[3] The problem is compounded by a "provincial" focus, a concentration on the geographic borders of Europe alone rather than a willingness to place the European case in its international context.[4] In the evolving industrial economy of the first half of the nineteenth century, the Oberlausitz region became entwined in a trade nexus ironically opened up by the very successes of British industrialization and competitive position. Importing mechanized yarns from Britain and exporting handwoven cloth to points east (particularly to areas such as Turkey and the Levant), Oberlausitz traders and commercial capitalists carved out a successful niche in the world market; they also actively sold cloth closer to home in Central Europe. For its turn, rising per capita cloth consumption as part of the growing involvement of the Ottoman Empire in the cash economy accounts for the lively demand for Oberlausitz cloth in Bursa, Damascus, and Aleppo. By the 1860s, the improved standard of living of the agricultural population in the eastern parts of Germany fanned a sufficiently vibrant internal market for Oberlausitz cloth to help propel the province toward mechanization. Then the Saxon Oberlausitz became linked to the wider German industrial economy by the specialized function it performed within the whole. But that is getting ahead of the story.

The critical period of challenge for hand-manufacturing interests in the Oberlausitz lasted well over a half a century, from roughly 1780 to 1860. Three major forces worked together to bring out the region's potential to seize a variety of market opportunities. The first involved the multiple economic advantages that accompanied the introduction of cotton weaving into the margravate while simultaneously perpetuating the area's historic involvement in linen goods manufacture. The second was the extent of state efforts in capital expenditures for adoption of new hand technology. And the third involved the local small producers themselves. The combination of manufacturing and agrarian involvements in the small family enterprise rested on highly flexible gender work roles. Householders responded to the challenges of competition by turning to inceasingly intricate combinations of work, by extensive hawking, and by bold efforts at smuggling.

Linen exports from the Oberlausitz Margravate had reached their high point in the decade of the 1780s at the precise moment when machine-spun cotton yarn from Britain began to infiltrate the Saxon market.[5] At the time there was no cotton industry of note in the Oberlausitz land itself. Other regions of Saxony long had been involved in cotton manufacture, however. Along with the Swiss and the subcontinental Indians, the Saxons stood at the center of world cotton production at the end of the eighteenth century.[6] Saxon businessmen, therefore, could ill afford to be indifferent to the newfangled inventions in cotton textile manufacture occurring in England. The growing influx into Saxon markets of machine-made yarns and quality cloth from across the channel elicited worried responses. It prompted a Plauen distributor named Baumgärtel to make a trip to England in the summer of 1791 to observe firsthand changes in the cotton industry which were affecting his profits adversely. His comments are worth repeating in some detail, for they capture the dramatic sense of challenge posed by the new mechanized technology which infected far-thinking continental businessmen.

> There had been recently in England unbelieveable progress in machine spinning, and the efforts of late by the rich English manufacturers to multiply yarn output and make it less expensive had such dimensions and were of such quality that they created well-warranted concerns that the British, with their volume, grade, and cheapness of production, would soon displace other manufacturers who lacked mechanized equipment of equal efficiency. Already, the Swiss muslin producers were beginning to sense the overwhelming competition of their English counterparts, and after a while they would probably no longer be able to cope with it. The same outcome was threatening muslin manufacture in the Voigtland district [of Saxony] unless the producers could succeed in acquiring yarn-spinning machines of the same quality as the English—which would be very difficult because the British keep this machinery extraordinarily secret.[7]

Baumgärtel's style, his determined language, betrays a keen appreciation of the pressing need to deal with rapidly changing economic conditions. Embedded in his imagery of the new age—machinery, competition, progress—were simultaneous promises of extraordinary benefits and devastating hardships.

Baumgärtel was right to stress the competitive pressures, for in the subsequent decade and a half after his trip to England, British exports of muslins, calicoes, piqué, and wallis rose rapidly, sending shock waves throughout the whole Saxon textile industry. The British materials were being purchased in increasing amounts because buyers substituted the cheaper cotton ware for more expensive silk and fine wool cloth. At the Leipzig fair alone in the early nineteenth century, the total value of imported English cotton goods nearly doubled in five years, rising from 2.5 million Thaler in 1800 to 4.1 million Thaler in 1805. It was merchants from Russia, Moldavia, Poland, and Turkey—presumably based in northern Ottoman lands close to the border between German and Slavic-speaking peoples—who most actively promoted this trade in fashionable cotton goods. In exchange, the eastern traders brought wool, tallow, Lithuanian hare pelts, and other furs. Earlier they had bought Saxon cotton cloth, but by the turn of the nineteenth century they shifted enthusiastically over to British manufactured textiles for their "superior quality, originality, and moderate price."[8]

Unquestionably, British cotton yarn and cloth exports posed a real threat to the indigenous Saxon cotton industry between roughly 1793 and 1806, and economic historians agree that the Continental Blockade essentially saved it.[9] Prohibitions on British imports gave the industry a much-needed breathing spell, without which it largely would have been destroyed; protection simultaneously permitted the shift to machine yarn spinning, and the number of spindles in Saxony rose from 612 in 1806 to 97,006 in 1812.[10] But there were costs as well. Protectionism was, after all, an artificial respite, permitting noncompetitive growth; it slowed down the importation of British machinery, and at the end of the blockade, the technological gap between Central Europe and Britain had increased significantly. Furthermore, after 1815, British-manufactured yarn and cloth returned to Saxon markets with a vengeance. If the economic impact of the blockade on the Saxon cotton industry was mixed, Napoleon's continental system was an unmitigated disaster for the Oberlausitz linen industry, which depended so heavily on exports. One traditional market after the other was lost; indeed, in 1813 at the once-vital Hamburg trade fair, most of the linen export houses from the Oberlausitz simply did not appear.[11] The protectionist policies of the Continental System, however, encouraged a temporary shift to cotton weaving that proved permanent just as the long-term results of the Napoleonic wars, disruptions of trade, and redrawing of the European map after 1815 spelled a significant change in the axes of the continental economy, which also affected the economic fortunes of the Oberlausitz Margravate. In the case of the continent, its active hub shifted from the Atlantic seaboard to the Rhineland, from the coast to the heartland. Thenceforth, the explosive area of growth of the continental industrial economy was northern and eastern France, Belgium, and northwestern Germany. But there had been significant developments as well in Saxony, Bohemia, Austria, and Hungary. Industrial growth in these lands was spurred on by evolving trade relations with the east, which also solidified at the time of the blockade.[12] Revival of manufacture in the Saxon Oberlausitz after 1815 owed its major stimulus to these new trade links to the east, and the main products of export were different kinds of woven cotton cloth.

The serious disruption of linen production in the Oberlausitz during the Continental Blockade had been met by the introduction of cotton weaving into the area on a large and increasingly successful scale. The first products were calicoes and cotton prints and raw and colored nankeens. Both were a simple flat weave which could be manufactured on the same loom used for linen with the same skill level, so weavers initially moved interchangeably between the two branches of textiles. Protected by the Continental System, these cotton cloths replaced banned British equivalents in the Turkish and Levant trade, which was being mediated successfully at the Leipzig and other Saxon fairs. After 1815, Oberlausitz manufacturers continued to provide a variety of cloth to Turkish and Levantine markets. To some extent, these entrepreneurs benefited from earlier established trading ties to the Ottoman Empire. The Ottomans had exported red yarn to the Oberlausitz on a rather large scale in the decades following the Seven Years' War.[13] This yarn was the last major manufacturing export of the empire, except for carpets and raw silk. At one time, Ottoman-made cloth had been sold throughout Europe, but by the mid-eighteenth century these textiles no longer were competitive, so some Oberlausitz firms began to manufacture an "Oriental" cloth that sold well in Europe. After 1815, they began to export a similar cloth to the Orient (the Near East) itself.

The history of weaving in the Oberlausitz of Ebersbach is largely the story of the special trade relationships between the south Oberlausitz and parts of the Ottoman Empire that played such a vital role for a time in the economic survival of the old Saxon hand-weaving region. The village, described as "beautiful, large, and densely populated" in 1815, became the most important center for so-called colorful (*bunt*) Greek or Oriental tweed.[14] A set of documents prepared by officials concerned with the growing socioeconomic crisis of the mid-1840s provides sufficient details to reconstruct these hitherto neglected exchange relationships. In the eighteenth century, Ebersbach had been a significant contributor to overall linen production in the margravate. In 1777, for example, of 84,000 pieces of linen from the Zittau area exported through Herrnhut, the village of Ebersbach alone contributed 8 percent, or 6,745 pieces. But this once-vibrant linen industry suffered irreparable damage in the early nineteenth century, as occurred elsewhere throughout the land. According to government reports, manufacturers then turned to finishing pure cotton cloth "in large volume." Through connections with "solid Viennese businesses," this expansion was directed toward the Levant.[15] Thus, Ebersbach entrepreneurs became integrated directly into the Levantine component of the historic trade nexus between Europe and the wider Orient. Viennese firms had long-standing commercial relations with the Near East; in the peace of 1718, the victorious Hapsburg government had concluded trade agreements with the Ottoman Porte, giving its citizens free access to markets within the empire and around the Mediterranean basin as well. It even founded the Eastern Trading Company, which directed the exchange of goods and established warehouses in Vienna and Belgrade.[16] So Ebersbach manufacturers moved into an existing structure that once had contributed measurably to the commercial development of both territories. But now, with ongoing industrialization, exchange became more one-sided, if its contribution to sustained economic growth is the object of inquiry. The Oberlausitz economy obtained raw materials and foodstuffs from the Ottoman provinces for its cloth furnished with imported European machine-made yarns.

Ebersbach businessmen saw new market opportunities open up and moved in.

Provincial officials in the capital of Bautzen with some exaggeration asserted that "there was a time when Ebersbach supplied the whole Oriental market almost by itself." The two leading entrepreneurs in the export business, Henke and Freude, were geographically more specific and in a report referred to Turkey—that is, the Turkish and Arab provinces of the Ottoman Empire—as the chief consumer of the colorful, flat-woven tweed cloth.[17] In this transition period, however, village weavers did not abandon linenmaking completely; a proportion continued to finish especially fine linen cloth destined for Saxony and the states of the Customs Union, and some also wove half-linen goods which were sent to North America. All this activity gave the village of Ebersbach, according to a traveler in midcentury, who drew on new industrial imagery, "the appearance of a city: good houses with lightning rods, many professionals, doctors. . . ."[18]

Oriental tweed became an essential export branch of the Saxon Oberlausitz. Growth of the specialty compensated for a continuous decline in the competitive position of Oberlausitz raw calicoes and colorful nankeens and shirtings, the original cotton products introduced into the margravate. These simple cotton weaves had been the first to be mechanized in England, and starting in the 1820s and accelerating thereafter, Oberlausitz hand producers simply were unable to compete with the same British cloth made on power looms. The growing reliance on colorful Oriental tweeds was part of a more general shift to handmade cotton textiles that at the time were not amenable to mechanization. During the decades of transition, the Saxon Oberlausitz came to specialize in so-called *Buntweberei*, a hand-manufactured colored cloth which remained competitive in a wide range of market settings. Not until the very late 1840s were the steps involved in the complicated alternation of various colored yarns first mechanized.[19] One essential strategy for survival became the manufacture of cloth which established its own competitive niche in the evolving world market. If this criterion explains in good measure the supply side of production, what accounted for the demand side in the exchange of goods? Why would a growing market for such colorful tweeds manufactured in Europe open up in the Ottoman Empire?

Economic historians of the Ottoman Empire note two important commercial trends in the early nineteenth century that may shed light on some aspects of the wider exchange relationships between Europe and the Near East during the early Industrial Revolution. First, the empire was increasingly using imported European-made cotton yarn to weave its own cloth locally, and second, it was purchasing growing amounts of European cloth. In the standard interpretation, rising yarn imports signaled the destruction of the once-vibrant hand-spinning industry of the empire, confirmation of ongoing deindustrialization in light of technological changes in Europe. By contrast, in a revision of this established wisdom, new research shows that yarn imports should be taken as a measure of added value. And the history of the Ottoman silk industry holds the key in this new interpretation. Between 1810 and 1850, silk cloth production declined significantly in the empire. Yearly output in the production center of Bursa fell from a high of 100,000 pieces to between 20,000 and 30,000, and the livelihoods of large numbers of silk spinners

and weavers were threatened. But the switch away from silk was met by a corresponding shift to production of high-quality cotton cloth (made from imported
yarn) and a simultaneous growing consumption of European-made cloth. Ottoman
consumers had been introduced to cotton textiles in the eighteenth century when
moderate amounts of Indian-made cloth created new tastes in the upper part of the
market. Initially, the British were able to satisfy the new preference as Ottoman
traders bought large amounts of cloth in fairs such as Leipzig; eventually, the Oberlausitz trader actively stepped into the market. For Ottoman consumers, high-quality cotton cloth began to displace their traditional reliance on silk. British mechanization of yarns encouraged a transformation of industrial manufacturing in the
Ottoman Empire. It altered the place where Ottoman labor was being used, away
from silk to cotton and away from cotton spinning to weaving. Revisionist historians, thus, speak not of absolute decline but of transformation of manufacturing activities.[20] The availability of cheaper-quality cloth changed consumption patterns,
and the empire's greater involvement in the wider cash economy spelled rising levels of per capita cloth consumption generally. It accounted for the sustained demand for Saxon handmade cotton textiles in the 1810s, 1820s, and 1830s. Trade
remained strong until the late 1840s, when fashions changed once again and Ottoman buyers, responding to the fickle tastes of consumers, showed a growing preference for decorative cloth resembling damask rather than the original flat-woven
product. Worried Oberlausitz officials correctly feared that much of the business of
the Viennese houses now would be taken over by Swiss producers shifting over to
the decorative motifs.

The Saxon Oberlausitz never relied solely on Oriental tweeds as its major export
commodity, however. Another kindred specialty blossomed at the same time, destined mainly for markets closer to home, in Saxony, the states of the Customs
Union, Bohemia, and other parts of Central Europe. Into the nineteenth century,
most central and northern Europeans essentially used wool material for their clothing; it was, however, relatively expensive, although extremely durable. It is not surprising that the lower classes increasingly turned to the less expensive cotton material for their attire; this cloth became the staple export article of the Oberlausitz
and, given the relatively low wages of local rural producers with their ongoing ties
to subsistence agriculture, the cheaper handmade ware came to dominate the markets of Central Europe, displacing the same cloth which originally had been made
in the mills and workshops of the lower Rhine.[21] Coincidental with the decline in
demand for Oriental tweed came a turn to another product, the manufacture of Orleans cloth, based on a mix of cotton and wool yarn, which for a time remained
competitive on hand looms. It was precisely the stages of production of both the
colorful cotton and Orleans wares that were mechanized starting in the 1850s. A
successful sequence of cloth manufacture—from monocolored nankeens to white
calicoes to colorful cotton and mixed Orleans cloth—had permitted capital accumulation for eventual investments in factory buildings and machine technology.[22]

The first five decades of the nineteenth century, then, were especially challenging for hand-weaving specialties in Europe and elsewhere. Machine-made cotton

yarns undercut their handspun equivalents in all but the finest grades, and cloth woven with the new threads was cheap, durable, and increasingly preferred by customers over linen, silk, and wool materials. Few areas of the world could escape for long the momentous consequences of these broad shifts in production and consumption patterns; but their impact was complex and multifaceted, and varied over time and region. For some areas, most notably India, British industrialization essentially destroyed the local manufacturing base.[23] For other areas, in contrast, the same technological changes opened up alternative productive and market opportunities, which historians only recently have come to investigate empirically. In the case of the Ottoman Empire, European industrialization on balance transformed the nature and extent of manufacturing in the nineteenth century rather than ruined it. And the old linen-weaving district of the Saxon Oberlausitz maintained its manufacturing profile by turning to new products that were competitive in the marketplace.

One key factor that sustained hand manufacturing in the Oberlausitz province during the early phases of factory industrialization was the introduction of cotton weaving into a historically linenmaking region. This same combination of productive activities helped explain the dramatic growth of Lancashire, "the classic industrial region" of England during the Industrial Revolution, as well as the economically vibrant Scheldt Valley of Belgium and the lower Rhineland in western Germany.[24] By contrast, contemporary European linen-weaving regions that deindustrialized, such as East Westphalia, Silesia, and Flanders, had failed to attract a viable cotton branch to their borders and were forced to rely on a single export for which markets were shrinking. But even the old hand-weaving districts of Normandy, which manufactured *siamoises*, a mix of linen and cotton yarns, could not remain competitive and suffered general depopulation. Earlier advantages such as cheap labor and market access became, in the new age, deterrents to technological experimentation.[25] In these cases, however, the consequences of deindustrialization varied. In areas of richer farmland, such as Upper Normandy or East Westphalia, that lost their industrial concentrations, smallholder labor was reabsorbed into agriculture; but in the case of Silesia and Flanders, their unfavorable location offered small manufacturers no employment alternatives, and labor was forced to move elsewhere for jobs. The regions were not located near substantial markets for finished goods, and their transportation costs were high relative to those of competitive regions.

The Saxon Oberlausitz was spared this fate. Starting in the early nineteenth century, as seen, cotton manufacture became an increasingly important source of livelihood in the region. The area continued to weave and export linen, though on a much smaller scale than a century earlier. What were the economic benefits of the linkages between cotton and linen manufacture? In essence, they worked to facilitate a slow but eventually successful transition to mechanized production in textiles and related industries. In the first place, cotton was the "strategic sector" of the region's economy at the time.[26] Given the elasticity of demand, it was the only product expanding rapidly, the one most suited to mechanization, and its development and technical improvement were the surest way eventually to introduce the new mechanized technology into the various stages of cloth production. Besides, cotton weaving spawned an important and related machine-making industry. Second, during the critical decades of competitive challenge, the Oberlausitz was able to sustain a dynamic export sector by shifting to the making of colored cloth and tweeds. In contrast, regions producing solely linen faced declining market opportunities. This growth in the cotton sector promoted ongoing capital accumulation, ever greater proportions of which eventually were invested in centralized mills, new types of machinery, and steam power. Third, there was much transference of labor and capital among the cotton, linen, and half-cotton branches of the local textile industry. These alternative production lines gave both small producers and the businessmen considerable flexibility to respond to the fluctuations of the business cycle. When demand fell off for cotton goods, there was a good chance for linenmaking to take up the slack. For example, in 1860 the businessman Wilhelm Meissner described how he shifted his business from Orleans weaving to the making of damask when there was a sudden drop in orders for the half-wool cloth. During the American Civil War, which disrupted raw cotton exports worldwide, the Oberlausitz linen industry experienced a growth spurt the likes of which had not been seen in decades.[27] The multiple employment and production options compensated for the differences in the timing and rate of mechanization of the heterogeneous textile industry. They bought time for the area's domestic linen industry until the later date at which it, too, began to shift over from hand to mechanized production.

Other factors, however, also contributed to the region's ability to preserve capital, labor, and markets. The Saxon Oberlausitz was never simply a one-industry region, a weakness that later often spelled deindustrialization. Early on, the presence of manufacturing work for export in the countryside had supported extensive population growth and the accumulation of a variety of skills, and it encouraged a lively local exchange economy, offering work for a wide range of village artisans and craftsmen. Already in the era of rural manufacture, the area exported textile tools and machinery as well as stones from its numerous quarries. Furthermore, there was considerable movement of labor between manufacturing and agriculture, which continued throughout the nineteenth century. On one occasion in October 1862, the Zittau entrepreneur Meissner himself wrote to local officials that his weavers had not yet experimented with new hand looms made possible by state subsidies because they were too busy doing the harvest work.[28] Local and state officials had been supporting businessmen in their efforts to raise the competitive position of hand manufacturing before the region was ready to sustain mechanized production. Saxon officials, overseeing the state's general economic health in the first half of the nineteen century, invested considerable capital in the Oberlausitz region. The transitional economy was strengthened in important ways by state expenditures for material and human growth.

Among economic historians of Central Europe, the Saxon state is reputed to have been "laissez faire" in its efforts to promote capitalist enterprise and industrial growth.[29] For example, Trebilcock, among others, writes that the Saxon rulers adopted a "near Smithian" posture toward business ventures, in marked contrast to their Prussian counterparts, seen as prime examples of official *dirigisme*, or active involvement in the economy.[30] Indeed, the theme of state involvement in economic development in the late eighteenth and nineteenth centuries long has engaged scholarly interest in European economic history. But as with many major interpretations of Europes' industrial past, judgments concerning the historic role of the states in recent years have been modified considerably. It was once common to note that pioneer England industrialized with minimal state assistance, in contrast to continental Europe, where the state played a more active role to compensate for its comparative backwardness. But scholars such as Immanuel Wallerstein who offer excellent synthetic discussions of the recent literature point to a significant shift in analysis: economic historians now recognize the role of the state in the British case after all, in offering protection for industrial growth, freeing markets for its goods, and supervising and safeguarding key industries.[31] Others stress, as did some earlier historians as well, the state's role in increasing the country's capital stock by adding to the infrastructure: investing in public buildings, transportation networks, and wider communication services.[32]

In the early nineteenth century, government priorities in Saxony began to include investments in the state's economic infrastructure. After 1815, officials for the first time included trade requirements, not only military contingencies, in their decisions to build new streets, roads, and highways.[33] The first route in Saxony to be upgraded to a highway for transit purposes was the Böhmische Strasse, a main artery connecting the industrial south Oberlausitz along the Bohemian border with the key market town of Leipzig; construction began in 1815. New trade routes also were planned that linked the south Oberlausitz with Dresden; other modernized routes went north-south and joined Löbau and Zittau together; and in the early 1830s, with an eye to promoting the sale of damask cloth, a smaller highway was built that tied Zittau with Gross-Schönau and on down to the Bohemian town of Rumburg.[34] Throughout the century, the state also acted in a timely and energetic fashion in the planning, negotiating, financing, and constructing stages of railroad building; it established a modernized postal service and encouraged all manner of new municipal construction beyond street renovations such as improvements in government structures and town halls as well as building orphanages, schools, and storehouses for grain. Official documents demonstrate unmistakably that the timing of this range of construction work in local Oberlausitz communities was designed partly to offer seasonal employment to a percentage of the *male* hand-weaving population caught in a business downturn.[35] (The policy never was defined explicitly in gender terms, however.) Such jobs helped diversify income for numbers of households and, as will be explored in more detail below, contributed to their survival during the difficult transition decades. State ends dovetailed with householder needs and worked to limit outmigration.

Equally characteristic was the government's investment in human capital through its efforts to further general literacy, training, and skill acquisition as well as professional growth. These commitments began in an earlier age, although they accelerated in the first half of the nineteenth century. In 1735, state officials had established a Commercial Deputation which was transformed thirty years later into a State Deputation for Agriculture, Manufacture, and Commerce, a visible and effective body offering advice on technical innovations and vocational training. In the nineteenth century, they fostered a variety of educational and technical institutions, including an academy for forestry, a polytechnical school in Dresden, and other trade schools; in 1835 they passed laws mandating primary education throughout the land and helped set up an annual industrial exhibition in Dresden (*Gewerbe-ausstellung*).[36]

Most economic historians, however, have something more specific in mind when turning to the issue of the "role of the state" in economic life. The phrase has become shorthand for an inquiry into the extent to which enterprises were founded on state or private initiative. In the Saxon case, Rudolf Forberger, the foremost economic historian of the kingdom's capitalist development, concludes that the state played a truly secondary role in the founding of manufactories and later factories; Saxon business history is tied up in the main with private capital.[37] But beginning in the second half of the eighteenth century and accelerating with greater urgency thereafter, government officials became increasingly preoccupied with new technology. On a continuous basis they sought to make available to enterprising businessmen the latest machines and work tools through subsidies, cash premiums, competitions, and prizes. Government interest and entrepreneurial needs coalesced to promote the acquisition of new work tools as well as construction of modern machinery to increase productivity. For example, officials offered "cash rewards" for introducing steam power in 1814, and beginning in the 1820s advertised "cash premiums" for the use of new looms for ticking, of machines for making reeds, shaping the teeth in the combs, and carding as well as for leathermaking, indigo dyeing, and fulling.[38] In this way, officials expected to benefit fiscally from the strengthened and more competitive position of the state's manufacturing and industrial base. In the Oberlausitz land, before the area could support power-driven machinery, state assistance specifically centered on making hand technology as competitive as possible. Archival materials furnish details on these official endeavors.

In their efforts to attract state funding, Oberlausitz businessmen were actively supported by local administrators worried about the region's overall economic health. This blend of private and administrative advocacy centered around efforts to obtain two types of "modern" presteam technology: the Jacquard loom for figured weaving in both damask and cotton cloth manufacture, and so-called regulator looms, which allowed hand weavers to make a more "regular" or even weave, introduced into the Orleans branch. In all the cases that were found in the archives, the businessmen obtained looms made in Saxony, and local officials spent considerable time investigating conditions in the industry to obtain the most suitable machinery. For example, in 1835 during long negotiations to introduce patterned cloth in the ticking industry in Waltersdorf, the district officer, Amtshauptmann von Igenhoeff, concluded that the best looms for the new purposes were being built by Gottlieb Friedrich Müller in the Saxon town of Chemnitz.[39] The arguments mustered by the local entrepreneurs and officials for state subsidies read like a catalogue of the great late nineteenth-century exhibitions extolling the fruits of industrial progress. In 1847, for example, Zittau administrators writing on behalf of the businessman Henke unquestionably favored the use of Jacquard looms for the Ebersbach tweed industry, which was then in some trouble. The new looms promised a "better product" and "better wages" and thus a way to achieve a more profitable industrial branch than "ordinary" cotton weaving. Echoing the perspective of the business community poised to adopt the new technology, officials wrote that "the introduction of Jacquard looms promises only advantages, not harm, and unquestionably represents progress in the industry. . . ."[40] That small producers might have a different point of view is not surprising. As hand weavers, they were deeply skeptical of the alien processes of mechanization going on around them. Indeed, weavers employed by the Zittau firm of Meissner and Haebler had actively resisted the initial efforts to introduce regulators into production. The workers feared that the new machinery somehow would hamper their custom of skimming off the extra yarn for personal use and lead to outside encroachment on the work processes by the distant employers.[41] But by the 1860s, these same businessmen were able to present the Dresden government with an impressive set of petitions signed by their workers in support of the innovations in hand technology. By then, the weavers apparently accepted the argument that only improvements in hand machinery would enhance their competitive position. In 1865, Orleans weavers of the firm of Meissner and Haebler called on government officials to consult the account books, which, they stated, showed unmistakably that "next to mechanized production hand weaving still can make money." Perhaps prompted by their employers, the weavers also noted that over the past two years, the firm had boasted a 15,000 RT profit.[42]

Public investments in hand technology in the Saxon Oberlausitz remained modest at best, however, although apparently no general survey of total government expenditures in the territory has yet been made. Archival documents offer the following picture of state support for technological experimentation. The first steps to encourage adoption of new hand technology occurred in the damask industry in Gross-Schönau, a coveted branch of manufacturing which long had received special government attention. In 1832, government officials offered cash premiums of 100 to 200 RT for the purchase of Voigtland-made Jacquard looms and doubling frames. Officials also were active in helping to introduce patterned weaving in the ticking industry in neighboring Waltersdorf in the mid-1830s.[43] During exceptional periods of crisis, as, for example, the one suffered by small producers in Reichenau as the result of a costly fire in 1848, state officials willingly gave subsidies to help defray the costs of starting the business up again. In the case of Reichenau, they offered 150 RT to ten weavers, including a woman by the name of Marie Rosine, to buy replacements for the damaged looms. The next sustained commitment of public monies, however, came in the Oriental tweed industry in the mid-1840s, when Levantine tastes shifted to patterned and figured cloth. State officials then hoped to improve the economic fortunes of the once-vibrant export branch by encouraging a shift to Jacquard-made cloth. Finally, in the 1860s, businessmen such as Wilhelm

Meissner convinced Dresden officials to underwrite part of their loan from the margravate regional bank for the purchase of the regulator looms for the Orleans industry. The timing of the request was critical because the finishing processes of dyeing and pressing in the branch had become fully mechanized with steam power. According to Meissner's logic, which proved quite persuasive, the industry was facing inexorable pressures also to mechanize the weaving stages of production, which would undercut the livelihood of large numbers of Oberlausitz hand producers. At the time, Meissner alone employed 1,000 people. But with the help of regulator looms, he argued, "we would be able to produce goods which could compete with those made on the mechanical looms." A 2,000 M capital outlay granted in 1862 enabled Meissner to dispense 151 such looms to eighteen neighboring villages and keep production going, at least in the short run. The ultimate outcome was not favorable, however. The firm went bankrupt in 1868 (a fate shared by numerous other Orleans businesses, as noted by local officials) and was bought two years later by the carpenter Pogge, after it had suffered further damages during a flood. The site ultimately was turned into a lumber mill.[44]

Public monies for the purchase of new technology easily shaded into financial support for the acquisition of new skills and tools. The final stage of government involvement in the hand manufacture of Orleans cloth came in the early 1880s in the villages of Ober- and Mittelweigsdorf and Dornhennersdorf. By then, power looms dominated the Orleans branch, but the hand weavers themselves had in no way shifted completely to factory production. The Zittau Chamber of Commerce was concerned with improving hand-weaving skills and dispensing new tools to hard-pressed weavers. Determined to help local hand producers learn to weave colored cotton material for dresses and aprons, the municipalities set up so-called workrooms (Arbeitsstuben). They explained to the Saxon Ministry of Interior, from which they were trying to obtain reimbursement for their expenses, that factory owners usually took the lead in establishing and paying for such instruction. But these small villages were some distance away from factory hubs, so the burdens had fallen on the townships. Through municipal efforts, a course was set up to teach new skills and dispense improved brushes to interested weavers. These brushes permitted a more "equal distribution" of the starch on the warp. Given the dispersed nature of the communities, one instructor also went into the homes of targeted weavers to teach the new skills on an individual basis and to give the weavers up-to-date tools. In their request, chamber officials estimated that forty-three men and women had been trained in their central location, while sixty-four men and women had been reached in their homes. The total cost came to 463 Marks 29 pennies for the salary of the instructors, purchase of seventy-one brushes, expenditure for rent, and other improvements of the looms.[45] The archival source has an added importance beyond its manifest intent of documenting expenses in order to obtain compensation. The report makes eminently clear that women weavers were involved in the educational process both in the central workroom and in their homes. But in the published record of the Chamber of Commerce activities that same year, only male weavers are mentioned in the discussion of the vocational training.[46] The printed account strikingly omits the participation of women in this textile branch, demonstrating clearly the pervasive gender bias at work, which was eliminating women's important role from the record of this changing world of industrializing manufactures.

In their effort to safeguard small-producer livelihood and the economic health of the hand-weaving province, Oberlausitz officials unintentionally provided extraordinary glimpses into the household gender dynamics of hand manufacturing in the first two-thirds of the nineteenth century. Their surveys and reports as well as the active and detailed exchange of information with local businessmen capture intriguing gender work relations that were operating beneath the level of public discussion and recognition. Indeed, these work roles offered small producers considerable economic flexibility during these difficult transitional decades. The impact of manufacturing in the countryside had important consequences for household gender relations, work roles, access to resources, and power, the nature of which historians are still exploring to good advantage.[47] But just as no single economic and demographic pattern characterizes the European regions undergoing extensive rural manufacture, so too local variables such as topography, inheritance customs, the nature and strength of manorial controls, and folk beliefs influenced the actual distribution of work among the men and women in small-producer families.[48]

In the Oberlausitz Margravate, the turn by rural people to linen weaving for export, which gathered momentum starting in the mid-seventeenth century, initiated a highly complex and continuously evolving set of gender dynamics shaping production. With the onset of mechanized competition beginning in the 1780s and the crisis years of war and blockade, small-producer households were able to develop their own strategies for survival, increasingly deploying adult men to do supplemental work outside of textiles and thus in many ways making women the year-round weavers in the district. They also carved out their own market strategies, exploring ways to sell and market cloth, both legally and, when necessary, through smuggling.

Rural manufacturing in the countryside of the Saxon Oberlausitz clearly had a profound impact on household formation and the work relations within the household. But since the economic and political forces organizing rural production itself were not static, the gender work roles were subject to considerable modification over time. The continuity in the location of production in individual households should not mask considerable change in the way householders balanced agricultural, manufacturing, marketing, and later other work over time. This pattern of change is difficult to capture, particularly for the pre-1780 era, but some of its broad outlines come through the often opaque source materials. Without a doubt, these shifting gender work roles helped maximize meager incomes in households tied to both agricultural and industrial pursuits.

The work generated by the manufacture of linen cloth in smallholder cottages of the south Oberlausitz—and the ancillary tasks of spinning, dyeing, and finishing that it gradually spawned—at the outset consolidated community ties to the land. Introduced into a feudal economy itself in considerable demographic and economic flux, textile production in many cases repositioned a mobile male labor force; it also opened wider opportunities for new household formation. The village of Oybin offers a classic example of these forces at work in the Oberlausitz. Prior to the introduction of linen weaving to the village after the Thirty Years' War, the local agricultural and wood products economy provided an insufficient basis for village livelihood in the face of population growth; some men of the village then trekked daily over the hills to the Bohemian town of Krombach for jobs in glassworks, while other toiled in nearby quarries. Women cared for the small subsistence plots that customarily came with a cottage; they grew corn and oats and watched over livestock as well, but many also worked in beekeeping for the local demesne, controlled in this case by the city of Zittau.[49] The new jobs in weaving, however, returned male workers to the home, and the added income permitted new family formation. Cottagers involved in textile production were the fastest-growing social group in the village economy of the south Oberlausitz. Indeed, these cottagers at the production end of a capitalist network became linked with local artisans, also expanding (although less rapidly) as a group, and peasants in a set of partially monetized exchange relations that underpinned community life for a time.[50]

Manufacturing drew women into its orbit more gradually as it continued to rearrange the balance between agricultural and industrial work. Long after the initial introduction of linen weaving into the countryside of the margravate, women apparently still focused much of their time on subsistence agriculture, raising crops that came to include vegetables and flax, and caring for the livestock. Evidence on the allocation of work in public spaces indicates that they also grazed livestock on common lands and picked berries, fruits, and nuts in summer and gathered fuel for household use in the forests.[51] By contrast, the allocation of work within the four walls of the household is difficult to determine with precision. But two types of indirect evidence suggest women's involvement in the manufacturing side of the cottage economy as well—a commitment that, indeed, became increasingly central to household livelihood. Scattered loom tax statistics in the eighteenth century record an increase in the number of households with two looms as well as looms operating throughout the year.[52] Admittedly, the gender of the weaver remains unspecified, but the numbers testify to the growing significance of manufacturing in the household economy still tied to agriculture. Indeed, by the early nineteenth century, in calculating time for rates per woven piece of cloth, the local custom included time spent by family members on "planting, hoeing, furrowing, and digging up" of potatoes in that overall calculation.[53] Clearly, by then, the continuation of women's earlier agricultural domain had become subsumed within the accounting formulas for textile production.

Second, and perhaps more directly to the point, contemporaries of a variety of persuasions—local and state officials, moralists and other religious figures, as well as angry urban guildsmen—all recognized at the time that rural manufacture promoted the independence of women. Through a variety of actions ranging from legal enactments to outright violence, they sought measures to curb that threatening autonomy by passing territorial decrees restricting women's work to agricultural service or, at best, spinning; by outlawing new expressions of wealth through sumptuary laws that defined proper dress for females in modest households; and by curtailing women's access to public spaces as well as their participation in village festivities. On occasion, guildsmen stormed outside the city gates to destroy the looms of village competitors, deriding the family work of cottage production as the work of women.[54] But the ongoing incorporation of women into clothmaking was not to be halted.

The wider economic changes associated with English industrialization acceler-ated the process of drawing women more fully into the weaving side of clothmaking, just as they eventually forced small producers to diversify their productive involve-ments, a process easier for men than women to undertake. Evidence is much more direct for these changing gender work roles in the decades of transition, and a broad brush can capture the larger picture. Mechanization of spinning in England and elsewhere increased the availability of yarn and led to a dramatic rise in demand for weavers. The secular trend is clear in the Oberlausitz, despite the momentary de-viations during the years of war and blockade. Women increasingly lost their work in hand spinning (indeed, so-called spinning villages which had "specialized" in an earlier age went over to weaving cloth in the 1820s) and increasingly found it in hand weaving.[55] Tandem agricultural changes underpinned this shift to manufac-turing, for industrial transformation was accompanied by significant agricultural re-forms, in Saxony accelerating at the end of the eighteenth century. Common lands were divided up, forests turned into arable land and ponds into meadows; the three-field system was transformed into a seven-year productive cycle, and fertilizers were introduced on a growing scale.[56] In the process women lost their customary rights to graze livestock and scavenge on common lands—important nonmonetary sources of livelihood. Consequently, women's household tasks came to include more cen-trally weaving cloth.

And yet, these very changes in household labor allocations, which greatly re-duced gender distinctions in the work of small producers, were themselves subject to serious strains as the transition decades deepened. Once the weaving process elsewhere had started its inexorable path toward mechanization, members of hand-weaving households in the Oberlausitz adopted other strategies to maximize dimin-ishing cash income. As noted earlier, they took alternative jobs—in municipal con-struction, in the laying of railroad beds, and in agriculture—but this seasonal work was opened only for men. Male availability for work outside the home, indeed, re-introduced gender work divisions into the family enterprise during certain seasons and stages of household growth. At other times, men and women worked together in weaving and selling cloth. In reality, the letters, petitions, and reports by local officials confirm that women had become the full-time weavers during these diffi-cult decades. For example, a Hirschfelde magistrate writing to the police chief in Zittau in the early 1880s about the activities of various local textile distributors noted almost parenthetically that since "the men typically sought work elsewhere, the women are employed."[57] This tenacious effort to perpetuate weaving reflected small-producer priorities to safeguard the family household with its ties to subsis-tence agriculture. In a survey remarkable for its inclusion of weaver voices, this priority was summed up admirably well—at least from the male perspective. The "single, unattached men" could pack up and move to factory villages or cities for work, but not "a family man, one who is tied to cottage, wife, and child."[58] Not only did this commitment ensure that small manufacturing households survived to once again make a complicated transition to capitalist industry, but the continued availability of a potential workforce in the villages, in turn, helped shape the subsequent dispersed character of factory industry in the area. Indeed, household survival had rested partly on a flexible mix of gender work roles; all evidence indicates that it often was women who met the hand-weaving contracts in the transition decades, while men were forced to take a variety of seasonal work elsewhere. It was women's work that permitted men to continue their primary identification in weaving. Gender structured class formation in highly significant ways in the Saxon Oberlausitz. But the official public discussion and presentation of work captured none of these complex, shifting, and constitutive gender roles: weaving remained a masculine occupation irrespective of the grassroots evidence of women's essential place within it.

Hawking self-made goods (and smuggling them as well) was a vital element in the economic activities of hand weavers in the Oberlausitz province. These market strategies also contributed in no small measure to the survival of many hard-pressed weaving households during the decades of transition to mechanized production. And these activities functioned best when men and women in family businesses shared work roles and alternated schedules. In the Oberlausitz, the widespread practice of selling cloth door to door was an official right confirmed by the state, and it underscores the importance of including the political context in economic and social analyses.[59] Oberlausitz weavers as well as those in Sebnitz had been given special rights to hawk goods throughout the Saxon kingdom in 1810; these rights, however, were not extended to guild weavers in the original lands of Saxony (*Erbland*). As the century unfolded, bringing new challenges to the Saxon textile industry, urban guildsmen launched a series of protests against the Oberlausitz rural peddlers who came to their doorsteps. For their turn, Oberlausitz hand weavers, aided by local officials safeguarding the economic interests of the province, successfully preserved these rights, although with some modification, until the new industrial code of 1862 opened up the job of hawker to all properly certified people.

Archival documents make clear that Saxon state officials by the early 1840s had intended to abolish the special hawking rights of Oberlausitz weavers in the name of rectifying a "legal inequality of producers." A resolution of the economic ministry to the king in 1840, prompted by the first protest of *Erbland* craftsmen, expressed its intention to end the "inequality" in the near future. But from the start, the ministers recognized that they could not abolish hawking in one blow without creating serious hardships. Indeed, they were not insensitive to the arguments forcefully made by Oberlausitz officials careful to document the significant place this informal trade nexus occupied in the economic life of the territory. "Not an inconsiderable part of the province's entire output was sold through hawking," provincial officials wrote in the 1840s, as the economic climate worsened. The local officers clearly recognized that hawking served as a critical safety valve. In their words, it gave the "less well-to-do weaver an opportunity to sell his goods," ensuring that the enterprise functioned at least part of the time independently of middlemen (in the *Kaufsystem*). But it also was important for those producers in the more classic "putting-out" system (*Verlag*). During the crisis year of 1848, for example, provincial officials recognized that the intertwining agrarian and industrial crisis was seriously threatening those weavers typically dependent on entrepreneurs for sales. "Since the majority of weavers who did no selling of their own but relied on manufacturers and wage income found employment no longer, it can easily be explained that many were pushed into hawking, for which they still had some cash to purchase materials for fabricating goods. In this manner they could care for both themselves and the members of their family." Hawking, indeed, permitted the weavers "to continue their customary work and thereby ensure their preference for this most-loved employment [in weaving]." This was particularly important, the officials pointedly noted, "for many, including the aged and wives and daughters, the so-called weavermaids who had few opportunities for other suitable employment."[60] The reference to women is doubly important. On the one hand, it underscores the point made earlier that women were integral to production; on the other, it distorts the picture through the label "maid," which implies an involvement only in the ancillary tasks of weaving.

Oberlausitz officials were not the only ones protecting the local hawking privileges; small producers themselves mounted a collective defense of their rights in petition after petition in the 1840s and 1850s. One such appeal in 1856, signed by concerned weavers in twenty-two industrial villages, made, in their words, the "indisputable" case that "if hawking had been prohibited we would have frequently heard of terrible events in our overpopulated province," an ambiguous point that contained a veiled threat of unrest as well as an image of destitution.[61] Indeed, Saxon officials were deeply concerned about the potential for disorder. At one point, in 1844, government officials had seemed intent on full abolition of the hawking privilege but backed away after an uprising of desperate weavers in neighboring Silesia in June of that year. The Silesian weaver revolt became a highly charged symbol in Central Europe, with its loss of life and arrest and sentencing of the destitute weavers; destruction of machinery, houses, and other property of businessmen; and extensive use of military force. It conjured up visions of an impending war of the poor against the rich and raised concerns among the more privileged groups of mounting threats to the existing social order. Perhaps the Saxon government feared a repetition of such unrest in its manufacturing villages without the margin of safety offered by hawking. Thus, in December 1844, it instituted only a series of modifications, restricting the criteria employed to issue the official passes which hawkers were required to carry.[62] Thenceforth, persons who earlier had hawked were required to reapply every six months (and make a persuasive case for continuation), and new passes were to be given only to persons or their immediate family members who would hawk goods that they themselves had woven on their own looms. The original law had been ambiguous about whether passes could also be obtained to peddle goods made by others locally and seemed to underwrite the existence of a petty trading group in the village. But after 1844, requests for new passes for people not involved in weaving the cloth themselves were turned down regularly. Thus, for example, Zittau officials rejected the effort of a widow, Johanna Gröllich of Eibau, to obtain a hawking pass because "she had neither hawked earlier nor did she plan to hawk either self-made cloth or that made by a family member."[63]

The petitions by weavers seeking hawking privileges offer an extraordinary glimpse into small-producer households, as members sought to justify and perpetuate their role in selling cloth door to door. Husbands were given passes, but so were wives and daughters. For example, at the sudden death of her father, Jocob Hättig, in Bertsdorf in 1858, his married daughter, Christiane Rössler, petitioned for permission to hawk his goods and settle his business for two years. She had accumulated enough experience as daughter and later as wife working in her own home. The request was granted. Karl Gottlieb Korselt's case also is revealing. Complications with his eyesight meant that his wife singlehandedly, in his words, "produced, commissioned, contracted as well as hawked" the cotton cloth made at home. He petitioned to obtain the right to help her sell the goods. But government officials "smelled" something irregular about the cloth that was to be sold and denied his request.[64] Through the lens of hawking, then, work roles were exchangeable among men and women in small-producer households and were not gender-specific. When the husband was away, the wife ran the family work unit, continuing to weave and meet work contracts; conversely, when the wife was out hawking, the husband took care of the home, looking after children and tending the small garden. The documents, in fact, affirm the importance of such role sharing, ironically in part by reverse example. A few cases exist (although they are not typical) in which a survivor petitioned the Saxon government to assume the peddling rights of a wife who had died unexpectedly. Johann Scholze from Heinewalde was such an individual. In his petition of 1850, he described a gender division of labor in his home: he "finished the goods and [his] wife alone undertook the selling and hawking." While the municipal officials supported Scholze's request, they predicted the family's imminent downfall. Due to rigid gender-role division, Scholze was ill informed about customers along the hawking circuit and would be unable to support the household.[65] Role sharing was a matter of practical necessity in this era of high mortality and economic deprivation.

The lack of an official pass did not necessarily deter people from hawking, however. The same documents contain a number of cases, which might be only the tip of an iceberg, in which Oberlausitz residents were arrested by police elsewhere and charged with illegally selling goods. In 1850, for example, Johanna Grosser from Opprach was sentenced to 10 RT or four weeks' imprisonment for violating the law; first she claimed she was not hawking at all, but she later recanted and pleaded leniency on the basis of dire poverty. Similarly, Johanna Christiane Gacht from Ebersbach was arrested in Spremberg also for hawking without a pass; but she fought the charge, saying she simply was bringing cloth to customers who had commissioned the goods. She mentioned the peasant households of Schindler, Thomas, and Freund as her customers and also a local fruit grower and a widow, who would testify on her behalf. Gacht, poor and indebted, was desperate to win her case and get back her confiscated cotton goods.[66]

Hawking goods illegally, an activity difficult to document anyway, easily shaded into smuggling, which, by all impressionistic accounts, also was widespread, particularly between Saxony and Bohemia, but also in places farther east. During the Napoleonic era, with its bewildering shifts of territory and tariff agreements, goods evading the tolls regularly were smuggled through the moutain passes from the Saxon Oberlausitz to points south. Business firms also used their own form of subterfuge to get around the laws. For example, they neglected to stamp the finished cloth with the company's insignia so that they could export the goods to places otherwise off-limits to Saxon-made wares.[67] The decision by Saxony to join the Customs Union in the early 1830s raised public debate among south Oberlausitz officials about the future of such theretofore profitable and winked-at smuggling activity across the border with Bohemia. Oberlausitz small producers, correctly as it turn out, feared that Austria would impose crippling tariffs on imported goods and patrol the border much more effectively; only in 1853, with the easing of trade relations between Austria and the German states of the Customs Union, did the markets to the south again become more open to wares made in the Saxon Oberlausitz.[68] Smuggling produced its own legends. One of the great popular heroes of the era of rural manufacture was Johannes Karasek, a deserter from the Austrian army known as the Prague Tease (*Prager Hansel*), who plied his form of social banditry in the decades between 1780 and 1810. Karasek was the Oberlausitz counterpart to Robin Hood and, in the weavers' version of the tale, stole cloth from rich distributors and producers in towns such as Niederoderwitz or Sohland and hid out with his supporters in Leutersdorf, then under Austrian jurisdiction. At first he sold the stolen goods at a cheap price, but later he gave them away to impoverished linen weavers. The different laws, customs, tariffs, and rates of exchange in the borderlands opened up semilegal economic niches which some used to make easy profits, others to purchase goods at a just price, and still others to promote their version of social justice. Even Adam Smith linked smuggling with popular justice, recognizing that the smuggler was a "respected" member of the community: "a person who, though no doubt highly blameable for violating the laws of his country, was frequently incapable of violating those of natural justice, and would have been, in every respect, an excellent citizen, had not the laws of his country made that a crime which nature never intended to be so. . . ."[69] During the early decades of the nineteenth century, smuggling had a particular economic logic which helped account, perhaps, for its popularity. Given the interregional gaps in European development between areas which had begun to mechanize (such as England and Belgium) and those still operating according to customary techniques (such as Bohemia or Eastern Europe), Saxony enjoyed the advantage of geographic proximity in competition with otherwise cheaper, equivalent British-made goods. Smuggling short distances was highly profitable because British cloth, given transport costs and higher wages at home, was not competitive in the interior of the continent.

The Saxon Oberlausitz has offered a rewarding perspetive from which to view the concrete impact of many of the broader changes propelling the European economy as a whole. Its significant place in the networks of production and exchange in the prefactory era was seriously threatened by the transition to mechanized production. Yet the margravate made the slow and painful transition to industrial capitalism, and its particular course adds rich and necessary details to the composite narratives of industrialization that are reshaping economic and social history.

A complex series of strategies worked to ensure the survival of small manufacturers until the area could accommodate factory industry on a large scale. Some were a function of more global and impersonal forces, linking regions for a time in sets of new trade relations; indeed, as the Oberlausitz case had shown, an intense exchange developed between it and Ottoman Turkish lands that proved economically rewarding for both sides in the 1820s and 1830s and, from the perspective of the ongoing industrialization of Saxony, bought precious time. Others reflected entrepreneurial initiatives, a willingness to chance a new exchange or a new product. Not only did these entrepreneurs operate in a political and legal context overseen by the state, they also benefited from more active state aid. In the Saxon case, state officials had their own agenda, to encourage technological innovations in hand production for fiscal and social reasons, that underwrote some entrepreneurial designs for a time. And small producers were equally important agents in their efforts to meet drastically changing economic contexts. Their survival rested in good measure on the complex set of gender relations that came to characterize domestic arrangements in manufacturing households tied into subsistence agriculture. These shifting gender roles offered cottagers considerable flexibility in maximizing incomes in cash and kind and developing ways to sell goods, including hawking them illegally if necessary.

Transition decades often are lost in narratives with a particular end in sight. Yet the evolving interaction of the transition period directly alters the very present and thus shapes the context within which future events and decisions occur. On one level, the final outcome of the separate yet often interconnected strategies of state officials, businessmen, and small producers achieved the ultimate objective of the initiators: mass outmigration and deindustrialization did not occur. This outcome was not without costs, including numerous bankruptcies and seriously deteriorating incomes of manufacturing households. Furthermore, it brought to the surface, though never explosively, the economic conflict that underlay relations among state officers, businessmen, and small producers. Time and again, weavers simply disregarded the law in their efforts to ensure their livelihood, and for a time they actively resisted technological innovations; for their part, weakened businessmen complained that state aid was insufficient. Women's essential participation in these survival strategies remained beneath the surface, invisible under the patina of public discourse. On another level, these overlapping systems of values and beliefs generated in confrontation with changing economic fortunes carried forward into the new era of industrial capitalism. They set the stage for ongoing interaction once again among state decision-makers, industrialists, and men and women workers. Indeed, they gave rise to the particular set of class and gender features that marked the distinctive nature of industrial capitalism in the Saxon Oberlausitz.

<hr>

Notes

1. On the importance of the Atlantic trade, see Immanuel Wallerstein, *The Modern World-System III: The Second Era of Great Expansion of the Capitalist World Economy, 1730-1840* (San Diego, New York, and Berkeley, 1989), pp. 67-73; François Crouzet, "Wars, Blockades, and Economic Change in Europe, 1792-1815," *Journal of Economic History* 24, no. 4 (1964): 568-69; Paul Mantoux, *The Industrial Revolution in the Eighteenth Century: An Outline of the Beginnings of the Modern Factory System in England* (Chicago and London, 1905; reprint, 1983), p. 99; Phyllis Deane, *The First Industrial Revolution* (Cambridge, 1967), pp. 52-53.

2. The inability to ascertain with certainty a region's place in ongoing industrial transformation was a major shortcoming of Mendel's so-called "protoindustrial" theory that saw rural manufacturing as the first phase of capitalist industrialization. Crucial variables such as proximity to coal beds or key railroad lines, which played no role in the theory, proved quite decisive. See D. C. Coleman, "Proto-industrialization: A Concept Too Many," *Economic History Review*, 2nd ser. 36 (1983): 435-48, and Jean H. Quataert, "A New View of Industrialization: 'Protoindustry' or the Role of Small-Scale, Labor-Intensive Manufacture in the Capitalist Environment," *International Labor and Working-Class History* 33 (Spring 1988): 3-37.

3. Sidney Pollard, *Peaceful Conquests: The Industrialization of Europe, 1760-1980* (Oxford, London, and Glasgow, 1981), p. 170.

4. Goodman and Honeyman in their useful survey of work history recognize that most analyses of Europe's so-called industrial revolution exclude an international dimension. See Jordan Goodman and Katrina Honeyman, *Gainful Pursuits: The Making of Industrial Europe, 1600-1914* (London, 1988), p. 210. But their work typifies another problem. Their own preference for the broad synthetic picture means they devote insufficient attention to the historical specifics of how, why, and where hand technologies proved most resilient. By contrast, Wallerstein's contribution lies precisely in its world perspective; his methodology seeks to reconstruct, for example, export-import statistics illustrative of the evolving world economy. His is a global approach, but he too readily adopts a facile deindustrialization model for regions outside the core industrial economies. In his schema, the mark of a country's involvement in the world economy after 1780 becomes inevitably the "decline of the manufacturing sector in the zones being incorporated." Wallerstein, *The Modern World-System III*, p. 149.

5. For a breakdown of Oberlausitz linen exports in the late eighteenth century, see, particularly, Wilhelm von Westernhagen, "Leinwandmanufaktur und Leinwandhandel der Oberlausitz in der zweiten Hälften der achtzehnten Jahrhunderts und während der Kontinentalsperre" (Ph.D. diss., University of Leipzig, 1932), pp. 6-7. Also, Edmund Gröllich, *Die Baumwollweberei der sächsischen Oberlausitz und ihre Entwickelung zum Grossbetrieb* (Leipzig, 1911), pp. 14-16.

6. Heinrich Gebauer, *Die Volkswirtschaft im Königreiche Sachsen. Historisch, geographisch und statistisch dargestellt* (Dresden, 1893), vol. 2, pp. 535-36, and vol. 3, pp. 1-5; Albin König, *Die Sächsische Baumwollenindustrie am Ende des vorigen Jahrhunderts und während der Kontinentalsperre* (Leipzig, 1899), p. 2.

7. Found in König, *Die Sächsische Baumwollenindustrie*, pp. 3-4.

8. König, *Die Sächsische Baumwollenindustrie*, pp. 29, 46-49.

9. Crouzet, "Wars," p. 577; Pollard, *Peaceful Conquest*, pp. 40-41; W. O. Henderson, *The Industrialization of Europe, 1780-1914* (New York, 1969), pp. 27-28.

10. Westerhagen, *Leinwandmanufaktur*, p. 24.

11. König, *Die Sächsische Baumwollenindustrie*, pp. 20-21, 36, 56, 69-73; Gröllich, *Die Baumwollweberei*, pp. 14-15.

12. Crouzet, "Wars," p. 587.

13. C. A. Pescheck, "Geschichte der Industrie und der Handel in der Oberlausitz," *Neues Lausitzisches Magazin* 29 (1850): 12-13.

14. August Schumann, *Vollständisches Staats-Post und Zeitungs-Lexikon von Sachsen* (Zwickau, 1815), vol. 2, pp. 318-19.

15. Staatsarchiv Dresden (hereafter StD), Ministerium des Innern (MdI), No. 5928, Den Notstand der Weber in der Oberlausitz und Maasregeln zur Abhülfe, Bl. 1-5. Also, August Weise, *Nachrichten aus der Vergangenheit und Gegenwart der Gemeinde Ebersbach nebst Einblicken in die Natur ihrer nächsten Umgebung* (Ebersbach, 1988), p. 100.

16. A. Klima, "Industrial Development in Bohemia, 1648-1781," *Past and Present* 11 (1957): 95-96.

17. Staatsarchiv Dresden, Aussenstelle Bautzen (hereafter B), Amtshauptmannschaft Zittau (hereafter AZ), No. 8080: Anlegung von Jacquard-Schlag-Maschinen, 1835-51, Bl. 46-47 and 59-60.

18. E. W. Richter, *Beschreibung des Königreiches Sachsen in geographischer, statistischer und topographischer Hinsight nebst geschichtlichen Bemerkungen zum Gebrauche für Schule und Haus*, vol. 3 (Freiberg, 1852), pp. 563-65.

19. Gröllich, *Die Baumwollweberei*, pp. 17-18, as well as his article "Die Baumwollweberei der sächsischen Oberlausitz und ihre Entwicklung zum Grossbetrieb," *Der Textil-Arbeiter* 24, no. 6 (February 9, 1912). Also, Gebauer, *Die Volkswirtschaft*, pp. 26-27.

20. For the more traditional views, see Charles Issawi, *An Economic History of the Middle East and North Africa* (New York, 1982), and Sevket Pamuk, *The Ottoman Empire and European Capitalism, 1820-1913: Trade, Investment and Production* (Cambridge, 1987). For more recent revisionist assessments, consult Donald Quataert, "Machine Breaking and the Changing Carpet Industry of Western Anatolia, 1860-1908," *Journal of Social History* (Spring 1981): 474-89; Sarah Shields, "An Economic History of Nineteenth-Century Mosul" (Ph.D. diss., University of Chicago, 1986), and Roger Owen, *The Middle East in the World Economy* (London, 1981). I want to thank Donald Quataert for discussing and clarifying many of these issues and for providing me with appropriate reading and reference materials.

21. Gröllich, *Die Baumwollweberei*, pp. 17-18; G. Korschelt, "Beiträge zur Geschichte der Webindustrie in der sächsischen Oberlausitz," *Oberlausitzer Rundschau* 2, no. 19 (1867; reprint, October 5, 1964): 293-94.

22. The earliest mechanized weaving mills in the Oberlausitz typically began as hand-manufacturing businesses dealing in colorful cotton and Orleans cloth. See, for example, the various business histories in *Die Deutsche Industrie. Festgabe zum 25 Jährigen Regierungs-Jubiläum seiner Magestät des Kaisers und Königs Wilhelm II*, Dargebracht von Industriellen Deutschlands (Berlin, 1913). Village histories are also extremely informative about the growth and development of local firms. Among many other citations, see, for example, Carl Melzer, *Chronik von Neugersdorf* (Neugersdorf, 1903). Archival documents reveal unusual details about the efforts to train the weavers in the new branches of production. For example, StD, MdI, No. 5928, Bl. 128-30: Gesuch des Kaufmanns Wilhelm Meissner in Zittau um Geld Unterstützung zu einen industriellen Unternehmen. Meissner, a Zittau businessman, had been absolutely key in the introduction of Orleans weaving into the region in the mid-1840s. He linked his interest in Orleans weaving explicitly to the crisis in hand calico making, due to the "competitive pressures of mechanized production."

23. Wallerstein, *The Modern World-System III*, p. 150, speaks of a deliberate policy of destroying India's manufacturing base.

24. Pollard, *Peaceful Conquests*, pp. 16, 18, 90-91; Peter Kriedte, Hans Medick, and Jürgen Schlumbohm, *Industrialisierung vor der Industrialisierung. Gewerbliche Warenproduktion auf dem Land in der Formationsperiode des Kapitalismus* (Göttingen, 1977), pp. 366-67; Gerhard Adelmann, "Die Ländlichen Textilgewerbe des Rheinlandes vor der Industrialisierung," *Rheinisches Vierteljahresblatt* 43 (1979): 260-88.

25. Gay Gullickson, "Agriculture and Cottage Industry: Redefining the Causes of Proto-industrialization," *The Journal of Economic History* 43, no. 4 (December 1983): 831-50, and David Landes, *The Unbound Prometheus: Technological Change and Industrial Development in Western Europe from 1750 to the Present* (Cambridge, 1969; reprint, 1979), pp. 161-63.

26. The term is Crouzet's, "Wars," pp. 579-80.

27. StD, MdI, No. 5929, Bl. 144-47. The point also is made by Korschelt, "Beiträge," pp. 293-94. For shifting work opportunities in textiles during the American Civil War, see StD, MdI, No. 5630: Den durch die Baumwollenkrisis herbeigrführten Nothstand: Generalia.

28. I explore the issue of rural manufacturing supporting a local exchange economy in another context below. For information on additional exports beyond textiles, see Werner Beyer, "Das Verkehrswesen der sächsischen Oberlausitz in der ersten Hälfte des 19. Jahrhunderts" (diss., University of Leipzig, Dresden, 1931), p. 16. The Meissner correspondence is in B, Kreishauptmannschaft Bautzen (hereafter KB), No. 8105: die Einführung von Regulator-Webstühlen, 1860, Bl. 54-56.

29. Rudolf Forberger, *Die Manufaktur in Sachsen vom Ende des 16. bis zum anfang des 19. Jahrhunderts* (Berlin, 1958), and also his *Industrielle Revolution in Sachsen: Die Revolution der Produkrivkräfte in Sachsen 1800-1830*, 2 vols. (Berlin, 1982). Also Wolfram Fischer, *Wirtschaft und Gesellschaft im Zeitalter der Industrialisierung. Aufsätze-Studien-Vorträge* (Göttingen, 1972), p. 472; Pollard, *Peaceful Conquest*, pp. 102-103; Clive Trebilcock, *The Industrialization of the Continental Powers, 1780-1914* (London and New York, 1981).

30. Trebilcock, *Industrialization*, p. 75.

31. For the classic view of England, see Henderson, *The Industrial Revolution*, pp. 10-11. Also, Trebilcock, *Industrialization*, pp. 16-17, and Dean, *The First Industrial Revolution*, p. 2. The reevaluation is in Wallerstein, *The Modern World-System III*, pp. 19, 78, and an earlier version is also in Karl Polanyi, *The Great Transformation: The Political and Economic Origins of our Time* (Boston, 1944; reprint 1957).

32. Dean, *The First Industrial Revolution*, pp. 152-53; Landes, *The Unbound Prometheus*, pp. 135-36, 151, 157.

33. Beyer, *Das Verkehrswesen*, pp. 2, 27.

34. Beyer, *Das Verkehrswesen*, pp. 36-37, 47.

35. StAD, MdI, No. 5630: Den durch die Baumwollenkrisis herbeigeführten Nothstand, Bl. 7-9. Also, *Bautzener Nachrichten*, April 17, 1848.

36. Forberger, *Industrielle Revolution*, p. 76; Rudolf Kötzschke and Hellmut Kretzschmar, *Sächsische Geschichte. Werden und Wandlungen eines Deutschen Stammes und seiner Heimat im Rahmen der Deutschen Geschichte* (Frankfurt/Main, 1965), pp. 292-93.

37. Forberger, *Industrielle Revolution*, pp. 72, 458-59.

38. Forberger, *Die Manufaktur*, p. 146.

39. B, KB, No. 8080: die Anlegung von Jacquard-Schlag-Maschinen, Bl. 5-7, 1835.

40. Ibid., Bl. 39-41, Einführung von Jacquardwebstühle in Ebersbach.

41. StAD, MdI, No. 5928, Bl. 257-58, August 24, 1864.

42. Ibid., Bl. 215-22.

43. StAD, MdI, No. 5928, Den Notstand der Weber in der Oberlausitz und Maasregeln zur Abhülfe, Bl. 1-5. Also Forberger, *Industrielle Revolution*, pp. 148-49. For a history of damask weaving and its privileges, see Friedrich Theodor Richter, *Geschichtlich-statistische Darstellung der Damastmanumfactur-Orte Gross- und Neu-Schönau in der Königlichen Sächsischen Oberlausitz* (Leipzig, 1837). For information on Waltersdorf, see B, KB, No. 8080, Bl. 2-3.

44. StAD, MdI, No. 5928, Bl. 1-5; 128-30; 164; 181-83; 317-19. And B, KB, No. 8080, Bl. 33-34, for the specifics about the Reichenau fire; Bl. 39-41, for efforts to introduce Jacquard looms into the tweed industry in Ebersbach.

45. StAD, MdI, No. 5928, Bl. 342-44, November 8, 1881.

46. *Jahres-Bericht der Handels- und Gewerbekammer zu Zittau* (Zittau, 1881), p. 39.

47. An early article that inspired considerable new inquiry and research was Hans Medick, "The Protoindustrial Family Economy: The Structural Function of Household and Family during the Transition from Peasant Society to Industrial Capitalism," *Social History* 3 (1976): 291-315.

48. The empirical case studies demonstrate considerable variation in household allocation of work by gender. See, among others, Gay Gullickson, "The Sexual Division of Labor in Cottage Industry and Agriculture in the Pays de Caus: Auffay, 1750-1850," *French Historical Studies* 12, no. 1 (Fall 1981): 177-99; Pat Hudson, "Proto-industrialisation: The Case of the West Riding Wool Textile Industry in the 18th and Early 19th Centuries," *History Workshop* 12 (1981): 34-61, and her "From Manor to Mill: The West Riding in Transition," in Maxine Berg et al., *Manufacture in Town and Country before the Factory* (Cambridge, 1983); Jean H. Quataert, "Combining Agrarian and Industrial Livelihood: Rural Households in the Saxon Oberlausitz in the Nineteenth Century," *Journal of Family History* (Summer 1985): 145-62; Rudolf Braun, *Industrialisierung und Volksleben. Die veränderungen der Lebensformen in einem ländlichen Industriegebiet vor 1800 (Züricher Oberland* (Erlenbach-Zürich, 1960); and, finally, Bernd Schöne, *Kultur und Lebensweise Lausitzer Bandweber 1750-1850* (Berlin, 1977).

49. Fritz Hauptmann, *Woher wir Kommen. Ein Buch von Heimat und Vorfahren*, 2 vols. (Marburg, 1970 and 1976). The example is in vol. 2, *Das Zittauer Land*, pp. 157-58. Also *Die Südöstliche Oberlausitz mit Zittau und dem Zittauer Gebirge* (Berlin, 1970), pp. 230-32.

50. See, particularly, Arno Kunze, "Vom Bauerndorf zum Weberdorf: Zur sozialen und wirtschaftlichen Struktur der Waldhufendörfer der südlichen Oberlausitz im 16., 17., und 18. Jahrhundert," in *Oberlausitzer Forschungen: Beiträge zur Landesgeschichte* (Leipzig, 1961), pp. 165-92. Also Helga Schultz, "Die Ausweitung des Landhandwerks vor der industriellen Revolution. Begünstigende Faktoren und Bedeutung für die 'Protoindustrialisierung,' " *Jahrbuch für Wirtschaftsgeschichte* 3 (1982): 79-90. For a graphic example of the way in which rural manufacture created symbiotic relationships in the countryside, see Eckard Schremmer, "Das 18. Jahrhundert, das Kontinuitätsproblem und die Geschichte der Industrialisierung: Erfarhungen für die Entwicklungsländer?" *Zeitschrift für Agrargeschichte und Agrarsoziologie* 29, no. 1 (1981): 58-78.

51. Pescheck, "Geschichte," pp. 173-83, 196, 205; Willi Boelcke, *Bauer und Gutsherr in der Oberlausitz* (Bautzen, 1957), and Walter von Boetticher, *Geschichte des Oberlausitzen Adels und seiner Güter, 1635-1815* (Görlitz, 1912).

52. Arno Kunze, "Der Weg zur kapitalistischen Produktionsweise in der Oberlausitzer Leineweberei im ausgehenden 17. und zu Beginn des 18. Jahrhunderts," in *E. W. von Tschirnhaus und die Frühaufklärung in Mittel- und Osteurpa* (Berlin, 1960), p. 210. *Zittauer Geschichtsblätter* 82 (November 6, 1912).

53. Friedrich Schmidt, *Untersuchungen über Bevölkerung, Arbeitslohn und Pauperism in ihrem gegenseitigen Zusammenhange* (Leipzig, 1836), p. 299.

54. Korschelt, "Beiträge," pp. 293-94; Pescheck, "Geschichte," pp. 6-7; and also his *Handbuch der Geschichte von Zittau* (Zittau, 1837), 2 vols., pp. 732-33 (vol. 1) and 70-71 (vol. 2). Also, Gröllich, *Die Baumwollweberei*, pp. 115-16, and von Westernhagen, *Leinwandmanufaktur*, pp. 10-11.

55. Pescheck, "Geschichte," pp. 3-6; Nathanael Gotfried Leske, *Reise durch Sachsen in Rücksicht der Naturgeschichte und Ökonomie* (Leipzig, 1785), p. 502; Richter, *Damastmanufaktur*, p. 291; G. Korschelt, *Geschichte von Oderwitz* (Oderwitz, 1871), p. 202.

56. Boelcke, *Bauer und Gutsherr*, pp. 169-76; Hermann Knothe, "Die Stellung der Gutsunterthanen in der Oberlausitz zu ihren Gutsherrschaften, von den ältesten Zeitem bis zur Ablösung der Zinsen und Dienste," *Neues Lausitzisches Magazin* 61, no. 2 (1885): 293-304;

Siegmund Musiat, *Zur Lebensweise des Landwirtschaftlichen Gesindes in der Oberlausitz* (Bautzen, 1964). Also, Lothar Schneider, "Arbeits- und Familienverhältnisse in der Hausindustrie," in Heidi Rosenbaum, *Seminar: Familie und Gesellschaftsstruktur. Materialien zur den sozioökonomischen Bedingungen von Familienformen* (Frankfurt/Main, 1978), p. 277.

57. B, AZ, No. 3645, Die Erwerbs- und Nahrungsverhältnisse der arbeitenden Bevölkerung betr., Bl. 147-48. For other examples of household diversification, see, among others, the archival collection Nr. 3643, Die Erwerbs- und Nahrungsverhältnisse . . . , 1877, which catalogues wages in a variety of alternative work undertaken by men. Also, Korschelt, *Oderwitz*, pp. 205-206, and Hauptmann, *Woher wir Kommen*, p. 149.

58. B, AZ, No. 3645, Mittelweigsdorf, April 20, 1880.

59. Too often in the literature, economic and social analysis fails to connect back to the relevant political contexts, thus slighting a significant and rewarding layer of interpretation. This is espcially true for much of the work on "protoindustry," and recently a new trend has emerged in historical sociology to encourage new thinking and "bring the state back in." For an exception to the tendency to slight the political context of rural manufacture, see Hans Medick, "Privilegiertes Handelskapial und 'Kleine Industrie,' " *Archiv für Sozialgeschichte 23* (1983): 267-310. See also the collection by Peter Evans, Dietrich Reuschemeyer, and Theda Skocpol, *Bringing the State Bank In* (Cambridge, 1985).

60. The archival documents on the hawking controversy are found in StAD, MdI, No. 6257: Den Hausirhandel der Oberlausitzer, Sebnitzer und Zwönitzer Weber betr. 1840.

61. StAD, MdI, No. 447: Die Soziale Lage der Arbeiterfamilie, 1856-1860, Bl. 989-91.

62. *Gesetz und Verordnungsblatt für das Königreich Sachsen vom Jahre 1844* (Dresden, 1844), p. 300: Verordung den Hausirhandel der Oberlausitzer und Sebnitzer Weber betr. December 5, 1844.

63. B, KB, No. 11237: die den Oberlausitzischen Leinwebern ertheilte Gestaltung zum Hausiren mit ihren Fabricaten, Bl. 25, January 12, 1848.

64. StAD, MdI, No. 6259, Bl. 56-58, March 26, 1858: petition by Rössler; B, Kreishauptmannschaft Bautzen, No. 11237, Bl. 38-39, October 10, 1847: petition by Korselt.

65. B, KB, No. 11237, Bl. 171-75, March 2, 1850, the Scholze materials. For an assessment about the nature of gender role sharing in small-producer households, see an earlier piece of mine, Jean H. Quataert, "Teamwork in Saxon Homeweaving Families in the Nineteenth Century: A Preliminary Investigation into the Issue of Gender Work Roles," in Ruth-Ellen B. Joeres and Mary Jo Maynes, *German Women in the Eighteenth and Nineteenth Centuries: A Social and Literary History* (Bloomington, Ind., 1986), pp. 3-23.

66. B, KB, No. 11238, Bl. 1, 10-12, July 19, 1850, and September 2, 1850: case of Grosser; Bl. 144-46, April 4, 1851, for the case of Gacht.

67. Von Westernhagen, *Leinwandmanufaktur*, pp. 23-24.

68. Beyer, *Das Verkehrswesen.*

69. Quoted in Deane, *The First Industrial Revolution*, pp. 206-207.

Tessie P. Liu **10**

The Commercialization of Trousseau Work: Female Homeworkers in the French Lingerie Trade

No other kind of work is more regularly represented as women's work than is sewing. Our image of the activity focuses attention on the seamstress's hands—her nimble fingers, their agile and precise gestures. Unlike so many other activities represented as feminine and perceived as belonging to nature and biology, sewing is broadly recognized as an acquired mastery, an expression of social identity. Comments about a woman's facility with needle and thread are but thinly veiled judgments of her upbringing and character. The bourgeois lady of leisure who knits intently among the embroidered birds and satiny flowers adorning her table linens, dresser scarves, and chair covers testifies that she has perfected the arts of womanhood. Her activity places her at the emotional center of her world.[1] She earns the respect of a society which values domesticity, and the admiration of her friends.

As a feminine activity, sewing is overloaded with meaning. Knots and all, it signifies the whole of our confusion and struggles over the concept of femininity and, implicitly, over that of masculinity as well. In studying needlework, we encounter all the difficult questions which seem peculiar to women's oppression. The battle over the place of sewing in women's education, for example, is not waged over needles, pins, and cloth: the social relations between the sexes are at stake. The appropriateness of sewing as metaphor and the power of its representations rest on the familiarity of their referents, the ordinariness of women laboring with needle and thread. Quite apart from the society which expects women to sew, for many women sewing is a pleasurable activity. It is also an ability in which they take pride. Needlework crafts objects which are used to adorn the self, to decorate the home, and to provoke admiration. Through needlework, some women find a medium of self-expression. Indeed, sewing is women's art as well as women's work.[2]

Yet why is it that when needlework is a labor of love, women's hand-stitched creations are treasured as artifacts, but when women perform the same tasks for wages, the same ability pays barely enough to support the seamstress? Women's skills, or, more accurately womanly skills, are transformed and devalued when they enter the marketplace. Unraveling the twisted relationships between women's social value and market value is one of the most difficult problems that historians of women's work must resolve. We must account for the intimacy of the power over women and the fact that oppression seems so near the female construct of identity and self.

The evolution of the lingerie trade in France offers a particularly appropriate case study for examining these questions. Definitionally, lingerie denotes undergarments, shirts, collars, sheets, towels, napkins, and tablecloths. It has always included the intimate clothing and household items which brides brought into marriage, that is, the bride's trousseau. Closely identified with the woman herself, the unity of *linge de corps* and *linge de maison* expressed the merging of her personal body with her social, domestic, body.

By the late nineteenth century, trousseau work was commercialized. Mass production of household linens and undergarments replaced much of the embroidery, sewing, and hemming done for personal use and the bespoke trade of seamstresses working for a limited local clientele. It was a mass industry which employed women to produce for women. The commercialization of trousseaux was part and parcel of a more extensive revolution in the production and retailing of ready-to-wear items. Pioneered by department stores in the mid-nineteenth century, this revolution in selling and buying became the foundation of mass consumer culture in Europe.[3]

Like other fashion trades, lingerie work was a "sweated trade." The industry paid notoriously low wages. Despite the possibility for factory organization, production was dominated by outwork. Rather than investing capital in machinery to increase productivity, the industry relied on "sweating" greater productivity out of handworkers by lowering piece rates. The notoriety of work conditions in this trade occasioned several extensive government inquiries. From these we have a wealth of information on work hours, types of tools and machinery, the location of work and markets, as well as the observations of wholesale merchants, subcontractors, and workers.

For women's historians, industrial homework seems to typify the fate and the value of women's labor in an industrial society—that 150 years after the Industrial Revolution which supposedly established the hegemony of machine labor and the factory system, women wage earners continued to depend on the speed and agility of their fingers and do their stitching at home. How are we to explain this phenomenon? Did the prior association of sewing with female gender and the resulting socialization influence the way the trade became organized when it was commercialized? Did it affect the location and organization of work, as well as the choice of technology? Are there special characteristics to the organization of women's work which are peculiarly suited to women's social identities and roles?

This essay begins with a survey of the lingerie trade in France in the early twentieth century, paying particular attention to the organization of production: the types of production techniques employed, the locations of work, the geographic distribution of the industry, and the type of workers recruited. My basic question is: What makes sweated work a viable production strategy? How does the logic of its organization reflect the nature of its product market on the one hand, and the dynamics of labor markets on the other? My purpose is to offer an empirical framework to test how different sets of ideas about women's proper sphere and proper activities become actualized. In particular, I will focus on the tension between the entrepreneurs' expectations of finding their ideal labor force among married women, and the circumstances under which these conditions were realized.[4]

The French Lingerie Trade

Sometimes stereotypes about a culture are based on observable realities. The French bourgeoisie has always taken great pride in the quality and elegance of its manufactured goods because they reflected the refinement of their national culture.[5] While the French have set the international standards for grace in styling home furnishings, glassware, and the like, certainly it was in the fashionable needle trades that French distinction excelled.[6] In the later decades of the nineteenth century, German, Swiss, Austrian, and Belgian producers with cheaper versions of French designs began to make inroads into the French domestic market and compete with France internationally. French production, however, prevailed in both domains. Between 1898 and 1900, French retailers imported about 700,000 francs' worth of lingerie articles every year from Germany, England, Switzerland, and Belgium, while French exports, including exports to these same countries, amounted to 23 million francs a year.[7]

The varieties and subspecialties offered to customers at home and abroad stretched the limits of imagination. First there were men's shirts: white shirts and colored shirts in cottons, in linen, in flannel, in plain and fancy weaves; men's drawers made of linen, silks, and flannel; vests, shirt fronts, collars, and cuffs. Then there was the branch of the trade specialized for women and children. Lingerie for women incorporated an endless variety of articles available in an equally vast array of fibers and weaves: for wearing, *chemises de jour* and *chemises de nuit*, camisoles, slips, dressing gowns, collars, sleeves, cuffs; and for household linens, pillowcases of all shapes and sizes, sheets, napkins, tablecloths, hand towels, bath towels, dish towels, and the like. For children, there was an equally sophisticated array of garments and infant "layette."[8]

With its many subbranches, this trade was among the most complex of the needle trades. Specialties differed from one region to the next. Paris and its suburbs produced the entire range from skirts to baby layettes, from coarsest grades to finest. The center of France, the departments of Cher, Indre-et-Loire, and Loire-et-Cher, specialized in men's shirts and undergarments for women and children. In the east, in the departments of Vosges and Meurthe-et-Moselle, lingerie work was a solution to the problems of the region's famed embroidery industry.[9] In the west and in the north, specialization in household linens grew out of the crisis of older textile-manufacturing regions, particularly the linen districts of the Choletais in Maine-et-Loire, and the linen- and fine woolen-producing areas of the Cambrésis in the department of the Nord.

Lingerie production alone employed a significant proportion of the female working population. At the turn of the century, according to the employment census of 1896, this trade employed a total of 1,234,916 women, of whom nearly 56 percent (688,098 workers) worked at home. The number of women engaged in the lingerie trade represented about 57 percent of all women employed in industry. Women lingerie workers were three times more numerous than women occupied in textile industries.[10]

The perfection and mass marketing of the sewing machine aided the rapid expansion of the mass-market fashion industries all over Europe. Sewing machines transformed the fashion trades by changing their pace. Capable of 1,000 to 2,000 stitches per minute, compared to the average 35 stitches per minute by hand, sewing machines sped up production from six to eleven times, depending on the article and the quality of the work required.[11] The increase in the pace of stitching encouraged greater subdivision of tasks, making simpler and smaller tasks, and changed the technology of pattern cutting and design to accommodate the increasing demand. After the 1860s, the band saw was adapted for cutting patterns in bulk. Adding more stitches, such as the zigzag, the simple sewing machine was used to make buttonholes and to do embroidery. Other modifications revolutionized the stitching of leather uppers in the shoe trade.

The general-purpose sewing machine was highly portable. These machines greatly increased productivity without taking up plant space with heavy, bulky machinery. Even specialized machines such as the buttonhole machine were no larger than the average simple machine. The adaptation of electric motors as well as small kerosene and petroleum motors made the machines even faster than those driven by hand cranks and foot pedals but did not alter their flexibility. So although it was possible to group high-speed and specialized sewing machines into factories and to incorporate all the various tasks under one roof, garment factories existed but were quite rare.[12]

The high risks involved in fashion markets influenced production arrangements. The logic of factory production did not always match the demands of this industry. For the factory system to be adopted effectively, the demand for a particular style or for a particular decorative design had to be great enough to justify a long-run series. Highly specialized, product-specific machines could be operated profitably only if the mounting and specifications did not change and machines were not idled often. For these reasons, men's clothing, especially army clothes and work clothes, for which style changes were less frequent and demand was more constant and predictable, became and has remained one of the few branches of the cloth industry to be located in factories. Often, the demand for variety and seasonal changes in materials and styles went against the logic and economic advantages of factory-based mass-production strategies. The extreme seasonability of the industry and the constant changes in style tended to favor smaller workshops and homework.[13]

This is the conventional wisdom for explaining the "persistence" of small-scale dispersed production into the age of factory manufacture. Yet when the French Office du Travail conducted a national survey on the conditions of the lingerie trade between 1905 and 1908 (the results of the survey were published in five volumes between 1909 and 1911),[14] the *enquête* showed that nationally, entrepreneurs used homework and shopwork in almost equal proportions regardless of product specialty.[15]

When the investigators of the Office du Travail asked manufacturers in various regions whether they preferred to group workers into factories or to put work out to homeworkers, they were of mixed opinions. Those who favored workshops and factories argued that the pace of production was more rapid and regular when work was centralized. The entrepreneur had greater control over the quality of the work, and could supervise the work more closely, ensure that mistakes were repaired, and guard against waste. With centralized production, there were fewer problems with uncertain delivery dates, and with irregular and faulty work. Partisans of workshops and factories argued that, in addition, centralized production was better for workers. They earned more money, worked shorter days, and labored under more hygienic conditions.[16]

Manufacturers who favored outwork primarily argued that homework was more economical for the business managers. Overhead costs were significantly lower. Capital was not immobilized in equipment and materials, and during the slack season, the entrepreneurs did not risk their investments in idled plants. They could reduce work to a minimum more easily than if they had workers regularly employed. These manufacturers claimed that workmanship was not necessarily inferior, but often superior. In addition, outwork gave entrepreneurs more flexibility in organizing production. They did not have to follow state legislation on work hours and work conditions. Moreover, because workers were dispersed, there were fewer strikes and no unions to challenge the authority of the entrepreneurs, they said. Homework, they argued, provided women a way to combine work and home life. Hence, it was more moral than factory work.[17]

Tallying the advantages and disadvantages, the investigators of the Office du Travail were surprised to learn that the important factor governing the choice between homework and shopwork seemed to be location: "The geographic situation of the establishments—the conditions which include the particular industrial and social situation—exerts more influence on whether homework or factory work is preferable than the type of articles made."[18] Given the efficiency arguments for matching production strategy to product markets, one might expect preferences for work organization to be divided along specialties. The importance of regional variations, however, points to the fact that entrepreneurs had to pay attention not only to the nature of product markets but also to differences in the conditions of the local labor market.

For example, in the department of Cher, one of the most important centers for the lingerie trade, manufacturers told investigators that they increasingly resorted to factories and small workshops because competition from other industries and from agriculture made it difficult to recruit homeworkers. At Bourges, many women homeworkers left the lingerie trade to work for higher wages in an establishment making army clothes. At Aubigny a men's shirt factory competed against lingerie, and at Vierzon a porcelain factory was the chief competitor.[19] The situation was the same in the department of Indre. At Villedieu (Indre), the installation of a shirt factory by Parisians and the development of a porcelain works attracted workers away from the lingerie trade.[20] Facing these difficulties, local entrepreneurs searched the countryside for homeworkers but found the rural situation unsatisfactory. As one of them explained,

> All the finishing work is done in the countryside, [and] that is the inconvenience. The workers work only when they have nothing better to do. They do their lingerie work between All Saints' Day and May, most often when watching over their goats. In summer they work in the fields; they work in the harvest and gather grapes, which lasts a long time because there are so many large vineyards. Between the rush season and the slow season in manufacturing, which depends on many factors, from time to time we are blocked by the mismatch between our need for workers and times when we have enough labor.[21]

Many rural entrepreneurs complained that it was difficult to push farm women to work sufficient hours. Farm women sewed only when they had nothing more pressing to do. Between the seasonal demands in field work and for the harvests and the daily demands of the farmyard animals and dairying, many would do needlework for only an hour a day, and that was not enough for the needs of the industry.

Similar difficulties explain why the industrial northeast never became an important center for the lingerie trade. In the town of Saint-Quentin, for example, there were too many competing industries which hired female workers. In the surrounding countryside, entrepreneurs complained that the work rhythm was too irregular. Women abandoned needlework for farm work; in particular, the extensive beet culture took female labor away from needlework.[22] In one center, Villers-Outreaux in the department of the Nord, most of the year there was a sufficient female population for the lingerie trade, but the situation was untenable because during the harvest season most families migrated to the Soissonais.[23]

Indeed, finding the appropriate workers was much more problematic than many urban merchants, and historians of the sweated trades, might have imagined. Many manufacturers thought married women provided an ideal labor force. Women wanted homework because it allowed them to combine and balance reproductive activities with wage earning. The nature of handwork and piecework was such that women could work when they liked. They were not obliged to meet the regimen of machines and an established workday. They could allow the necessities of day-to-day family life to interrupt their labor and turn their empty hours into cash. Since manufacturers argued that many women worked for supplemental incomes, "une salaire d'appoint" or "pin money," they thought that these women would be relatively indifferent to low wages. The fact that all women were presumed to know how to sew, thus requiring no training at the entrepreneur's expense, added to the vision that women with domestic responsibilities were ideal homeworkers.

However, there was not an inexhaustible reservoir of workers ready to be tapped. Reality did not mesh with such wishful thinking. The volatile character of fashion markets may have encouraged entrepreneurs toward dispersed production, in order to minimize investments in capital and product-specific machinery and to emphasize flexibility in the production process. We should not underestimate the tremendous problems which dispersing production incurs, however. The geographic successes and failures of the French lingerie trade lead to several observations about the nature of labor relations peculiar to outwork which many researchers in the field have overlooked.

First, even though the fashion trades were highly seasonal and the conditions of retail markets favored outwork and even part-time workers, business succeeded only when the entrepreneur controlled the work season and the slack seasons and when the entrepreneur could reasonably regulate the hours and the productivity. In other words, workers had to be flexible according to the needs of the entrepreneur and not according to their own needs. This distinction is crucial because it gives a different meaning to the "matching" of labor demand and supply. The usual analysis of homework presents it as an adaptive strategy for unstable markets but does not stress enough that homework is a production strategy for minimizing risks for the merchant entrepreneur.[24] This is accomplished by passing on the consequences of risks to workers. Recognizing this fact points to the necessary power imbalances in the social relations of production that allow this strategy to be viable economically. Thus when workers had many choices, or could impose their own priorities onto the work routine, as was the case with women in agricultural households, manufacturers who had the capital resources felt that centralized production was preferable to homework. Manufacturers closer to the edge of survival, and unable to afford the capital investment this production strategy demanded, probably had to abandon the trade.

Second, while gathering workers together introduces problems of collective action, homework is not free of disciplinary problems. For dispersed production to function effectively, entrepreneurs must hold even greater disciplinary power than factory foremen because homeworkers must be regulated without direct supervision. Here we must be careful not to exaggerate the power of the entrepreneur. This power to enforce sweated conditions did not necessarily derive from the relations of production. More often, entrepreneurs were benefiting from other, more intimate forms of discipline.

Third, many studies of sweated work have argued that the key to its success was cheap labor, but they do not examine or treat as problematic the conditions which render labor cheap.[25] In these explanations, "cheapness" appears as an inherent quality of rural labor or female labor. My examples argue against these assertions empirically. Counterexamples alone do not resolve this problem, though. Unless we can specify those processes which render labor cheap and exploitable, most labor segmentation theories are redescriptions of existing inequalities and not explanations of them.

A Regional Case History

An examination of a region where entrepreneurs in the lingerie trade did not complain of labor shortages will be instructive. The manufacturers and subcontractors in the region around the town of Cholet in the department of Maine-et-Loire favored outwork. The obstacles which blocked the successful organization of outwork in the fashion trades in other regions, such as the center or the northeast, did not impinge on the entrepreneurs of the Choletais. The workforce was available consistently year-round and could be depended on to work at its trade as a primary occupation. Local entrepreneurs enjoyed a high degree of control over a decentralized production process.[26] What characteristics of this labor supply sustained sweated work in the region? How did these conditions come about?

By their own testimony, many entrepreneurs began with workshops and small factories for finishing work, but soon abandoned them in favor of outwork.[27] Putting out did create problems for distributing and collecting work, and some merchants complained that the quality of work suffered. One subcontractor noted that he could not produce the finer decorations which required detailed supervision.[28] The benefits of outwork, however, outweighed the difficulties.

Although in principle homeworkers could work as much or as little as they wanted or needed, most homeworkers in the Choletais worked between eleven and thirteen hours a day. This was far longer than the regulated ten-hour workday in factories. Moreover, workers in the Choletais on the average worked the longest workdays of all the *lingères* surveyed in the national inquiry.[29] While no one obliged them to work these hours, their low piece rates served as the disciplinarian. Piece rates were extremely low in the Choletais, and as everywhere else, lingerie work was highly specialized. Tasks in the finishing trade were extensively subdivided. One piece often passed through five, sometimes six, seven, and even eight workers. Finishing pillowcases was divided into the following tasks, with a different specialized worker performing each task: drawing threads paid ninety centimes per dozen; basting and quilting paid about seventy centimes per dozen; making buttonholes by machine paid about forty centimes per dozen; and sewing buttons by hand paid about ten centimes for every six dozen buttons. For a final finishing, the pillowcases were distributed for embroidery. Hand embroidery and machine embroidery were yet another special subbranch of the finishing trades with its own elaborate divisions and pay scale. A similar division of tasks and piece rates existed for sheets. Napkins paid thirty-four to forty centimes a dozen, but often it required twelve to fourteen hours for a worker to realize that dozen. Hemming hand towels and dish towels by hand required almost ten hours of labor to finish a dozen. This task, however, paid only thirty-five centimes a dozen. Finishing handkerchiefs paid forty to sixty centimes per dozen depending on the style. On a good day, working by hand, one worker reported that she could finish eighteen kerchiefs.[30] Others reported a productivity of two dozen kerchiefs a day.[31]

Typically, after twelve- to fourteen-hour workdays, needlewomen could earn as little as ten, fifteen, or twenty francs a month. Rarely did a woman earn seventy to eighty francs a month.[32] These wages could not support a family. Many of the daily salaries could not support even a single wage earner. Of the twelve workers interviewed by the investigators, on the average each contributed about a third of the household resources. Individually, the contributions of the yearly wages differed dramatically, ranging from 8 percent to as high as 53 percent.[33] Clearly this was part-time pay for full-time work. Women did not fill the empty hours after housework and family duties with a little stitching. Sewing invaded family life. Stray threads littered the floors. Patterns, finished pieces, material, scissors, and pins covered the family table. Children helped with this work, and sometimes even husbands.

Here we see that domesticity and wage work, even done at home, placed contradictory demands on women's time and energies. Some women may have wanted to balance motherhood with wage earning at home, but the actual constraints and organization of the trade meant that neither the dreams of entrepreneurs nor the dreams of workers were simultaneously realizable. When homework is a tenable organization of production from the perspective of the entrepreneur, it does not permit women to actually satisfy the reasons for their preference to stay home. Why, then, were these women willing to accept this kind of work?

In the last decades of the nineteenth century, two kinds of homework moved into the Choletais. In addition to the lingerie trade, there was also shoe production. Both these industries hired primarily women, but not all rural women were potential recruits for lingerie work. Employment patterns were socially specific and reflected the broader trends in the regional economy. The village of Villedieu-la-Blouère, typical of the inner *bocage*, provides a useful case. Examining the background of the workers reveals that approximately 72 percent of the shoeworkers came from weaving and artisanal households, whereas only 6 percent came from agricultural households; 73 percent of the needleworkers came from weaving and artisanal households, and less than 4 percent came from agricultural households.[34] Not all women in the Choletais were available for homework. Explaining this pattern requires an examination of the situation in weaving households.

By the early twentieth century, the Choletais, like the Cambrésis, which was also a center of the lingerie trade, was one of the few remaining centers of hand-loom weaving in France. The Choletais had a long history of small-scale rural manufacturing. Superficially, at least, the lingerie and shoe industries appeared to continue the tradition. In the eighteenth century, the region was famous for its linen cloths and linen kerchiefs, with the work organized as cottage industries. The nineteenth century was marked by protracted struggles over mechanization of textiles in which hand-loom weavers were remarkably successful at holding onto their domain. Since the 1880s, when linen weaving was first mechanized on an extensive scale in the main towns of the region, hand-loom weavers as small-scale independent producers had tried to prevent the rapid decline of their standard of living by negotiating standard piece rates with local merchants and wholesalers. In a series of bitter strikes, hand-loom weavers were able to slow the decline but were powerless to stop mechanized production from taking the lion's share of the market. By the early twentieth century, a new division of labor between machine production and handwork had emerged. Power looms produced the median grades of linen which formerly were produced on hand looms, pushing handwork to the margins of the linen market, as it specialized in the fine counts which machines could not reproduce technically as well as the coarse counts which were not remunerative enough to justify the investment in expensive machinery.[35]

While the number of hand-loom weavers in the region declined, the losses were not as significant as one might have expected. For example, in the commune of Villedieu-la-Blouère, in 1881, when linen weaving was first mechanized, there were 128 households in which the head of the household was a hand-loom weaver. After thirty years, in 1911, the census taker listed 114 weavers as heads of households. However, while in 93 percent of these weaving households in 1881 every member of the household held some occupation connected to cloth production, either as weavers or in an ancillary task, in 1911 only 44 percent of the 114 weavers were heads of family production units. In 46 percent of the households where a weaver was the head of the household, children and wives were employed in another profession.[36]

Clearly male weavers did not respond to declining piece rates by switching occupations or even looking for other jobs. Equally, they did not leave the region to look for work elsewhere.[37] In fact, these weavers refused work in the shoe industry even when jobs were offered. As one disgruntled and perplexed shoe entrepreneur explained, he had initially conceived of slippermaking as a good venture, anticipating the number of weavers who would flock to this new trade. He discovered to his dismay, however, that hand-loom weavers did not want new jobs. A few tried their hand at shoemaking for a while, but soon returned to weaving. Shoe entrepreneurs solved their problem by hiring women instead.[38]

As their livelihood was threatened, hand-loom weavers reacted by organizing and trying to hold onto their status as independent producers. They battled against proletarianization. This conflict must be understood as a struggle over the technical arrangements of production in the region's textile industry. Power looms and hand looms represented different social relations of production. In essence hand-loom weaving survived only as the occupation of fathers, whose position as head of a family production unit was increasingly becoming the memory of another era.

The accommodation between the two types of weaving technology, that is, the ability of hand-loom weaving to survive in relation to power-loom production, rested on particular family dynamics. The most pressing problem was the collective survival of household members. Rapidly declining piece rates no longer paid for the subsistence of all those who worked in the household production unit. Weaving families received diminishing returns for the same and perhaps even greater effort.

Additional income was required if these families were to survive as units. Yet, if the object was supplemental income alone, why should declining piece rates in hand-loom weaving affect men and women differently? Why should a crisis in income lead to women taking extremely low-paying work? Many more sons of hand-loom weavers continued in weaving than went into other occupations. The crisis of hand-loom weaving brought more women—wives and especially daughters—into the wage labor market. This process, which reshaped the regional labor market by creating a new group of people who sought employment and the process on which the new outwork industries subsisted, was gender-specific. In this case, understanding the content of gender and generational identities is the key to the puzzle.

In weaving households, the organization of work and family life and to a large degree individual identities as well was grounded in clothmaking. We can distinguish a division of labor between male and female tasks. Male heads of households were "weavers" or "master weavers," younger males were "apprentice weavers" or called simply "weavers." Female members of the household were identified by ancillary tasks in clothmaking, such as mounting the warp and skein winding as *ourdisseuses* and *dévideuses*. Within this division we can discern a notion that male "skills" were linked to craftsmanship—that is, knowledge and adeptness at making cloth, and that female "activities" were linked to helping and aiding the main productive activities of the household, but that women were not directly responsible for the quality and production of the actual product.

It mattered little that in day-to-day production, who performed which tasks was solved in flexible ways.[39] Occupation titles did not necessarily govern or limit the kinds of tasks people performed. Rather, it is more important to conceive of occupational titles, in this case, as signifying relationships. That is, although *ourdisseuse* and *dévideuse* denote specific activities, the names actually specify the relationship of those who carry these titles to those who are named *tisserand* (weavers). It is *tissage* which gives the household its social identity, not *ourdissage* or *dévidage*. The notion of male craftsmanship or skill in clothmaking integrated members of the household into the production process along a particular authority structure. This underlying logic subdivided tasks by sex and generation, affirming the power of men over women, of older men over younger men.

The equation between masculinity and skill was not unique to the male hand-loom weavers of the Choletais. Sally Alexander and Barbara Taylor have observed that Chartist tailors and bootmakers in nineteenth-century England made the same claims about their activities, especially when they wished to exclude women from their trades.[40] The frequency of this pattern has led John Rule to conclude that most artisans believed that they held "property" in their skills but that this property was thought to inhere in men exclusively.[41] Extending the analogy further, skill is not just any possession: I would liken it to patrimony. Like patrimonial property it is not just about an individual's ownership. Patrimony orders kin relations around the patriarch as well as the relationship of individual family members to each other.[42]

This arrangement rested on a concept of moral order. Like all these constructs, it describes the "ought" in the system rather than the "is." The belief system did not ensure the actual authority of fathers as heads of households, nor did it describe how compliance and cooperation were actually achieved. Nor was it a matter of personal gain that fathers should assume responsibility for the family enterprise. Certainly not all fathers lived up to or even welcomed this responsibility. However, the patriarchal division of labor was very real in the moral self-perception of hand-loom weavers. We witness a telling expression of this moral economy in the language of protest. In the words of hand-loom weavers in Saint-Léger-Sous-Cholet in a strike in 1904:

> What does the honest and hard-working worker want? It is to live by the work of his profession, to raise his family honestly, to give to our beloved France soldiers robust in body and spirit, and mothers who possess the moral energy to raise their children. It is greed that grows in society, and perhaps (in all) humanity, all society should be based on the three grand words of human thought, Duty in all things, Justice, and Reason. For us, the cost of labor must be raised to where the worker has a proportional part of the boss's profits because they contribute to the wealth of the latter.[43]

Interestingly, the hand-loom weavers of Saint-Léger-Sous-Cholet placed profession first. They did not indicate that their first duty was to family, and consequently they would take any work to support their families. For many hand-loom weavers, the struggle to maintain and raise piece rates was a battle for justice. In their view, a just society would give to the weaver his fair share. A just society would allow him in the exercise of his profession to adequately fulfill his duty to his family.

The above passage suggests an order of priorities which subsumes family interest into the individual professional identity of the father. This is a subtle distinction but one that takes on greater significance if we think about who took wage work in weaving households. The significance of this connection for authority within the family is clear when the equation begins to break down under outside pressures. If the head of the household entered another profession, it was a sign of defeat, marking the end of the struggle he had waged collectively. Women, however, could become wage earners in order to supplement the family income because their work roles were less central to the social identity of the household. These were not gender identities of a predictable sort. Women were not defined by their reproductive abilities, although they clearly performed them. Instead, they were defined as producers, but secondary producers whose specific activities were not crucial to family identity.[44] The indivisibility of masculinity, skill, and status as head of a household defined the family interest around the prerogatives of the father. The majority of male weavers continued in their trades, but the struggle against proletarianization was a victory only for the *père de famille*. Wives and daughters were called upon to maintain the fiction. Obviously, there is another story embedded here, one which articulates the understanding and the experiences of the women involved. It is particularly important to tease out how these women might have thought of themselves and whether they articulated a notion of individual interests in relation to the collectivities in which they lived. The difficulty of finding appropriate sources to recount experiences from their perspectives often seems insurmountable. Finding ways to illuminate the questions about consent, cooperation, and sacrifice is equally daunting. While I do not yet have adequate answers, we can find a point of departure in the folklore of women's work. Although the rich set of associations between needlework and femininity do not explain why women end up sewing for a living, the prominence of textile metaphors in female storytelling traditions suggests that perhaps the language women use in their needleworking activities becomes metaphors for articulating their experiences as well as commenting on their fate and life chances as women.[45]

It is evident that women are oppressed by both capitalist and patriarchal structures, but the two systems do not act as one. The precapitalist handicraft economy was organized by particular sets of patriarchal principles. Capitalists did not simply take over these patriarchal principles, as some feminist theorists have argued.[46] In fact, this was not possible because patriarchal authority was inseparable from the market-based autonomy of small-scale producers, their knowledge of manufacturing processes (what we would call skill), and from the sexual division of labor which allowed the household to function as a production unit. To proletarianize artisans was to attack precisely those aspects of artisanal production where patriarchal authority was embedded. Thus the artisanal struggle against capitalist relations of production was at the same time a struggle for their notion of the father's prerogatives.

In retrospect, the resistance of hand-loom weavers may seem doomed to fail, but the fact that many of these weavers who were in the prime of life in the 1880s finished their days as hand-loom weavers thirty or forty years later should indicate the tenacity of their grip on this identity and their notion of craft and skill. Small-scale producers have a remarkable degree of staying power. Their decision to stay rather than migrate, to remain hand-loom weavers and not to search out new jobs, however, was predicated emotionally and materially on the acceptance of the same set of associated meanings by the women in the households. The final link in the chain rested on the ties which bound these women as family members—bound in by the interlacing of fragile threads. Indeed, we can appreciate the accuracy and power of textile metaphors to capture the quality of these social ties. It may very well be that the women and men in these families never articulated the terms of their relations. The ultimate power of these meaning systems and the personal identities constructed within them is that the assumptions implicit in their actions are not consciously, or at least not fully, questioned.

The emotional and economic complexities of women's oppression in this struggle came from the unspoken demand on women to fill in the gaps—the shortfalls in money and ideology. In the end, the fabric must be strong. Women in weaving families stood at the juncture of the entrepreneur's search for cheap labor and the male weavers' struggle for craft identity and independence. They stood at the point where the demand for labor and the supply of labor converged. Holding these disparate strands, they bore the costs passed on by others and absorbed the consequences of other people's priorities.

The term "women's work" is ambiguous. It can be interpreted as a purely descriptive phrase, as the work that women end up doing in any particular context. Alternatively, it can also be interpreted as work which belongs to women, work which expresses female social identity or some kind of female essence. Sewing is often thought of as women's work in the sense of expressing women's social identity. As a prescription for the work that women should do, the activity signifies a field of meanings centered around notions of domesticity, linked to the process of becoming female socially. In terms of appearances, the work that women end up doing seems neatly to replicate the cultural prescriptions of the kind of work which is quintessentially female. It is thus tempting to assume that there is a causal connection between the two different meanings of women's work.[47]

This essay has shown that these causal links are mostly illusory. The line of inquiry following from this assumption usually misspecifies how gender as a social phenomenon shapes historical processes by posing the question in essentialist terms. A more fruitful approach disentangles the questions analytically, distinguishing the logic behind the organization of production in the sectors of the economy where women workers tend to concentrate from questions about why it is that women performed these kinds of jobs. In this essay I have used two sets of research strategies, one for understanding how entrepreneurs use labor and the other for understanding the social processes which create the supply of female labor.[48]

Following the dominant social ideologies about women's domesticity, many entrepreneurs and subcontractors in the lingerie trade expected to find their workforce among married women with children. The realities of maintaining control over the production process and of finding a steady labor supply, however, quickly taught them otherwise. Economically, the viability of producing by hand in the homes of workers depended on finding a group of workers desperate enough to work the long hours for what were the lowest possible wages. As a production strategy, sweating exposed the blatant power imbalances which existed between entrepreneurs and homeworkers. Creating these "appropriate" conditions and structures in the labor supply, however, was not under the control of individual entrepreneurs. As I have shown, the processes which created the supply of female labor must be examined separately. In the Choletais, this process was one of the unintended consequences of the protracted struggles over proletarianization in the local textile industry. Gender systems which were part of the organizing principles of precapitalist household economies became the divisions along which the local labor market was segmented. A contextual understanding of the meaning of these gender identities is the critical link in explaining why men's resistance to the establishment of capitalist relations of production in weaving would lead to the development of proletarianized outwork for women.

There can be no simple answer for understanding the "technology of women's work" because both production technology and gender ideology are flexible systems which must be understood contextually. At times, gender ideology affects the demand for female labor, but equally, gender affects the conditions under which there is a "supply" of female labor. It is important to apply gender analysis to both domains, but each is subject to a different order of intervening circumstances, conflicts, and contingencies which together produce the outcomes we observe. These outcomes cannot be derived simply from an examination of the ideology around women's work and family roles. Rather, as I have demonstrated in this essay, the outcome depends on a series of complex historically and geographically specific interactions.

Notes

1. Bonnie G. Smith, *The Ladies of the Leisure Class: The Bourgeoises of Northern France in the Nineteenth Century* (Princeton: Princeton University Press, 1981).

2. See Judy Chicago, *Embroidering Our Heritage: The Dinner Party Needlework* (Garden City, N.Y.: Anchor Books, 1980).

3. During the late nineteenth century, consumption as an activity was explicitly sexualized. For example, in Emile Zola's novel about a department store, *Au Bonheur des dames*, the dominant metaphor representing women's experiences of shopping and buying in department stores was seduction. For a more general study of the reception of mass consumption in the late nineteenth century, consult the work of Rosalind Williams, *Dream Worlds: Mass Consumption in Late Nineteenth Century France* (Berkeley: University of California Press, 1982). For a detailed study of the workings of department stores, see Michael B. Miller, *The Bon Marché: Bourgeois Culture and the Department Store, 1869-1920* (Princeton: Princeton University Press, 1981). Theresa McBride, "A Woman's World: Department Stores and the Evolution of Women's Employment," *French Historical Studies* 10 (1979): 664-83, and Susan Porter Benson, *Counter-Cultures: Saleswomen, Managers, and Customers in American Department Stores, 1890-1940* (Urbana: University of Illinois Press, 1986), have studied the lives of saleswomen employed by department stores.

4. The role of the state in structuring the labor force, and in particular the complex actions of protective legislation, is an important line of analysis which I will not consider in this essay. Joan W. Scott, in her article "L'Ouvrière! Mot impie, sordide . . . ," in *The Historical Meanings of Work*, ed. Patrick Joyce (Cambridge: Cambridge University Press, 1987), pp. 119-42, and Marilyn J. Boxer's article "Protective Legislation and Home Industry: The Marginalization of Women Workers in Late Nineteenth–Early Twentieth Century France," *Journal of Social History* 20 (Fall 1986): 45-65, have shown how the language of moral endangerment and the sexual vulnerability of women became the basis for the legislative debate on protective legislation for working women. Enacted into law, these notions limited women's access to certain jobs. Mary Lynn Stewart has studied the unintended effect of protective legislation on the organization of the French textile trades. Often legislation affecting factory work enhanced the attractiveness of homework as a production strategy. See Mary Lynn (Stewart) McDougall, "The Economics of Regulation: French Labor Legislation in the Textile Industry, 1892-1914," paper presented at the Social Science History Association meetings in Washington, D.C., October 1983.

5. For a study of the role of feminine sensibility in shaping production priorities and particularly the role of bourgeois women as consumers, see Whitney Walton, " 'To Triumph before Feminine Taste': Bourgeois Women's Consumption and Hand Methods of Production in Mid-Nineteenth-Century Paris," *Business History Review* 60 (Winter 1986): 541-63, and *France at the Crystal Palace: Bourgeois Taste and Artisan Manufacture in the Nineteenth Century* (Berkeley: University of California Press, 1992).

6. In part this reputation originated with the popular image of the power of French aristocratic women. For these women, known for their charm, wit, sexual license, the "power" of the boudoir centered on the privileges and rituals of attending the ladies' long *toilette*. See Vera Lee, *The Reign of Women in Eighteenth Century France* (Cambridge, Mass.: Schenkman, 1975).

7. Alfred Picard, *Le Bilan d'un siècle*, vol. 5 (Paris: Imprimerie Nationale, 1906), p. 429.

8. Ibid., pp. 426-29.

9. Ministère du Commerce, Office du Travail, *Enquête sur le travail à domicile dans l'industrie de la lingerie*, vol. 5 (Paris: Imprimerie nationale, 1911), p. 17. See also chapter 6 in this volume.

10. The total active female population in 1896 was 6,382,658, of whom 2,750,364 were employed in agriculture and 2,178,894 were employed in industry. Ministère du commerce, Office du Travail, *Résultats statistiques du recensement des industries et professions (le dénombrement général de la population du 29 mars 1896)* (Paris: Imprimerie nationale, 1901).

11. James A. Schmiechen, *Sweated Industries and Sweated Trades: the London Clothing Trades, 1860-1914* (Urbana: University of Illinois Press, 1984), pp. 25-26.

12. Interestingly, the important transformation of artisanal needle trades took place before Isaac Singer introduced his machine to the European public in the Great Exhibition of 1851. The greater technical efficiency of the sewing machine translated into higher profits only within the appropriate social relations of production. As Christopher H. Johnson's study of the Parisian tailoring trades, "Economic Change and Artisan Discontent: The Tailors' History, 1800-1848," in *Revolution and Reaction: 1848 and the Second French Republic*, ed. Roger Price (London: Croom Helm, 1975), pp. 87-114, indicates, the changes pushed through by merchant clothiers early in the nineteenth century—extensive subdivision of labor and taking the task of coordinating production away from master tailors—were far more corrosive of the artisanal organization of the garment industry than the introduction of machine work. In fact, the latter was possible only after the proletarianization of the trade. For a study of women workers in the Parisian garment trades, see Joan W. Scott, "Men and Women in the Parisian Garment Trades: Discussions of Family and Work in the 1830's and 1840's," in *The Power of the Past*, ed. Pat Thane and Geoffrey Crossick (Cambridge: Cambridge University Press, 1985), pp. 67-93.

13. Albert Aftalion, *Le développement de la fabrique et le travail á domicile dans les industries de l'habillement* (Paris: L. Larose et L. Tenin, 1906), especially pp. 65-96 and 144-56. For a recent version of the same argument, see Michael J. Piore, "Dualism as a Response to Flux and Uncertainty" and "Technological Foundations of Dualism and Discontinuity," in *Dualism and Discontinuity in Industrialized Societies*, ed. Suzanne Berger and Michael J. Piore (Cambridge: Cambridge University Press, 1980).

14. Ministère du Commerce, Office du Travail, *Enquête sur le travail à domicile dans l'industrie de la lingerie*, 5 vols. (Paris: Imprimerie nationale, 1908-11).

15. *Enquête sur le travail à domicile, lingerie*, vol. 5 (Paris: Imprimerie Nationale, 1911), pp. 60-62.

16. Ibid., pp. 58-60; see also Aftalion, pp. 165-214.

17. Ibid., see also Aftalion, cited above in note 13.

18. Ibid., p. 62.

19. Ibid., p. 39.

20. Ibid., p. 43.

21. Ibid.

22. Ibid., p. 46.

23. Ibid., p. 47.

24. The most common explanation in the current literature is the match between women's preference to work at home given their family responsibilities, and the entrepreneurs' expectation to hire women because of the volatile nature of demand in the fashion industry. For example, Barbara Franzoi has noted in her study of the homework in Germany in the

early twentieth century that "for women it was the rhythm of work that gave domestic industry its uniqueness as an industrial work form. Homework intruded into the time and energy a woman could devote to household tasks, but the intrusion was perceived as less harsh
than factory work. More importantly, homework served as a base for the preservation of the
family economy, especially for women and children in which members not only contributed
wage but frequently worked together to secure that wage. Women attempted to make the job
fit their family circumstances instead of the reverse. This is a primary reason for the continuation of traditional work choices. It is also a fundamental explanation of how women endured the impact of industrialization without profound disruption. Women's family roles defined their work identity. Decisions were made within this framework governed by a constant
attempt to balance family needs with economic demands." "Domestic Industry: Work Options and Women's Choices," in *German Women in the Nineteenth Century*, ed. John C. Fout
(New York: Holmes and Meier, 1984), p. 262. As Sheila Allen and Carol Wolkowitz have
pointed out, these explanations perpetuate certain myths about why homework exists. "The
widely accepted assumptions about the characteristics of homeworkers have come to be seen
as an explanation for homeworking itself. It is all too easy to move from possible explanations
of why individuals are constrained to work at home to using these to explain why homeworking is so extensive. By so doing, the belief is fostered that homeworking is a function of
the needs and preferences of its work-force, a burden they have brought upon themselves, or
a choice they have made freely, rather than a form of production in which they participate."
Homeworking: Myths and Realities (London: Macmillan Education Ltd., 1987), p. 59.

25. For an example of such arguments, see the study of Duncan Bythell, *The Sweated
Trades: Outwork in Nineteenth Century Britain* (London: Batsford, 1978).

26. Ibid., pp. 43, 127.

27. *Enquête sur le travail à domicile, lingerie*, vol. 2 (Paris: Imprimerie Nationale, 1908), pp.
693, 695, 696.

28. Ibid., p. 695.

29. *Enquête sur le travail à domicile, lingerie*, vol. 5, pp. 80-84.

30. *Enquête sur le travail à domicile, lingerie*, vol. 2, pp. 695-96.

31. Ibid., pp. 700-15.

32. Ibid., p. 696.

33. Ibid., pp. 700-15.

34. Archives Communales de Villedieu-La-Blouère, Listes nominatives du recensement
de la population, 1911.

35. This explanation for the survival of hand weaving along with machine weaving follows the logic of Aftalion's analysis, which notes that the profitability of machine production
rests on understanding the segmentation of product markets. See note 13 above. For a study
of hand-loom weaving families in the Cambrésis, see Louis A. Tilly, "Linen Was Their Life:
Family Survival Strategies and Parent-Child Relations in Nineteenth Century France," in
Interest and Emotions: Essays on the Study of Family and Kinship, ed. Hans Medick and David
Sabean (Cambridge: Cambridge University Press, 1984), pp. 300-16. See also Serge Graft-
eaux, *Mémé Santerre, A French Woman of the People*, trans. Louise A. Tilly and Kathryn L.
Tilly (New York: Schocken, 1985), for a biographical account of a woman from a hand-loom
weaving family of the Cambrésis.

36. Archives Communales Villedieu-la-Blouère: Listes nominatives du recensement de la
population 1881, 1911.

37. There were few opportunities for men to earn supplemental income from agriculture.
The commercialization of livestock farming increased the demand for year-round agricultural
labor, which farmers solved by hiring more farm servants and reducing their reliance on the
seasonal labor which weavers had formerly provided. In addition, weavers owned a minuscule
proportion of the land in the region. Most rural weavers owned their house and a small garden plot. In exceptional cases, the better-off weavers owned a small meadow or several fields.
For the Choletais, at least, there is little evidence to support the explanation offered by many

economic historians that handicraft production survived in the French countryside as seasonal employment for an agricultural population. A more extensive discussion can be found
in my book, *The Weaver's Knot: The Contradictions of Class Struggle and Family Solidarity in
Western France, 1750-1914* (Ithaca, N.Y.: Cornell University Press, 1994).

38. Réné Chené, *Les débuts du commerce et de l'industrie de la chaussure dans le region de
Cholet* (Maulévrier, Maine-et-Loire: Herault, 1980).

39. Francois Simon, a schoolteacher whose father and brothers were hand-loom weavers
in the Choletais, noted that both men and women wove. In addition to weaving, women also
prepared the yarn for weaving. *Département de Maine-et-Loire, la commune de La Romagne*
(Angers: A. Bruel, 1927), p. 58. Mémé Santerre (see note 35), who also came from a weaving
family and wove as a young girl, observed the same flexibility of activities in her father's
house.

40. Sally Alexander, "Women, Class, and Sexual Differences in the 1830's and 1840's:
Some Reflections on the Writings of Feminist History," *History Workshop Journal* 17 (Spring
1984): 125-49; Barbara Taylor, " 'The Men Are As Bad As Their Masters': Socialism, Feminism, and Sexual Antagonism in the London Tailoring Trade in the 1830's," in *Sex and Class
in Women's History*, ed. Judith I. Newton, Mary P. Ryan, and Judith Walkowitz (London:
Routledge and Kegan Paul, 1983), pp. 187-220.

41. John Rule, "The Property in Skill in the Period of Manufacture," in *The Historical
Meaning of Work*, ed. Patrick Joyce (Cambridge: Cambridge University Press, 1987), pp. 99-
118.

42. Pierre Bourdieu, "Marriage Strategies as Strategies of Social Reproduction," in *Family
and Society*, ed. Robert Forster and Orest Ranum (Baltimore: Johns Hopkins University Press,
1976), pp. 117-44.

43. Archives Nationales C7318: Chambre des députés, Enquête sur l'industrie textile en
France 1903-04, régions non-visités, Maine-et-Loire. Réponse de la Chambre syndicale des
ouvriers tisserands de Saint-Léger-Sous-Cholet.

44. Joan W. Scott has found that skilled Parisian tailors in the 1830s and '40s held similar
conceptions about maleness and femaleness in relation to family identity. As with the Choletais, these arguments about the nature of gender identities became salient in a period of profound transformations in the basic social relations of production in the garment industry. See
note 12 above.

45. Not surprisingly, literary theorists and folklorists have explored this theme most ex-
tensively. See Nancy K. Miller, "Arachnologies: The Woman, the Text, and the Critic," in
The Poetics of Gender, ed. Nancy K. Miller (New York: Columbia University Press, 1986), pp.
270-95; Patricia Kleindienst Joplin, "The Voice in the Shuttle Is Ours," *Stanford Literature
Review* 1 (Spring 1984): 25-53; J. Hillis Miller, "Ariadne's Thread: Repetition and Narrative
Line," in *Interpretation of Narrative*, ed. M. J. Valdes and O. J. Miller (Toronto: University of
Toronto Press, 1976), pp. 148-66; idem, "Ariachne's Broken Woof," *Georgia Review* 31
(Spring 1977): 44-60; Karen E. Rowe, "To Spin a Yarn: The Female Voice in Folklore and
Fairy Tale," in *Fairy Tale and Society: Illusion, Allusion, and Paradigm*, ed. Ruth B. Bottig-
heimer (Philadelphia: University of Pennsylvania Press, 1986), pp. 53-74; Ruth B. Bottig-
heimer, "Tale Spinners: Submerged Voices in Grimm's Fairy Tales," *New German Critique* 27
(1982): 141-50; idem, *Grimm's Bad Girls and Bold Boys: The Moral and Social Vision of the
Tales* (New Haven: Yale University Press, 1987); Marta Weigle, *Spiders and Spinsters: Women
and Mythology* (Albuquerque: University of New Mexico Press, 1982). For the most part,
these studies have been concerned with locating the "female voice," but this notion is usually articulated as a universal voice of women's condition, rather than analytical voices reflecting the intelligence of the poor and powerless who must make their way through the
world. For an interesting analysis of folktales with the tools of social history, see Peter Taylor
and Hermann Rebel, "Hessian Peasant Women, Their Families, and the Draft: A Social-
Historical Interpretation of Four Tales from the Grimm Collection," *Journal of Family History*
(Winter 1981): 347-78, and Hermann Rebel, "Why Not 'Old Marie' . . . or Someone Very

Much like Her? A Reassessment of the Question of Grimm's Contributors from a Social His-torical Perspective," *Social History* (January 1988): 1-24. Following a similar perspective, I am preparing a study on textile metaphors and women's magical implements based on tales taken from the Cinderella cycles.

46. For an overview of this debate, see the essays in *Women and Revolution: A Discussion of the Unhappy Marriage of Marxism and Feminism*, ed. Lydia Sargent (Boston: Southend Press, 1981). My own position is closest to that of Ann Ferguson and Nancy Folbre, who emphasize the tensions and contradictions between patriarchy and capitalism.

47. Conservative social reformers of the late nineteenth and early twentieth centuries, in fact, saw just such a connection. For example, in 1909, when the Academy of Moral and Social Sciences of the Institut de France deliberated about the problems of female home-workers, one participant, the Count of Haussonville, who was an advocate of protective leg-islation for female homeworkers, linked women's economic plight to the nature of their skills. Paraphrasing Voltaires's "Toute Française, ce que j'y imagine, sait bien ou mal faire un peu de cuisine," he added his own: "toute Française sait, bien ou mal, faire un peu de cou-ture." In their youth, he observed, all women learned to use the needle and thread. Haus-sonville reasoned that it was because all women possessed these skills that wages were so low. Women undermined each other through competition, he argued. Because women of all dif-ferent stations in life and of different economic needs would sew to earn a little extra, one woman might accept sewing at a rate that another woman deemed too low. Meager wages resulted from the endless supply of women who could perform these tasks.

This notion of "supply outstripping demand" makes sense only if one assumed distinct and separate spheres in which particular activities were inherently male or female. Thus when women needed to earn wages, because of their sexual identity, they were suited only for a prescribed number of occupations. One could argue, of course, that seamstresses could restrict access to the trade as a way to demand higher wages. But for Haussonville, it was precisely because sewing was so closely bound to femaleness that to restrict that knowledge was in-conceivable. A woman who did not sew, like a woman who did not cook, was not a woman at all. The resemblance to Rousseau's views on sewing can hardly be accidental. Sewing, like other female vocations, embodied the totality of a woman's social being. Ultimately, his ex-planation for low wages placed the burden on femininity itself. Destined to sew because they are so formed, women were exploited because they sewed. By this account, the female wage earner was disadvantaged by her sex. "Celles qui travaillent à domicile," Séance et travaux de l'Académie des sciences morales et politiques, Compte rendu 71 (1909): 703-827.

48. In neoclassical economic analysis, it is unnecessary to investigate the two questions separately because it is assumed that a single mechanism, price, will explain both. For an alternative analysis similar to the approach developed in this essay and an excellent critique of neoclassical models, see Jane Humphries and Jill Rubery, "The Reconstitution of the Sup-ply Side of the Labour Market: The Relative Autonomy of Social Reproduction," *Cambridge Journal of Economics* 8 (December 1984): 331-46.

CONTRIBUTORS

Reed Benhamou is Associate Professor in the Department of Home Economics at Indiana University. Her studies on furniture production, the craft of gilding, and eighteenth-century culture have appeared in *Technology and Culture*, *European Studies Journal*, *Studies in Eighteenth-Century Culture*, and *Studies on Voltaire and the Eighteenth Century*.

Pierre Caspard is Director of the Service of the History of Education, one of six research laboratories of the National Institute of Educational Research (Institut National de Recherche Pédagogique) in Paris. His work focuses on demographic structure and technology in the cotton-printing industry.

Walter Endrei lives in Budapest and does research on early European textile techniques. Trained as an engineer at the University of Budapest, he has applied his education to the analysis of hand spinning machines. His book *L'Évolution des techniques du filage et du tissage au moyen âge à la revolution industrielle* was the first to measure hand-spinning productivity with modern methods.

Daryl M. Hafter is Professor of History at Eastern Michigan University. Her work on French women in preindustrial technology has appeared in *Business History Review*, *Annals of the New York Academy of Sciences*, and *Dynamos and Virgins Revisited: Women and Technological Change in History*.

Inger Jonsson is studying economic history in the graduate program of the University of Uppsala, Sweden. Her dissertation analyzes the role of women in protoindustrialization, focusing on the flax industry in Hälsingland, Sweden, 1700-1850.

Tessie P. Liu, Assistant Professor in the Department of History at Northwestern University, has just published *The Weaver's Knot: The Contradictions of Class Struggle and Family Solidarity in Western France, 1750-1914*.

Rachel P. Maines owns a museum curatorial services firm and is the author of articles on material culture and the history of technology.

Jean H. Quartaert is Professor and Vice-Chair of the Department of History at Binghamton University. She is author of *Reluctant Feminists in German Social Democracy, 1885-1917* and coauthor of *Socialist Women* and *Connecting Spheres: Women in the Western World*.

Patrizia Sione earned her Ph.D. in American History at Binghamton University. She is conducting research in Italian archives on the late nineteenth-century migration of northern Italian textile workers to the silk district in New Jersey.

John F. Sweets, Professor of History at the University of Kansas, is the author of *The Politics of Resistance in France* and *Choices in Vichy France: The French under Nazi Occupation*.

Whitney Walton is Associate Professor in the Department of History at Purdue University. She has written about the connections between technology, culture, and the history of women in articles and in *France at the Crystal Palace: Bourgeois Taste and Artisan Manufacture in the Nineteenth Century*.